A Necessary Consequence

Monographs in Baptist History

VOLUME 33

SERIES EDITOR
Michael A. G. Haykin, The Southern Baptist Theological Seminary

EDITORIAL BOARD
Matthew Barrett, Midwestern Baptist Theological Seminary
Peter Beck, Charleston Southern University
Anthony L. Chute, California Baptist University
Jason G. Duesing, Midwestern Baptist Theological Seminary
Nathan A. Finn, North Greenville University
Crawford Gribben, Queen's University, Belfast
Gordon L. Heath, McMaster Divinity College
Barry Howson, Heritage Theological Seminary
Jason K. Lee, Cedarville University
Thomas J. Nettles, The Southern Baptist Theological Seminary, retired
James A. Patterson, Union University
James M. Renihan, Institute of Reformed Baptist Studies
Jeffrey P. Straub, Independent Scholar
Brian R. Talbot, Broughty Ferry Baptist Church, Scotland
Malcolm B. Yarnell III, Southwestern Baptist Theological Seminary

Ours is a day in which not only the gaze of western culture but also increasingly that of Evangelicals is riveted to the present. The past seems to be nowhere in view and hence it is disparagingly dismissed as being of little value for our rapidly changing world. Such historical amnesia is fatal for any culture, but particularly so for Christian communities whose identity is profoundly bound up with their history. The goal of this new series of monographs, Studies in Baptist History, seeks to provide one of these Christian communities, that of evangelical Baptists, with reasons and resources for remembering the past. The editors are deeply convinced that Baptist history contains rich resources of theological reflection, praxis and spirituality that can help Baptists, as well as other Christians, live more Christianly in the present. The monographs in this series will therefore aim at illuminating various aspects of the Baptist tradition and in the process provide Baptists with a usable past.

A Necessary Consequence

The Use of Confessional Language to Affirm
the Trinity Among English Particular Baptists
as Evidenced by Bristol Baptist Academy in
the Eighteenth Century

Steven Olsen

☙PICKWICK *Publications* • Eugene, Oregon

A NECESSARY CONSEQUENCE
The Use of Confessional Language to Affirm the Trinity Among English Particular Baptists as Evidenced by Bristol Baptist Academy in the Eighteenth Century

Monographs in Baptist History 33

Copyright © 2025 Steven Olsen. All rights reserved. Except for brief quotations in critical publications or reviews, no part of this book may be reproduced in any manner without prior written permission from the publisher. Write: Permissions, Wipf and Stock Publishers, 199 W. 8th Ave., Suite 3, Eugene, OR 97401.

Pickwick Publications
An Imprint of Wipf and Stock Publishers
199 W. 8th Ave., Suite 3
Eugene, OR 97401

www.wipfandstock.com

PAPERBACK ISBN: 979-8-3852-4157-6
HARDCOVER ISBN: 979-8-3852-4158-3
EBOOK ISBN: 979-8-3852-4159-0

Cataloguing-in-Publication data:

Name: Olsen, Steven, author.

Title: A necessary consequence : the use of confessional language to affirm the trinity among english particular baptists as evidenced by bristol baptist academy in the eighteenth century / Steven Olsen.

Description: Eugene, OR : Pickwick Publications, 2025 | Series: Monographs in Baptist History 33 | Includes bibliographical references and index.

Identifiers: ISBN 979-8-3852-4157-6 (paperback) | ISBN 979-8-3852-4158-3 (hardcover) | ISBN 979-8-3852-4159-0 (ebook)

Subjects: LCSH: Baptists—Great Britain—History—18th century. | Reformed Baptists—Great Britain—History—18th century. | Particular Baptists—Creeds. | Particular Baptists—Doctrines. | Baptists—Doctrines. | Baptist Confession of Faith (1644).

Classification: BX6335 .O45 2025 (print) | BX6335 .O45 (ebook)

To the eighteenth-century Particular Baptists who passed on an orthodox heritage by standing in an orthodox lineage.

Contents

Abbreviations ix

Chapter 1: Introduction 1
    Research Problem 1
    Thesis 2
    Literature Review 3
    Delimitations 7
    Definition of Terms 7
    Organization of Study 9

Chapter 2: "The Bible Only Is the Religion Of Protestants!": Seventeenth-Century Answers to Eighteenth-Century Questions 11
    Anti-Trinitarian Presence in Seventeenth-Century England 12
    The Protestant Principle 25
    Conclusion 30

Chapter 3: Ambiguous and Amicable: How Seventeenth-Century General Baptists Responded to Antitrinitarianism 31
    The Antitrinitarian Dispute with Matthew Caffyn 32
    The Response of the General Baptists 40
    Conclusion 60

Chapter 4: Confessional and Confrontational: How Seventeenth-Century Particular Baptists Responded to Antitrinitarianism 61
    The Antitrinitarian Dispute with Thomas Collier 61
    The Response of the Particular Baptists 77
    Conclusion 90

Chapter 5: An Orthodox Heritage: History of Broadmead Church, Bristol Academy, and the Salters' Hall Debates 91
    The History of Broadmead Baptist Church 91
    The History of Bristol Baptist Academy 103
    The History of the Salters' Hall Debates 113
    Conclusion 125

Chapter 6: "Teach What Accords With Sound Doctrine": Trinitarian Teaching at Bristol Baptist Academy 126
    The Trinitarian Library of Bristol Baptist Academy 127
    The Trinitarian Curriculum of Bristol Baptist Academy 130
    The Trinitarianism of Caleb Evans 141
    Conclusion 152

Chapter 7: "You Will Save Both Yourself and Your Hearers": The Trinitarianism of Bristol Baptist Academy Alumni 153
    Alumni Who Affirmed Orthodox Trinitarianism 154
    Robert Hall Jr. and Accusation of Trinitarian Downgrade at Bristol Academy 163
    Job David, an Alumnus Who Denied Orthodox Trinitarianism 166
    Conclusion 169

Chapter 8: Conclusion 171
    Review 171
    Reflections 173
    Recommendations 176

Bibliography 179
Subject Index 195

Abbreviations Page

1LCF44	*1644 First London Baptist Confession of Faith*
1LCF46	*1646 First London Baptist Confession of Faith*
2LCF	*Second London Baptist Confession of Faith*
Alcester Confession	*A Short and Compendius Confession of Faith Held by the Church of Christ Meeting at Aulcester in the County of Warwick*
BES	Bristol Education Society
Bristol Academy	Bristol Baptist Academy
Broadmead	Broadmead Baptist Church
AHEB	*A History of the English Baptists*
THEB	*The History of the English Baptists*
HEGB	*The History of the English General Baptists*
KJV	King James Version
MGA	*Minutes of the General Assembly*
Salters' Hall	*Salters' Hall Debates*
SD	*Savoy Declaration*
WCF	*Westminster Confession of Faith*

1

Introduction

> And from what has been suggested, it is I think very evident that a minister's giving a confession of his faith previous to his ordination, is so far from interfering with the right of private judgment . . . that it is rather on the other hand a necessary *consequence* of the natural exercise of this right, betwixt a minister and the people to whom he is called to minister.[1]

Research Problem

THE DOCTRINE OF THE Trinity came under considerable pressure in the 1700s, specifically the deity of Jesus as the Son of God. Baptist churches were under pressure to disavow confessional trinitarian language and to only uphold scriptural language that referenced the deity of the Father, Son, and Holy Spirit. A specific event in England demonstrates the pressure of the day. That event is the Salters' Hall Debates of 1719.

The Salters' Hall Debates consisted of the three dissenting denominations: Presbyterians, Congregationalists, and Baptists. The material cause of the debate was how local Presbyterian churches in Exeter should respond to ministers who denied classical trinitarianism, specifically the deity of the Son. While most present at the debates upheld classical trinitarianism,

---

1. Evans et al., *Charge and Sermon*, 17. Caleb Evans's conviction that confessional statements are a necessary consequence of private judgments in doctrinal matters because others have a right to know what a person actually believes. Evans gave this declaration at his ordination service as associate pastor at Broadmead Baptist Church on August 18, 1767.

there were opposing views as to how churches ought to respond. One group, the subscribers, argued that ministers ought to affirm the first article of the Thirty-Nine Articles of Religion[2] as well as the fifth[3] and sixth[4] questions of the Westminster Shorter Catechism. The other group, the nonsubscribers, argued that ministers ought to affirm only the language of Scripture as related to the Trinity. This discussion led to the formal cause of the debate, which was whether churches ought to require ministers to subscribe to confessional statements.

The story of the Salters' Hall Debates will be told later, for now it should be known that the nonsubscribers narrowly won the debate. Initially, it might appear as a positive outcome that the Scriptures, the words of God, won over confessions, the words of men. However, the history proceeding from Salters' Hall conveys a different outcome. Many Baptist churches that affirmed only scriptural trinitarian language began to adopt antitrinitarian positions such as Arianism, Socinianism, or Unitarianism.[5]

Thesis

The argument of this book is that Bristol Baptist Academy in the eighteenth century helped to secure English Particular Baptist churches from drifting toward antitrinitarianism by teaching orthodox trinitarianism to the students in response to the Salters' Hall Debates.

The question is whether Bristol Baptist Academy responded to the debate of Salters' Hall, and, if so, whether the response had an effect on the preaching and application of theology by its students in eighteenth-century Baptist churches of England. This question pulls together four separate topics: the Salters' Hall Debates, Bristol Baptist Academy, the history of eighteenth-century English Baptists, and the antitrinitarian doctrine

---

2. "Of Faith in the Holy Trinity: There is but one living and true God, everlasting, without body, parts, or passions; of infinite power, wisdom, and goodness; the Maker, and Preserver of all things both visible and invisible. And in unity of this Godhead there be three Persons, of one substance, power, and eternity; the Father, the Son, and the Holy Ghost."

3. "*Are there more Gods than one?* There is but one only, the living and true God."

4. "*How many persons are there in the Godhead?* There are three persons in the Godhead; the Father, the Son, and the Holy Ghost; and these three are one God, the same in substance, equal in power and glory."

5. "The approach to the Salters' Hall debates [was] marked by the desire to be faithful to Scripture as the arbiter. Doctrinally, it left a lot of room for creative thinking, as some long-established beliefs and practices could not be unmistakably proven from Scripture." Copson, "General Baptists," in Copson and Morden, *Challenge and Change*, 48.

of the eighteenth century. Others have researched each of these four areas resulting in considerable publication of books, dissertations, and articles. However, there are no published works that consider these topics all together.[6] With that said, there are several works that do address a portion of these four topics.

Literature Review

Trinity, Creed, and Confusion, edited by Stephen Copson, is a collection of essays that explores the historical event of the Salters' Hall Debates. The book also evaluates the outcome of the debates in relation to the Particular and General Baptists. The essays as a whole attempt to demonstrate that all present at Salters' Hall agreed on classical trinitarian doctrine. What the attenders did not agree upon was the use of confessional language to express trinitarian doctrine. Those who would be known as the nonsubscribers refused to subscribe to confessional trinitarian language. They argued that the Trinity ought to be expressed only in scriptural terms. Those who would become known as the subscribers claimed scriptural terms are not adequate enough because many antitrinitarians affirmed such language. Therefore, the subscribers argued that churches and ministers ought to affirm trinitarian doctrine as specifically stated in certain confessions. Among the Baptists at Salters' Hall, twelve General Baptists and two Particular Baptists did not subscribe, and eleven Particular Baptists and one General Baptist did subscribe. The subscribers suspected that nonsubscription either meant one was antitrinitarian or would become antitrinitarian.

The idea for the thesis of this book derives from *Trinity, Creed, and Confusion*. In the introduction, Copson provides four areas of needed research regarding the Salters' Hall Debates and eighteenth-century English Baptists, prompting the formation of this thesis. One area of research he calls "echoes of the Salters' Hall Debates."[7] Copson asks whether the subscribers were suspicious that Arminianism would lead to Arianism. He suggests that the academies, such as Bristol Baptist Academy, would be a place of study to answer this question.

Roger Hayden published his 1991 dissertation, *Continuity and Change*. The question addressed by Hayden is whether Particular Baptists in eighteenth-century England accepted high (or hyper)-Calvinism. Hayden

---

6. This statement should be qualified with the acknowledgment that there are no published works that consider these topics together as far as this writer is aware at this time of writing.

7. Copson, *Trinity, Creed and Confusion*, 5.

challenges the notion that *most* Particular Baptists adopted and practiced high-Calvinism. He contends that most Particular Baptists adopted and practiced Evangelical Calvinism throughout the eighteenth century. Whereas men like John Skepp, John Gill, and John Brine were influencers among Particular Baptists for high-Calvinism, Evangelical Calvinism had its influencers as well. These influencers were Bernard Foskett, Hugh Evans, and Caleb Evans. These three men were the first three principals of the Bristol Baptist Academy. Hayden argues that the Bristol Academy under the leadership of Foskett and the Evanses helped to anchor Particular Baptist churches in Evangelical Calvinism. The academy did this, in part, by upholding the *Second London Baptist Confession of Faith* of 1689. The students who then pastored local Baptist churches preached and practiced Evangelical Calvinism.

The focus of this book and that of Hayden's are similar. Both look to the Bristol Baptist Academy as an anchor against a drift in theology, either toward high-Calvinism or toward antitrinitarianism, among Baptist churches. Hayden's method serves as a model for this work. He establishes how Bristol Baptist Academy was an antithesis to the high-Calvinism of the day and also how the academy actively worked to teach and practice Evangelical Calvinism. This book will do the same but in regard to orthodox trinitarianism and antitrinitarianism. Hayden's focus is on the two forms of Calvinism, High and Evangelical, whereas the focus of this dissertation is on the two forms of trinitarianism, confessional and scriptural. Hayden references the Salters' Hall Debates three times in his writing, and only one of those times does it receive an extended treatment of three pages. Though little mentioned, what Hayden demonstrates is that the debates at Salters' Hall were known by Foskett and that he responded with implementing the *Second London Confession* at the Western Association and the academy.

In Essence One, edited by Haykin and Paul, provides a beneficial discussion of various Particular Baptists and how they defended trinitarian doctrine amidst an antitrinitarian society. The book is a collection of essays presented in 2019 at the Andrew Fuller Center for Biblical Studies.[8] The purpose of the book is to demonstrate how Particular Baptists in the United Kingdom from the seventeenth to the nineteenth century defended trinitarian doctrine against Socinianism and Unitarianism by use of both scriptural and confessional language. Particular Baptist figures who defended orthodox trinitarianism include William Collins, Benjamin Keach, John Gill, Anne Dutton, and Alexander Carson. Among Baptist antitrinitarians referenced in the articles are Thomas Collier and Matthew Caffyn. As to the

---

8. The final two chapters were not essays presented at the conference.

use of confessional language to articulate trinitarian doctrine, the *Second London Confession of Faith* and the *Orthodox Catechism* are discussed as Particular Baptist responses to antitrinitarianism. Also included is a chapter on the Salters' Hall Debates that argues the main issue at the debates was subscription to confessional trinitarian language rather than rejection of trinitarian doctrine.

This work and *In Essence One* have several topics in common. Both argue that Particular Baptists maintained trinitarian doctrine through the use of and subscription to orthodox confessions of faith. Common figures include Caffyn, Collier, and Gill. The Salters' Hall Debates also serve as an event to highlight how churches in the eighteenth-century England were divided over subscription to confessions.

Though both works have similar arguments, there are differences that make this work distinct. *In Essence One* accurately assumes much of the antitrinitarian context of the seventeenth and eighteenth centuries in England. This work will attempt to provide a clearer context by considering the rise of Socinianism in England and the development of the Protestant Principle that supported Socinian exegesis. *In Essence One* includes Particular Baptists over the course of three centuries in and around the United Kingdom. This work will look at the trinitarian debates among English Baptists in the seventeenth century only as a means to understand the trinitarian context in the eighteenth century. Also, this work will focus prominently on faculty and alumni of Bristol Baptist Academy in the eighteenth century.

Cross wrote a masterful work on the influence of and need for ministerial education among Baptists in *"To Communicate Simply."* He calls to modern-day Baptist colleges in England to recover the value of theology held by Baptist colleges in the eighteenth and nineteenth centuries. His book demonstrates the historical necessity and influence dissenting academies have had upon local churches. Cross argues that Baptists have historically held that a theologically educated ministry is a necessity, and not optional, for effective ministry in the local church. He does not focus exclusively on Bristol Baptist Academy, but he does appeal to the academy as one example of ministerial training that had a positive influence in local Baptist churches of England.

"To Communicate Simply" and this book have in common that the health of local churches is, in part, dependent upon well-trained ministers. And well-trained ministers come from academies and colleges who educate them in right doctrine and provide needed learning. Cross affirms that the Bristol Academy is one such place. So, Cross provides warrant for the argument that doctrinally sound academies produce ministers who then pastor doctrinally sound local churches.

What Cross does not address in his book is the issue of classical trinitarian doctrine. He primarily focuses on the topics of language studies, Bible translations, and missions as examples of how local Baptist churches benefitted by the Baptist colleges. This work will focus exclusively on the topic of the Trinity, and will further support Cross's argument by demonstrating how the Bristol Academy positively influenced the local Baptist churches.

Stephen Holmes addresses the failure of why just reading the Bible does not inevitably lead one to orthodoxy in his chapter "Dangers of Just Reading the Bible" in *Exploring Baptist Origins* edited by Cross and Wood. The context he uses to demonstrate this failure is the Salters' Hall Debates, and specifically the General Baptists. The General Baptists present at Salters' Hall, except for one, refused to subscribe to a trinitarian confessional statement that used nonscriptural terms. Their conviction was that Scripture alone is sufficient for such matters of doctrine. Holmes accepts the position that General Baptists adopted views more similar to Socinianism than to classical Christology.[9] Holmes argues that the General Baptists' isolationism is what caused them to veer toward Socinian views.[10] "What needs to be stressed, though, is that the churches [General Baptists] were generally extremely closed, conservative, and biblicist."[11] This isolationism was in part isolation from the ecclesiastical community. By ecclesiastical community is meant the traditional teaching of the church throughout church history. Holmes is attempting to explain why just reading the Bible in isolation is no guarantee that a person or church will come to orthodox belief. The General Baptists refused to appeal to tradition as a means to understand and explain Scripture. Such persons or churches are capable of coming to orthodox beliefs through reading of Scripture under the guidance of the Holy Spirit.[12] However, the guidance given by the Holy Spirit will not deviate from the guidance given to the churches in the past.

Holmes provides support for an underlying assumption of the thesis of this book by way of giving a negative example. An assumption of the thesis is that classical confessions are useful to guide one's reading of Scripture along orthodox beliefs. The negative example is that of the General Baptists' isolation from such confessions. Though Holmes rarely refers to the Particular Baptists, he does affirm that they held to a Christology "from

---

9. Holmes, "Dangers," in Cross et al., *Exploring Baptist Origins*, 131.

10. For further evidence of the General Baptists' isolationism, see Brown, *English Baptists of the Eighteenth Century*, 29–55.

11. Holmes, "Dangers," in Cross et al., *Exploring Baptist Origins*, 130.

12. Holmes, "Dangers," in Cross et al., *Exploring Baptist Origins*, 137.

the earliest confessional material."[13] Their acceptance of such confessions allowed them to not only subscribe to the trinitarian confession at Salters' Hall, but also to ward off a Socinian reading and understanding of Scripture.

Delimitations

There are five parameters encompassing this work. The first parameter is *time*—the seventeenth and eighteenth centuries. These centuries are chosen not because they were the only centuries to face trinitarian debates, but rather because the eighteenth century was a time when many churches within denominations that had once affirmed orthodox trinitarianism now denied such beliefs.

The second parameter is *location*—England. Just as antitrinitarianism is not restricted by time, neither is it by borders. However, England is the focus because it was the location where Baptists were flourishing the most.

The third parameter is *denominational*—Baptists. In eighteenth-century England, Presbyterians, Anglicans, and to a lesser extent Congregationalists faced antitrinitarian doctrine within their ranks. This dissertation will focus only upon the English Baptists, both the Particular Baptists and the General Baptists.

The fourth parameter is *doctrinal*—the Trinity and Christology. Other doctrines will be considered in this dissertation only as related to the doctrine of the Trinity.

The last parameter is *place*—the Bristol Baptist Academy. Bristol Academy was the first Baptist academy to be founded and it held great influence among Baptist churches in England.

Definition of Terms

Thirteen terms will appear regularly throughout the book. Here is the intended meaning of each term.

Antitrinitarian—the denial of classical trinitarianism.

Arianism—an antitrinitarian view that affirms the oneness of God as consisting of only God the Father. Arianism denies the Son is coeternal, coessential, and coequal with the Father. The Father created the Son before all of creation. Arianism affirms the Son possessed a divine nature as he was created by the Father before all of creation. Arianism affirms Jesus is the Son of God.

---

13. Holmes, "Dangers," in Cross et al., *Exploring Baptist Origins*, 127.

Classical Trinitarianism—the affirmation that God eternally exists in three persons—Father, Son, and Holy Spirit—and each person is fully God, and there is only one God. Classical trinitarianism is the affirmation of the early church councils and creeds that expressed the meaning of trinitarian doctrine. These councils and creeds include the Council of Nicaea 325, the Council of Constantinople 381, the Council of Chalcedon 451, and the Athanasian Creed.

Confessional Trinitarianism—the affirmation of nonscriptural language used to express the meaning of the Trinity that is not antithetical to classical trinitarianism. Examples include, but are not limited to, the Baptist Confessions of Faith in 1644, 1646, and 1677, the Westminster Shorter Catechism, and the Thirty-Nine Articles of Faith.

General Baptist—the designation given to Baptists who affirmed the theology of Jacob Arminius: General Atonement, Free Will, and the Possibility to Fall from Grace.[14]

Nonconfessional Trinitarianism—the denial of nonscriptural language used to express the meaning of the doctrine of the Trinity. This position only affirms scriptural language used in the explanation of the doctrine. This position does not necessarily deny classical trinitarianism, even as it is understood by confessional trinitarians.

Nonsubscribers—those at Salters' Hall who refused to subscribe to confessional language to express trinitarian doctrine and adhered only to scriptural terms to express trinitarian doctrine.

Orthodox Trinitarianism—an inclusive term used to express affirmation of both classical and confessional trinitarianism together.

Particular Baptists—English Baptists who affirmed the five conclusions set out by the Council of Dort in 1619: Particular Atonement, Total Depravity, Unconditional Election, Effectual Grace, and the Perseverance of the Saints.[15]

Protestant Principle—the declaration that the Bible is the only and the perfect rule of faith. Doctrines necessary to believe for faith and practice are only those that are clearly stated in Scripture. Doctrines that are unclear in Scripture are not necessary to believe and are to be given latitude in interpretation. The implementation of the principle is to only judge a person's orthodoxy by the clear doctrines in Scripture without the use of confessional language.

Socinianism—an antitrinitarian view that affirms the oneness of God as consisting of only God the Father. Unitarianism denies that the Son

---

14. McBeth, *Baptist Heritage*, 21.
15. Bebbington, *Baptists Through the Centuries*, 52.

is coeternal, coessential, and coequal with the Father. Socinianism is a form of adoptionism of Jesus as the Son of God. Jesus was a man whom the Father chose to be his Son and placed his Spirit upon him giving him divine authority.

Subscribers—those at Salters' Hall who subscribed to the first article of the Thirty-Nine Articles of Religion, as well as the fifth and sixth questions of the Westminster Shorter Catechism to express trinitarian doctrine.

Unitarianism—an antitrinitarian view that affirms the oneness of God as consisting of only God the Father. Unitarianism denies that the Son is coeternal, coessential, and coequal with the Father. Jesus was only a mere man whom God used as his messenger.

Organization of Study

Chapter 2 will set the stage for the trinitarian debates of the eighteenth century by exploring trinitarian discussions in the seventeenth century. First will be considered the rise of Socinianism in seventeenth-century England. Then will be considered the development of the Protestant Principle.

Chapters 3 and 4 provide the context of the trinitarian climate for Baptists in the eighteenth century. The Salters' Hall Debates exposed the need for a confessional trinitarianism among Baptists, but the issue did not begin in the eighteenth century with the Salters' Hall Debates. The chapters will first go back to the seventeenth century. In this century both Particular and General Baptists faced potential trinitarian heresy among their ranks. The difference is in how both groups of Baptists responded to the challenge. Chapter 3 focuses on the General Baptists' response to Matthew Caffyn. Chapter 4 concentrates on the Particular Baptists' response to Thomas Collier.

Chapter 5 relates the histories of Broadmead Baptist Church, Bristol Baptist Academy, and the Salters' Hall Debates. Broadmead will be shown to be a Particular Baptist church that had settled on the *Second London Baptist Confession of Faith* of 1689 prior to the close of the eighteenth century. From this church is started the Bristol Baptist Academy that then has the same conviction of confessional doctrine. Focus will be given to Bernard Foskett, the first principal of the Academy and particularly to his commitment to orthodox trinitarianism. Then, the history of the Salters' Hall will show that the primary issue was that of confessional trinitarianism.

Chapter 6 turns attention to the trinitarianism taught at the Bristol Baptist Academy. Bristol Academy was aware of the Salters' Hall Debates and responded by maintaining orthodox trinitarianism. The chapter will explore the trinitarian teaching of Bristol Academy as evidenced by its library, curriculum, and its third principal, Caleb Evans.

Chapter 7 will focus on four alumni of Bristol Academy. Two of the alumni will serve as an example of students who later pastored Baptist churches and maintained orthodox trinitarianism as taught at the academy. One alumnus, who also served for a time as a tutor at Bristol Academy, will be considered as he was accused of being antitrinitarian at the academy. And, finally, one alumnus will serve as an example that not all students maintained the teaching they had received at the academy.

Chapter 8 concludes with a review and then provides reflections on topics in the paper, along with recommendations for further study.

2

"The Bible Only Is the Religion of Protestants!"

Seventeenth-Century Answers to Eighteenth-Century Questions

WHY DID A THEOLOGICAL debate in a local Presbyterian church in Exeter become so public and heated in London by the three dissenting denominations? Why would ministers not subscribe to trinitarian confessional language if they sincerely affirmed classical trinitarianism? And why did Baptists at Salters' Hall divide roughly along Particular and General identity lines when it came to subscription? The answers to the first two questions are the subject of this chapter. The answer to the last question brings together the first two answers within the context of Particular and General Baptists in the seventeenth century, which will be considered in the next chapters.

The chapter will begin with an answer to the first question. The three denominations in London were concerned about the rise of antitrinitarianism among churches across eighteenth-century England. The concern was true of both subscribers and nonsubscribers at Salters' Hall. Antitrinitarianism was not a novel concept in the 1700s. Its emergence can be traced back to the preceding century. The Reformation had brought many doctrinal changes to the church, but trinitarian doctrine was left untouched. The reason was that both the Catholic trinitarian doctrine and Reformation trinitarian doctrine were in agreeance. And so, for a time, trinitarian doctrine was received by the Church of England and the dissenting churches as settled in the Nicene and post-Nicene eras. This is not to suggest that some of the dissenters did not hold antitrinitarian views. Rather, those who were antitrinitarian did not have a voice to express their opinions. At least they did not have a voice until the 1640s. "It was in this turbulent decade that the seeds of future trinitarian conflicts were sown."[1]

The second question will be addressed next. Sincere classical trinitarians at Salters' Hall would not subscribe to trinitarian confessions due to their profound respect for the sufficiency of Scripture. The Reformation's slogan and practice of sola Scriptura replaced the authority of church doctrinal tradition with the authority of Scripture within the Church. However, sola Scriptura was not intended to eliminate tradition from the Church. The Reformers affirmed and utilized traditional teachings of doctrine, such as trinitarian doctrine, in their own teachings. Nevertheless, some orthodox teachers in the seventeenth century developed the Protestant Principle. This principle transformed *sola* Scriptura into *nuda* Scriptura, meaning Scripture only. While well-intentioned, this principle disregarded the language of tradition and confessions regarding doctrine in favor of scriptural language alone.

Antitrinitarian Presence in Seventeenth-Century England

Antitrinitarianism, particularly Socinianism, found a foothold in England during the seventeenth century. Richard Muller provides the background for its arrival by tracing the evolution of trinitarian doctrine during the Reformation. Francis Cheynell then presents evidence of how Socinianism made its way into England.

Setting the Stage for the Debate

Antitrinitarian views were not new debates within the church. The church had antitrinitarian advocates since the Patristic era, during the Medieval era, and into the Reformation era. Yet, because their views were not broadly accepted by the church, the voices of these advocates remained largely silent. The antitrinitarian voice of seventeenth-century England, however, gained renewed interest with lasting consequences. Muller effectively sets the stage for the trinitarian debate of that era. He devotes his final volume of Post-Reformation Reformed Dogmatics to *The Triunity of God*. Muller helps modern-day listeners hear the voice of these characters.

---

1. Dixon, *Nice and Hot Disputes*, 35.

The Trajectory of Trinitarian Doctrine

Comparing the historical paths of church doctrines, Muller concludes that "the trajectory of trinitarian thought in sixteenth and seventeenth centuries is markedly different" from other doctrinal issues, such as the doctrines of Scripture and of God's divine essence and attributes.[2] He provides three reasons for the divergence of trajectories. The first reason is general and true of all doctrinal legacies, not just trinitarianism. The patterns by which doctrines are transmitted from one era to another, such as from the Middle Ages to the Reformation and then to early orthodoxy,[3] "remain as varied as the doctrines and many doctrinal nuances themselves."[4] Theologians in the different eras who would agree on the substance of a doctrinal issue would not necessarily use the same "formulae and patterns of argument."[5] The result was that doctrines were susceptible to diverging paths due to the diverse methods theologians employed to articulate and justify their positions.

The second and third reasons for the divergent trajectory of trinitarian doctrine are unique to the doctrine itself. Trinitarian doctrine is unique because it "stands as a carefully defined dogma of ecumenical orthodoxy" unlike other doctrines.[6] Muller's point is that the doctrine of the Trinity has an older and more widely accepted creedal definition than do other doctrines such as Scripture or the divine essence and attributes. The Reformers and the Roman Catholic Church both accepted the creedal definition of the Trinity as defined in the Patristic era. For this reason, the substance of trinitarian doctrine was not a matter of debate in the Reformation. Where the Reformers differed from the Roman Catholic Church was in the weight or degree of authority granted to the patristic creeds and church councils. The Reformers affirmed the traditional teaching regarding the Trinity; however, they did not regard the traditional teaching as on the same normative level as that of Scripture. Creeds could only have a derivative normality as they stood upon scriptural teaching. Muller concludes that the Reformers' contribution to trinitarian orthodoxy was "the grounding of the formulae and the traditional language more completely and explicitly on Scripture

---

2. Muller, *Triunity of God*, 17.

3. The reference to "early orthodoxy" is used by Muller to depict the time span of 1565–1640. Early orthodoxy "was the era of the confessional solidification of Protestantism." Muller, *Prolegomena to Theology*, 31.

4. Muller, *Triunity of God*, 17.

5. Muller, *Triunity of God*, 18.

6. Muller, *Triunity of God*, 18.

than had been done for centuries."[7] Trinitarian doctrine, therefore, entered the seventeenth century with a traditional and exegetical basis.

The Challenge of Traditional Trinitarianism

This traditional and exegetical foundation for the Trinity, however, faced a significant challenge in the seventeenth century. The challenge came not by way of denying the role of tradition nor by way of denying the normative standard of Scripture. The seventeenth-century challengers of the Trinity affirmed both tradition and Scripture. This is the third unique divergent trajectory of trinitarian doctrine. The defenders of the Trinity,[8] as defined by the church since the Patristic era, now had to develop trinitarian doctrine "in the context of fairly consistent denial of the doctrine by a number of highly insistent thinkers and groups who became increasingly adept at using both Scripture and early patristic tradition *against* the church's dogma" of the Trinity.[9] The trinitarian challengers had in essence taken the tools of the trinitarian defenders for use in their own antitrinitarian offense.

The defenders not only had to defend the doctrine of the Trinity but also defend their use of tradition and Scripture in distinction from that of their challengers. Regarding Scripture, the defenders of the Trinity explained their position in biblical and exegetical terms but had to avoid and deny the "starkly rational biblicism" as used by the challengers.[10] The defenders, therefore, could not just cite texts that affirmed their trinitarian beliefs because the challengers would also cite texts for their position. The defenders' exegetical task was all the more difficult because they were reluctant to use philosophical terminology that tended to speculation.[11] Scott Swain argues that because the Reformers struggled with the new exegetical tools of the Enlightenment to show the form of trinitarian theology from Scripture, they utilized both *analogia Scriptura* and *analogia fidei* to exhibit the Trinity in Scripture.[12]

The defenders of the Trinity, after stating their exegetical defense of the Trinity, would then turn to tradition; but even then they had to distinguish themselves from their challengers. Muller states, "The development of

---

7. Muller, *Triunity of God*, 19.

8. "Defenders of the Trinity" specifically meant those who defended orthodox trinitarian doctrine in the seventeenth century.

9. Muller, *Triunity of God*, 19 (emphasis added).

10. Muller, *Triunity of God*, 21.

11. Muller, *Triunity of God*, 21.

12. Swain, "Trinity in the Reformers," in Emery and Levering, *Oxford Handbook*, 227–39.

the Protestant orthodox doctrine of the Trinity can be described as a battle over the tradition or even as a battle between differing modes of reception of tradition."[13] The battle was over which church fathers the defenders and challengers would choose from. The reason is that the church fathers "if not necessarily different in fundamental intentionality . . . offered a rather different expression of the triadic nature of the Godhead than the teaching of Nicene and post-Nicene fathers."[14] Both defenders and challengers of the Trinity could find, seemingly, support for their different beliefs from among the church fathers.

Muller sums up his tracing of the trinitarian trajectory, "In short, the Reformed orthodox doctrine of the Trinity was no simple restatement of the patristic norms—rather it was a complex development of doctrine intended to recover, respect, and use the patristic definitions and arguments insofar as they could be argued anew exegetically, under the authority of the biblical norm."[15] His analysis of the course trinitarian doctrine traveled sets the stage for the seventeenth-century trinitarian debate in three ways. First, the trinitarian debate of the seventeenth century arose after a long period of silence. Trinitarian doctrine had been a near settled doctrine in the church throughout the previous centuries. Antitrinitarians had arisen within the church throughout these centuries before, but the seventeenth-century antitrinitarians arose in a way "not seen since the patristic period."[16] Second, the trinitarian debate of the seventeenth century agreed on the authority of Scripture. The antitrinitarians were not those who opposed Scripture but sincerely wanted to understand and rightly apply Scripture. Also, both trinitarians and antitrinitarians were committed to the use of Scripture language. This commitment will lead some trinitarians to only affirm scriptural language and avoid confessional language. And third, the trinitarian debate of the seventeenth century agreed on the use of tradition. The antitrinitarians saw themselves standing in the tradition of church teaching and not outside of it. Likewise, trinitarians, though committed to scriptural language, could and did utilize the confessional language of the creeds.

Francis Cheynell

While Muller reflects on the formation of the trinitarian debate in the seventeenth century, it would be beneficial to listen to someone who personally

---

13. Muller, *Triunity of God*, 21.
14. Muller, *Triunity of God*, 21.
15. Muller, *Triunity of God*, 22.
16. Muller, *Triunity of God*, 19.

experienced and participated in the debate. One such person is Francis Cheynell (*bap.* 1608, *d.* 1665).[17] Cheynell became anxious with the presence of Socinianism in England. Though Socinian beliefs were not widely accepted by those in the academies or churches of England, Cheynell suspected there were advocates of the belief, especially by the Archbishop of Canterbury, William Laud. In 1643, Cheynell wrote *The Rise, Growth and Danger of Socinianisme together with a Plaine Discovery of a Desperate Designe of Corrupting the Protestant Religion*. This was Cheynell's first entrance into the trinitarian debate and his way to refute and combat rising antitrinitarianism.[18] Cheynell's work served as a warning about the presence of Socinianism in England and the need for Parliament to address it.

The Rise of Socinianism

Rise, Growth and Danger is divided into six chapters. The first chapter is "The Rise of Socinianisme." Cheynell begins by demonstrating that Socinianism is not a new heresy. The Socinians have merely "refined or enlarged the ancient heresies."[19] Cheynell highlights, or lists, over a dozen trinitarian heresies with whom the Socinians are alike: Arians, Photinians, Samosatenians, Nestorians, Noetians, Macidonians, Valentinians, Marcionites, Cerdonians, Manichees, Pelagians, Apollinarians, Sabellius, and the Donatists.[20] Each of these heresies are distinct in their own way from one another. Cheynell's point is not that Socinians are equal in form with the ancient heresies.[21] Rather, Cheynell's point is that the Socinians agree in substance with each of these antitrinitarian groups; that substance being the denial of the Son to be "Consubstantiall with the Father."[22]

Although Socinianism isn't a novel heresy, Cheynell's primary concern in this introductory chapter is how the continental church in the recent past handled such a heresy with such carelessness and naivety.[23] In Cheynell's

---

17. Pooley, "Cheynell, Francis."

18. Seven years later, in 1650, Cheynell wrote *Divine Trinunity of the Father, Son, and Holy Spirit*.

19. Cheynell, *Rise, Growth and Danger*, 1.

20. Cheynell, *Rise, Growth and Danger*, 5.

21. At times, Cheynell admits that the ancient heresies are better than modern Socinianism. "The Socinians are farre worse then Nestorius, for they do not onlely deny, that the selfe same person who was borne of the Virgin, is the second person in the Trinity, but they utterly deny that there is any second Person, or third Person which is Consubstantiall with the Father." Cheynell, *Rise, Growth and Danger*, 5.

22. Cheynell, *Rise, Growth and Danger*, 2.

23. "I would willingly discourse at large of some later passages, and subtile

estimation, the sixteenth-century continental churches mistook these heretics as true Protestants, and their "vaine curiosity" into the subject matter made them "a mere prey to these subtle Hereticks."[24] Cheynell worried that churches in England in the seventeenth century would follow the continental churches and not take Socinianism seriously. Thereby, Socinianism would grow within the church and England as it did in the sixteenth-century continental churches.

Examples of heretics with whom the continental church dealt too lightly with are Valentinus, Lalius Socinus, and Faustus Socinus. By focusing on these three individuals, Cheynell traces the rise of Socinianism as a modern heresy back to sixteenth-century Italy. He begins with Valentinus Gentilis. In 1558, Valentinus was brought before a Genevan church senate to explain his teaching of the Trinity. Cheynell states Valentinus's understanding of the Trinity as "the God of Israel is the only true God the Father of Jesus Christ; and so by opposing the Father to the Son, and affirming that the Father only was the true God, he did clearly deny the Son to be the true God."[25] The issue at hand for Valentinus was that of essence. Valentinus held that the Father had a divine essence while the Son and Spirit "had an Essence different from the Divine Essence."[26] Upon the senate's correction of Valentinus's heretical views, Valentinus repented of his heresy.

Cheynell is disappointed, to say the least, with the senate's response.[27] The senate forgave Valentinus and freed him from prison only with the promise from him in return that he would not leave the city without permission. Valentinus did promise, but he soon then broke that promise. He fled to neighboring towns and countries, eventually spending time in Poland. For eight years, Valentinus disseminated his heretical teachings across Europe during his journey. In 1566, Valentinus found himself before another church senate under the jurisdiction of Bern.[28] Unlike his first appearance before a church senate, Valentinus would not repent of his teaching and the senate would not show him mercy. Valentinus was sentenced to death and

---

inventions by which Socinianisme was introduced in forraine parts, and in some parts established by the suffrage and subscription of too many eminent wits, and great Scholars." Cheynell, *Rise, Growth and Danger*, 5.

24. Cheynell, *Rise, Growth and Danger*, 7.
25. Cheynell, *Rise, Growth and Danger*, 8.
26. Cheynell, *Rise, Growth and Danger*, 9.
27. "Behold the mercy of Geneva to one that was but hopefull, though he had beene an Heretick, a Schismatick, a Seducer, they forgave him, and gave him leave to come forth of prison, without taking any Sureties." Cheynell, *Rise, Growth and Danger*, 10.
28. Cheynell, *Rise, Growth and Danger*, 12; Aretius and South, *Short History of Valentinus*, 27–28.

then executed. In Cheynell's estimation, this was a just and right decision by the senate. Death was the "deserved punishment" because Valentinus would "not by prayers, teares, arguments, entreaties, be wrought upon to change his mind: he had a faire warning given him before, by the Senate of Geneva, if he had had the grace to have taken it."[29]

Cheynell gives attention to Valentinus as an example to the English Parliament; the example being how not to handle cases of antitrinitarianism. The Genevan senate showed mercy at the beginning to Valentinus. Such mercy only led to the spread of antitrinitarian views across the continent. Cheynell recommends that "Socinians are not to be suffered in any State, for they will not shew any obedience or respect to Magistrates."[30] The Parliament should act decisively against Socinianism in England if they are not to suffer the same fate as Europe.

Cheynell moves his attention to the more popular of Socinian heretics from Italy, and for whom Socinianism receives its label. They are the uncle and nephew Lalius and Faustus Socinus. Lalius, the uncle, was the tutor and Faustus, the nephew, was the disciple. Though Lalius lived concurrently with Valentinus, he remained in the shadows with his heresy, while Valentinus lived in the light with his. Cheynell says that Lalius "most of this while [in the days of Valentinus], played least in light, till he went quite out of sight, in the yeare 1562."[31] Because Lalius "carried matters [his heretical views] thus closely" and employed "sleight of wit and hand," he was only suspected of being a "seducer" three years prior to his death.[32] Rather than Lalius's death bringing an end to the spread of his heresy, it became the catalyst for the advancement of his views, for Faustus was not to stay in the shadows with his uncle's teachings. Cheynell says, "Therefore certainly most of his [Lalius's] opinions would have died with him, had not this unlucky Faustus poysoned the world with them."[33]

Cheynell does not go into detail of Lalius's heretical views other than to say that "the heresy doth directly strike at the Nature, Person, Offices, Satisfaction, Sacraments of Christ."[34] Cheynell seemingly does not want to detail Lalius's views so as not to be guilty of propagating, even unintentionally, the Socinian heresy. The reason for this lack of detail appears to be Cheynell's concern of what is currently happening in England. A work

29. Cheynell, *Rise, Growth and Danger*, 13.
30. Cheynell, *Rise, Growth and Danger*, 33.
31. Cheynell, *Rise, Growth and Danger*, 13.
32. Cheynell, *Rise, Growth and Danger*, 15.
33. Cheynell, *Rise, Growth and Danger*, 15.
34. Cheynell, *Rise, Growth and Danger*, 14.

of Faustus had been translated into English and was being read by a Mr. Webberly at the Lincolne College.[35] The Socinian heresy will never die with its predecessors if their writings are kept alive. Not only should Socinian heretics be dealt with severely, as with Valentinus, but their works should also perish with them.

"So much for Lalius" and now on to Faustus.[36] If Lalius was the architect of Socinianism, then Faustus was the builder. "Lalius did contribute materials" but it was Faustus who "added form and method to that monstrous body of errours and blasphemies which we call Socinianism."[37] As with Lalius, Cheynell does not detail Faustus's teachings. Cheynell has already asserted that Socinianism is no new heresy but only an ancient one that denies the Son is of equal substance with the Father.

Cheynell's main concern with Faustus is his subtlety "to disgrace truth by scoffes and slanders."[38] He gives two examples. The first is Faustus's subtlety in evangelism. Faustus warned Christians that the doctrine asserting Christ's divinity rendered Christian religion absurd to Jews and Turks.[39] Cheynell worried that such sentiment for the conversion of Jews and Muslims would persuade Christians to abandon a core tenet of the Christian faith.[40] Cheynell's other example is Faustus's subtlety with Scripture. Though Faustus "pretended to be ruled by Scripture, it is most evident that all his [Faustus's] Art was to withdraw men from hearkening to the plainest Texts of Scripture which doe contradict blinde carnal reason."[41] This might be Cheynell's primary concern with Faustus. Cheynell worried that Christians would be lured by the appeal to reason to judge the revelation of Scripture.

Cheynell's opening chapter on the rise of Socinianism is not to give a detailed and historical account for how Socinianism came to fruition. His intent is to warn the churches of England of the rising tide of Socinianism into their country. The Socinian heresy is not a modern theory that

---

35. Cheynell, *Rise, Growth and Danger*, 46.

36. Cheynell, *Rise, Growth and Danger*, 17. Cheynell's curt transition from Lalius to Faustus reflects his contempt for Lalius and his wish to leave Lalius in the grave along with his teachings.

37. Cheynell, *Rise, Growth and Danger*, 13.

38. Cheynell, *Rise, Growth and Danger*, 18–19.

39. Cheynell, *Rise, Growth and Danger*, 19.

40. "Now the Socinians would have us to deny Christ to be God, that we may convert Turkes and Jewes to the Christian faith: as if the best way to convert men to the Christian faith, were to deny a prime article of our Christian faith; or as if Jews and Turks would have a better opinion of Christ, if the Christians should deny him to be God, and so harden them in their beloved blasphemies." Cheynell, *Rise, Growth and Danger*, 19.

41. Cheynell, *Rise, Growth and Danger*, 20–21.

should be considered—it is an ancient heresy. And as with all heresies, it is to be opposed and eradicated. If not, then England will go the way of other European countries that have been infected with such teaching. However, Cheynell fears the church in England has not acted swiftly against Socinianism but has been intrigued by its subtle teachers.

The Presence of Socinianism

Cheynell provides three men as evidence that a Socinian presence was taking hold in England: Mr. Webberly, the Archbishop of Canterbury, and William Chillingworth. In the preface to *Rise, Growth and Presence* Cheynell speaks of a Mr. Webberly. Parliament appointed Cheynell to the University of Oxford to "settle peace and truth" and to restore its "ancient order."[42] During this appointment, Cheynell recounts a notice issued about a "pestilent book that is highly prejudicial to both truth and peace."[43] The book was discovered in the possession of Mr. Webberly, a fellow at Lincoln College.[44] Cheynell does not name the book. He only describes it as a "Socinian Master-peece" translated into English from Latin.[45] Though Webberly claimed the book was only for his own personal study, Cheynell was convinced Webberly intended the book to be published in print "for the benefit of this Nation."[46] One may ask what danger there was in one Socinian book being published into English. For Cheynell, the translation of this book and the intent to publish it demonstrates how brazen Socinians had become in England. "Now they think they may own the businesse they dare appeare in their proper colours, and blaspheme Christ in plaine English."[47]

---

42. Cheynell, "Epistle Dedicatory," in Cheynell, *Rise, Growth and Danger*. Philip Dixon gives the date of this event as 1648. Dixon, *Nice and Hot*, 48. His date of the event, however, is five years after the publication date of *Rise, Growth and Danger* in 1643, which publication date Dixon affirms in his citation of the book. The question is whether the event in question occurred before or after the publication of Cheynell's book. In support of Dixon's later date is the fact that Parliament in 1648 appointed Cheynell as a reforming visitor to the University of Oxford. Pooley, "Cheynell, Francis," para. 4. If this is the appointment Cheynell refers to in his "Epistle Dedicatory" and therefore when he discovered this Socinian book, then the "Epistle Dedicatory" would have to have been written years after the book was published. However, "Epistle Dedicatory" in *Rise, Growth and Danger* is stated by Cheynell to have been written on April 18, 1643. Dixon does not address the discrepancy of dates.

43. Cheynell, "Epistle Dedicatory," in Cheynell, *Rise, Growth and Danger*.

44. Cheynell, *Rise, Growth and Danger*, 46.

45. Cheynell, "Epistle Dedicatory," in Cheynell, *Rise, Growth and Danger*.

46. Cheynell, "Epistle Dedicatory," in Cheynell, *Rise, Growth and Danger*.

47. Cheynell, *Rise, Growth and Danger*, 46.

While Mr. Webberly may have some influence as a fellow at the Lincoln College, Cheynell turns his attention to a man of greater role and influence—William Laud, the Archbishop of Canterbury. Cheynell has three concerns with the Archbishop: his tolerance of Arminianism, his appointment of Chillingworth, and his confidence in reason. Though the main title of Cheynell's work is *The Rise, Growth and Danger of Socinianism*, Cheynell constantly attacks Arminianism throughout the book. In fact, the very last line of the full title lists Arminian doctrines and practices as a reason for the rise of heretics and sectaries in England. In "The Epistle Dedicatory," Cheynell perceives Arminianism and Socinianism working together to weaken the church and state, "But there are other Philistines, namely Arminian and Socinian Philistines, by which Church and State are much endangered, and it is the businesse now in hand to lay open their mystery of iniquity to the publique view."[48] The two work hand-in-hand because Cheynell believes that "Arminianisme is a faire step to Socinianisme."[49]

Cheynell does not appear to claim Arminians are Socinian. He asserts that Arminians share common convictions with Socinians. Cheynell considers these common convictions as substantive enough to lead Arminians to the Socinian camp. The common connections are two: anti-Reformed doctrine and criteria for fundamental doctrine. Arminians and Socinians share anti-Reformed doctrine in common. "The Socinians have one Principle that draws a great party after them of all heretikes, & sectaries. Nothing (say they) is Fundamentally necessary to salvation but only Faith or obedience to the commands of Christ, for they make faith & obedience all one, *ut supra*."[50] Cheynell's point is that Arminians and Socinians do not adhere to the Reformed doctrine of the necessary work of the Holy Spirit to regenerate a person nor to illumine the truths of Scripture. A person is free to decide salvation for himself or by reason to determine truth for himself. "Nay Arminians and Socinians both tell us, that there is no need of preaching: saving Truths are sufficiently manifested."[51] For the Arminians, it is the supremacy of "universal grace" and for the Socinians it is "right reason" over the effective and necessary work of the Holy Spirit for salvation and illumination.[52]

Arminians and Socinians also hold in common that no doctrine is fundamental that is not agreed upon throughout church history:

---

48. Cheynell, "Epistle Dedicatory," in Cheynell, *Rise, Growth and Danger*.
49. Cheynell, *Rise, Growth and Danger*, 35.
50. Cheynell, *Rise, Growth and Danger*, 37.
51. Cheynell, *Rise, Growth and Danger*, 33.
52. Cheynell, *Rise, Growth and Danger*, 44.

> Must we then subscribe to that Arminian and Socinian principle, *Nullum dogma controversum est fundamentale?* When a point begins to be controverted shall it cease to be Fundamentall? By this meanes we may bring in an *Atheisticall Libertinisme* into the Church; we shall have no more articles of our Faith, then the *Arminians*, or *Socinians* please to leave us.[53]

The fundamental principle is that fundamental doctrine is not contested within the church. Fundamental doctrine for the Arminians would deny special grace. Fundamental doctrine for the Socinians would deny the deity of Christ. Cheynell's concern is that doctrine reduced to a common denominator is no saving doctrine.

With this connection made between Arminianism and Socinianism, Cheynell insinuates that the Archbishop has allowed Socinianism to spread throughout England by his tolerance of Arminianism: "All the Grand-Malignants, Arminians, Papifts, and Socinians are of one confederacy, all united under one head the Arch-Bishop of Canterbury, the Patriarch or Pope of this British world."[54] Cheynell does not directly label the Archbishop as an Arminian, but he does claim that the Archbishop has promoted Arminianism by his tolerance of it.[55] One example given by Cheynell is from the Archbishop's 1639 work, *Conference with Fisher*. This is an expanded version of his 1624 appendix to Francis White's account of his conferences with the Jesuit Fisher.[56] Anthony Milton describes the conference as discussing the relationship of salvation to local church membership and the authority of church and Scriptures, and how much erroneous belief might discount salvation.[57] In Milton's estimation, "Laud expounded a carefully moderate position, which displayed a notable reluctance to brand churches or individuals with heresy, or to speculate on which doctrines might deprive an individual of salvation."[58] Cheynell cites the Archbishop as stating

---

53. Cheynell, *Rise, Growth and Danger*, 45. The principle is, "*No controversial doctrine is fundamental.*"

54. Cheynell, "Epistle Dedicatory," in Cheynell, *Rise, Growth and Danger*.

55. John Goodwin believed that Laudian Arminianism was owed more to political reasons because Puritan theology was unpopular with most people in England. Coffey, *John Goodwin*, 211.

56. Cheynell does not totally discount the 1624 edition. "I must confesse there is good learning in that book of his, which was printed 1624. I should doe him wrong if I should deny it; and though there are some passages which found ill, yet I have charity enough to put a good construction upon most of them." But the later 1639 edition is really another book in which Cheynell believes the Archbishop "had altered his Religion in those 15 yeares." Cheynell, *Rise, Growth and Danger*, 40.

57. Milton, "Laud, William," para. 15.

58. Milton, "Laud, William," para. 15.

that confession of the godhead of the Son and the Holy Spirit as "nicities."[59] Cheynell interprets the use of "nicities" as follows, "If you will be exact, you may say that Christ is God, but that's but a nicety, somewhat more then needs, a man may be saved without it; for the Arminians say Athanasius was too bold to prefix that Proud Preface before his Creed, Whosoever will be saved, &c. and I make no doubt but his Grace was led much by them, he had such high thoughts of the Arminian conceits."[60] The Archbishop, according to Cheynell, is in agreement with the Arminians that a person should not be burdened with too much doctrine to confess in order to be saved, especially in confession of the godhead as affirmed by Athanasius.

The Archbishop is not only guilty of spreading Socinianism through his tolerance of Arminianism, but also by his appointment of William Chillingworth, "It is well known that the Arch-Bishop did highly favour, and frequently employ men shrewdly suspected for Socinianisme. Master Chillingworth, to speak modestly, hath been too patient, being so deeply charged by Knot for his inclining towards some Socinian Tenets."[61] Cheynell's critique of Chillingworth is Chillingworth's placement of reason above revelation, which is a Socinian principle.

The Reformed principle that reason is to submit to revelation is turned upside down by the Socinians. The Reformed principle posits that the Holy Spirit speaks through the Scriptures (and illuminates the hearts and minds of men with a radiant light, enabling them to comprehend the Scriptures) as the Judge of controversies. In response, the Socinians argue that the judgment of sound Reason becomes ineffective and lacks authority before the illumination of the Holy Spirit.[62] Cheynell considers Chillingworth as being nearer the Socinian principle than the Reformed principle. He cites Chillingworth from his *Religion of Protestants*, "The Scripture is not to be believed finally for itselfe, but for the matter contained in it, so that if men did believe the doctrine contained in the Scripture, it should no way hinder their salvation not to know whether there were any Scripture or no."[63] Chillingworth places high regard on man's reason to understand Scripture.

More will be said about Chillingworth and his *Religion of Protestants* in the next section, "The Protestant Principle." Whether Cheynell is correct in asserting that Chillingworth was a Socinian is a topic for debate. Contemporaries in Chillingworth's day considered him as such. Yet, Chillingworth

59. Cheynell, *Rise, Growth and Danger*, 42.
60. Cheynell, *Rise, Growth and Danger*, 43.
61. Cheynell, *Rise, Growth and Danger*, 34.
62. Cheynell, *Rise, Growth and Danger*, 27.
63. Cheynell, *Rise, Growth and Danger*, 28.

denied he was a Socininian. In *Religion of Protestants*, Chillingworth answers Edward Knott's argument that the rejection of the Roman Catholic Church's infallibility leads to Socinianism, "Neither is it possible for the wit of man by any good, or so much as probable consequence, from the denial of the Churches Infallibility to deduce any one of the ancient Heresies, or any one error of the Socinians, which are the Heresies here entreated of."[64] Chillingworth in this reply classifies Socinianism as a heresy and he rejects that he is leading others towards it. For Cheynell, however, this denial is not adequate since he places Chillingworth on the side of the Socinian principle and not the Reformed principle. Chillingworth is not in agreement, at least fully, with the Reformed principle. He advances what is a core tenet of Socinianism, that revelation is under the authority of reason. But that does not de facto make him Socinian. One could argue that the logical conclusion of his position leads one to Socinianism, but Chillingworth may have chosen not to go that far.

Chillingworth's Socinian principle of reason over revelation gained further ground in England by the Archbishop's support of him. This leads into Cheynell's third concern over the Archbishop. Like Chillingworth, the Archbishop places emphasis on reason to judge revelation. In reference back to the Archbishop's *Conference with Fisher*, Cheynell cites him as saying, "The Mysteries of Faith doe not contradict Reason, for Reason by her own light can discover how firmly the principles of Religion are true."[65] Cheynell is not negating the use of nor the validity of reason in religious matters. For had the Archbishop said "reason by the light of Scripture, or by the light of the Spirit," Cheynell would have gladly affirmed such a principle.[66] Reason, however, has limitations. Reason is unable to grasp by its own power the great truths of Scripture. Cheynell provides a list of these truths as the resurrection of the body, three persons in the godhead and yet one God, the Word made flesh, the virgin birth, and the atonement.[67] All these truths elude man's reason without the illumination of the Holy Spirit.

If reason is to be elevated above revelation, then the Christian faith would be reduced to what can only be substantiated by reason. Such a faith, says Cheynell, is not Christian, "In like manner the Arch Bishop, if he will be true to this Principle he hath laid down, must affirm that no man shal be daned for rejecting any Articles of the Christian Faith, which reason by her own light cannot discover to be true, and so manifestly true that

---

64. Chillingworth, Preface to *Religion of Protestants* sec. 10.
65. Cheynell, *Rise, Growth and Danger*, 40.
66. Cheynell, *Rise, Growth and Danger*, 40.
67. Cheynell, *Rise, Growth and Danger*, 41.

they ought to be firmly beleeved. If this be not Socinianisme in the highest, let the impartial Reader judge."[68] In effect, Cheynell is saying that the Archbishop cannot logically uphold all the Thirty-Nine Articles held by the Church of England because reason "by her own light" cannot comprehend all the statements contained therein.

Cheynell's *Rise, Growth and Danger* is one of the earliest works in England to call attention to the presence of Socinianism in the country. Though Cheynell's work is polemical and he argues more from comparison to show that one is guilty of Socinianism, he does demonstrate that Socinianism had a foothold in seventeenth-century England. Socinian advocates in a short time would become much bolder in advancing their position in print.[69]

The Protestant Principle

The nonsubscribers at Salters' Hall concluded the debates with a list of their own advices to the controversy at Exeter. These advices are found in the anonymous writing *An Authentick Account of Several Things Done and Agreed upon by the Dissenting Ministers Lately Assembled at Salters-Hall*. Among the eight advices, the nonsubscribers appeal to the "Protestant Principle." The whole of this fourth advice is as follows:

> If after all, a publick Hearing be insisted on, we think the Protestant Principle, that *the Bible is the only and the perfect Rule of Faith*, obliges those who have the Case before them, not to condemn any Man upon the Authority of Humane Decisions, or because he consents not to Humane Forms or Phrases: But then only is He to be censured, as *not holding the Faith necessary to Salvation*, when it appears that he contradicts, or refuses to own, the *plain and express Declarations of Holy Scripture*, in what is there made necessary to be believed, and in Matters there solely revealed. And we trust that All will treat the Servants of their common Lord, as they who expect the final Decision at his appearing.[70]

The Protestant Principle as defined by the nonsubscribers is that the Bible is "the only and perfect rule of faith." Whereas Scripture is the rule of faith in all matters, the Protestant Principle is limited only to the *use* of

---

68. Cheynell, *Rise, Growth and Danger*, 42.

69. In 1648 John Biddle (infamously referred to as "the father of English Unitarianism") published his antitrinitarian work *A Confession of Faith Touching the Holy Trinity, According to the Scripture*.

70. *Authentick Account*, 8–9.

Scripture as a rule of faith in all matters. That is, a person may judge the orthodoxy of another person only in the matters where scriptural declarations are "plain and express." Such matters that are plain have no alternative interpretations and are to be believed by all persons who claim the Christian faith. In matters where scriptural declarations are unclear, greater latitude in interpretation is to be granted.

Since the nonsubscribers limited the use of Scripture as a rule of faith in all matters, they excluded the use of confessions as a standard of faith in all matters. Confessions of faith come under the banner of "human decisions . . . human forms or phrases." In matters that are clear, confessional language is unnecessary as a standard due to the clarity of the truth revealed in Scripture. Scriptural language is sufficient to judge the orthodoxy of a person. The person should only be judged according to his affirmation or denial of the scriptural declaration. In matters that are unclear, confessional language is unjustified as a standard because no one person's conscience is to be the rule of another person's belief.

As Contrasted to Sola Scriptura

The Protestant Principle stems from the reformational principle sola Scriptura. Sola Scriptura is the appeal to Scripture as the ultimate authority in matters of faith and doctrine. The Reformers appealed to sola Scriptura as a means to controvert the Roman Catholic Church's appeal to church tradition as equal authority with Scripture. This is not to suggest that the Reformers appealed to Scripture alone in matters of faith and rejected classical confessions and teachings of the church. Muller maintains that, especially in the doctrine of the Trinity, the Reformers' greater work "was the grounding of the formulae and traditional language more completely and explicitly on Scripture than had been done for centuries."[71] The Reformers received the traditional doctrines, such as the Trinity, but then sought to secure the truth upon Scripture.

The Protestant Principle, however, is not the same as the Reformer's sola Scriptura. Sola Scriptura holds the Bible as authoritative over tradition. The Protestant Principle holds the Bible as exclusive to tradition. The Socinians used the Protestant Principle to overturn traditional teaching regarding the Trinity. They viewed trinitarian doctrine "as yet another manifestation of the anti-Christian designs of the Roman Church."[72] As perceived inheritors of the Reformation, many Socinians sought to fulfill the Reformation

---

71. Muller, *Triunity of God*, 19.
72. Dixon, *Nice and Hot*, 42.

by appealing to Scripture only over and against the tradition of the Trinity, as much as the Reformers did against transubstantiation.[73]

As Articulated by Chillingworth

William Chillingworth's 1638 *Religion of Protestants* shaped the understanding and application of the Protestant Principle for the seventeenth and eighteenth centuries.[74] Chillingworth is responding to Edward Knott's work *Mercy and Truth, or, Charity Maintain'd by Catholiques* written in 1634. Knott warns that the Protestant religion's rejection of the Roman Catholic Church's infallibility will lead them to Socinianism. Knott specifically cites and charges Chillingworth as one who had succumbed to Socinianism.[75] Chillingworth pinpoints Knott's charge:

> Your calumnies against Protestants in generall are set downe in these words, Chap.2.§.2. *The very doctrine of Protestants if it bee followed closely, and with coherence to it selfe, must of necessity induce Socinianisme. This I say confidently, and evidently prove, by instancing in one errror, which may well be tearmed the Capitall and mother Heresy, from which all other must follow at ease; I mean their heresy in affirming, that the perpetuall visible Church of Christ, descended by a never interrupted succession from our Saviour, to this day, is not infallible in all that it proposeth to be believed, as revealed truths.*[76]

The only space Chillingworth gives to address the charge of Socinianism is in his twenty-three page "Preface to the Author of Charity

---

73. "Thus a crucial component of completing the work of the Reformation was to completely dismantle the Babylonian ziggurat [the Roman Catholic Church]. Their [Socinians] battle cry can be summarized as three Ts: Tradition, Transubstantiation, and Trinity." Lim, *Mystery Unveiled*, 12.

74. "Chillingworth's works, especially *The Religion of Protestants*, were frequently reprinted during the seventeenth and eighteenth centuries." Chernaik, "Chillingworth, William," para. 22.

75. "In 1636 Knott cited Chillingworth's views on the role of reason in the interpretation of Scripture as evidence of his Socinian tendencies. Although Knott was very keen to press home the claim that Socinianism was the logical progression of Protestantism, a move that was to become a standard part of Catholic polemic, the tract itself is short of concrete evidence and slurs Chillingworth by inference and innuendo." Dixon, *Nice and Hot*, 42.

76. Chillingworth, Preface to *Religion of Protestants* sec. 9.

Maintained."[77] Chillingworth thought little of Knott's charge and evidence of Socinianism against himself and Protestants.[78]

Having dismissed the charge and danger of Socinianism in the preface, Chillingworth directs his attention at the substance of Knotts's charge, the rejection of the Roman Catholic Church's infallibility. Along similar lines as the Reformers, Chillingworth appeals to Scripture over and against the infallibility of the Roman Catholic Church. He clearly states his position in this statement, "The Bible. The Bible, I say, The Bible only is the Religion of Protestants! Whatsoever else they believe besides it, and the plain, irrefragable, indubitable consequences of it, well may they hold it as a matter of Opinion, but as matter of Faith and Religion, neither can they with coherence to their own grounds believe it themselves, nor require the beliefe of it of others, without most high and most Schismaticall presumption."[79] By this statement Chillingworth does not intend to divide Roman Catholics and Protestants with the Bible. Rather, he attempts to find common ground between Catholics and Protestants; that common ground being the Bible.[80]

That "the Bible is the religion of Protestants" is not an affirmation of the Protestant interpretation of Scripture as stated in confessions.[81] The religion of Protestants is the mere affirmation that the Bible is the Word of God. Nine sentences after the above declaration, Chillingworth gives this clarifying statement, "I am fully assured that God does not, and therefore that men ought not to require any more of any man then this, To believe the Scripture to be God's word, to endeavour to find the true sense of it, and to live according to it."[82] But for Chillingworth the discovery of the true sense of Scripture by one person is not to be imposed upon any other person. That would be a violation of the Protestant religion. Men may deduce clear and

---

77. According to a word search for "Socinian" or "Socinianism" in the PDF format of *Religion of Protestants*, the only appearances of these terms are in "Preface to the Author."

78. Chillingworth quips, "In all which discourse, the only true word you speak is, This I say confidently: As for proving evidently, that I believe you reserved for some other opportunity: for the present I am sure you have been very sparing of it." Chillingworth, Preface to *Religion of Protestants* sec. 9.

79. Chillingworth, *Religion of Protestants*, 375–76.

80. "Chillingworth's position is consistently eirenic: Roman Catholics and Protestants, he argued, agree in many of the fundamentals of faith, and this common body of belief is far more important than any 'diversity of opinions' among 'the severall Sects of Christians.'" Chernaik, "Chillingworth, William," para. 17.

81. "The Bible alone being the religion of Protestants he [Chillingworth] stood in contradiction to the growing confessionalism of contemporary Protestantism." Waller, "William Chillingworth," 186.

82. Chillingworth, *Religion of Protestants*, 376.

indisputable conclusions from Scripture. However, they are to hold such conclusions as "opinions" and not as matters of "faith and religion" to be believed by others.

The reason why one person's or church's conclusions drawn from Scripture were not to be imposed upon others is that men, and consequently churches, are fallible. *Religion of Protestants* was a "systematic rejection of infallibility" for both Protestants and Catholics.[83] Chillingworth says, "But that there shall be alwaies such a Church, which is an infallible Guide in fundamentalls, this we deny."[84] For Chillingworth, human presumption can be too closely joined with orthodox belief resulting in the repression of truth.[85]

Chillingworth ostensibly holds no truth of Scripture as universal or necessary for belief among Christians. Yet, he does distinguish between two types of truths in Scripture: fundamental and not fundamental. Fundamental truths are necessary to be believed by all who claim the Christian faith. Fundamental truths are "*evidently delivered* in Scripture and commanded to be preach't to all men."[86] Truths that are not fundamental are not required to be believed or agreed upon by Christians. Nonfundamental truths are those "which are *obscure*" in Scripture.[87] Later, Chillingworth summarizes his position, "In a Word, That all things necessary to be believed are evidently contain'd in Scripture and what is not there evidently contained, cannot be necessary to be believed."[88] Chillingworth equates truths necessary for salvation as those which are evident and therefore fundamental. If "truths *not necessary to the Salvation*, cannot be necessary to the being of a Church," then truths necessary to salvation are necessary to the being of a church.[89] This restricts the accessibility of fundamental truths in Scripture to what is readily comprehensible through reason.

Chillingworth's *Religion of Protestants* is different from that of the Reformer's sola Scriptura.[90] The Reformers sought to build doctrine from Scripture, while Chillingworth sought to limit doctrine in Scripture. And this limitation of doctrine influenced later generations of the church's practice of the Protestant Principle.

83. Wilmer, "Chillingworth on Infallibility," 100.
84. Chillingworth, *Religion of Protestants*, 150.
85. Waller, "William Chillingworth," 187.
86. Chillingworth, Preface to *Religion of Protestants* sec. 32 (emphasis added).
87. Chillingworth, Preface to *Religion of Protestants* sec. 32 (emphasis added).
88. Chillingworth, *Religion of Protestants*, 115.
89. Chillingworth, Preface to *Religion of Protestants* sec. 32 (emphasis added).
90. "Though conceived as a Protestant apologetic, there is throughout the whole work an apparent aloofness from and a critical modification of orthodox Protestantism on certain significant points." Waller, "William Chillingworth," 182.

Conclusion

This chapter has provided two key issues from the seventeenth century that carried over into the eighteenth century and were present at the Salters' Hall Debates. Antitrinitarian views and practices arose in seventeenth-century England that carried over into the next. Though orthodox trinitarian defenders continued the Reformers' grounding of the Trinity upon Scripture and tradition, the antitrinitarians wielded these same tools by the handle of reason to deny the Trinity. Also, the Reformed principle of sola Scriptura morphed into the Protestant Principle. Well-meaning trinitarians refused to affirm confessional language of the Trinity so as not to undermine the authority of Scripture and its language. In the next two chapters, it will be shown how the Particular Baptists practiced the Reformed principle and how the General Baptists practiced the Protestant Principle regarding the trinitarian controversy.

3

Ambiguous and Amicable

How Seventeenth-Century General Baptists Responded to Antitrinitarianism

THE PREVIOUS CHAPTER EXPLORED the rise of antitrinitarian thought in seventeenth-century England. The chapter left unanswered the third question posed at the beginning, why did Baptists at Salters' Hall divide roughly along Particular and General identity lines when it came to subscription? The responses of General and Particular Baptists at Salters' Hall in the eighteenth century are a demonstration of how both responded to antitrinitarianism in the seventeenth century.

General and Particular Baptists shared some things in common. Both groups of Baptists affirmed classical trinitarianism. Each of them had to deal with antitrinitarian advocates within their own circles. But the General and Particular Baptists addressed the matter from different convictions. The General Baptists responded with the writing of a confession that employed only scriptural terms to uphold and explain trinitarian doctrine. The Particular Baptists responded with the writing of a confession that employed both scriptural and traditional terms to uphold and explain trinitarian doctrine. In keeping with these convictions, the Particular Baptists at Salters' Hall were willing to subscribe to confessional trinitarian language and the General Baptists were unwilling to subscribe to such language. This chapter will focus on the General Baptist response.

The Antitrinitarian Dispute with Matthew Caffyn

The antitrinitarian dispute for the General Baptists began as early as their first or second General Assembly.[1] Matthew Caffyn is the one who stands at the beginning of the dispute and throughout the remainder of the seventeenth century. Joseph Wright, a messenger from the General Baptist church in Maidstone, Kent, in 1653 brought charges of blasphemy against fellow General Baptists Matthew Caffyn and William Jeffery to the second General Assembly meeting in Stone Chapel, London.[2] Wright recounts his charges against Caffyn and Jeffery in *Speculum Haereticis* (1691).[3] Wright accused Caffyn and Jeffery of denying the belief that Jesus took His flesh from Mary.[4]

Matthew Caffyn (*bap*. 1628, *d*. 1714), in his day, was a prominent General Baptist. At a time when General Baptists were not known to have many educated ministers, Caffyn was known as a man of "good natural abilities cultivated by a liberal education."[5] His parents sent him to a distinguished

---

1. The minutes of the first General Assembly are dated 1654. In his introductory note to the first minutes of the Assembly, W. T. Whitley says the General Assembly either occurred in 1654 or in 1653. Whitley, *MGA*, 1:2.

2. Wright remembers that he was not able to attend the first assembly due to sickness, but he did attend the second assembly in 1653. Wright, *Speculum Haereticis*, in Bass, *Caffynite Controversy*, 149 (6). If Wright is referring to the official General Assembly meetings, then he is mistaken when the first and second assemblies were held. The extant official minutes for the first General Assembly do not indicate that such an accusation was brought forward. Whitley asserts that the "only portion of the proceedings of 1654 that have come down to us" is a "brief manifesto, disavowing sympathy with the Fifth-Monarchy movement." Whitley, *MGA*, 1:2. Also, Wright is not recorded as being present at the first meeting; however, Caffyn and Jeffery were present. The next extant minutes for the General Assembly are dated the seventh month of 1656 and being held in London. These minutes do not record an accusation brought by Wright against Caffyn and Jeffery. However, all three men are recorded as messengers present at this assembly. Also, there is a statement on "How is Jesus Christ Dauids Roote & offspring" that was agreed upon by the messengers, which indicates that the topic of Christology was discussed by the messengers. The statement reads, "Thus he yt was wth God & was God as he was such was Dauids Root. And he that was wt God and was God yt same was made flesh made of or Borne of a woman of ye seed of Dauid and so was Dauids offspring." Whitley, *MGA*, 1:6.

3. The only extant copy of this work is held by the Württembergische Landesbibliothek, Stuttgart, Germany. Bass, *Caffynite Controversy*, 143. Bass includes a transcription of that text in Appendix B of *Caffynite Controversy*. Bass indicates the page numbers of the extant copy in the transcription. All citations to *Speculum Haereticis* will be according to the pagination of Bass, *Caffynite Controversy*, with the page number of Wright, *Speculum Haereticis*, in parenthesis.

4. Wright, *Speculum Haereticis*, in Bass, *Caffynite Controversy*, 148 (5).

5. Taylor, *HEGB*, 1:293.

grammar school in Kent and then he attended the university of Oxford.⁶ While a student at Oxford, he adopted and defended the principles of credobaptism. He was thereby expelled before graduating.⁷ Caffyn returned home and joined the General Baptist church in his hometown of Horsham, Sussex, pastored by Samuel Lover.⁸ Soon after joining the church, Caffyn was called to the ministry and co-pastored the church until Lover's death.⁹ Caffyn's theological education and giftedness to defend the Christian faith, especially the General Baptist faith, became evident. By 1655, Caffyn engaged in public disputes ranging from Quakerism, paedobaptism, and the doctrine of predestination.¹⁰ He had such success in these debates that General Baptists in the region of Sussex began to call Caffyn their "battle-axe and weapon of war."¹¹

The Alleged Heterodoxy of Caffyn

Extant works written by Caffyn are few, and what exists are not doctrinal in nature. The only exception is a 1654 refutation of Quakers, *The Deceived, and Deceiving Quakers Discovered*. This work, however, is too early for Caffyn to address the charges of heterodoxy made against him. In the other works, Caffyn does not declare and defend his Christology nor contest the charges of heterodoxy made against him. Therefore, what is known about Caffyn's Christology primarily comes from those who make accusations against him.¹²

Early in his conversion to the Baptist faith and practice, Caffyn did not hold unorthodox Christology. In fact, Wright acknowledges that Caffyn affirmed an orthodox Christology as late as 1650 or 1651.¹³ At his baptism, Caffyn professed that there is, "One God, the Father, Word, and Holy Spirit,

---

6. Crosby, *THEB*, 4:328.

7. Whitley, *MGA*, 1:xxii; Taylor, *HEGB*, 1:293. Credobaptism is defined as a person being baptized, normally by immersion, subsequent to his profession of faith in Christ Jesus.

8. Bass identifies the church as the Southwater church near Horsham. Bass, *Caffynite Controversy*, 35.

9. Taylor, *HEGB*, 1:293.

10. Bass, *Caffynite Controversy*, 34.

11. Taylor, *HEGB*, 1:168.

12. While it is possible that some of his accusers overstate or misstate Caffyn's position, there can still be truth found in what they say.

13. Wright indicates that forty years prior to the writing and publication of *Speculum Haereticis*, Caffyn affirmed orthodox Christology. Wright, *Speculum Haereticis*, in Bass, *Caffynite Controversy*, 148 (5) Wright wrote *Speculum Haereticis* in 1690 according to his introduction. It was published in 1691.

all Three of the same Substance; and Holy Trinity in Unity, from Everlasting unto Everlasting, and Unchangeable. And that the Second Person in the Holy Trinity did in time take our Nature in the Womb of the Blessed Virgin Mary, and was very God, and very Man, in one Person for evermore."[14] Wright was able to know the confessed faith of Caffyn as they were friends at one time. Thomas Crosby recounts Caffyn as placing "great confidence" in Wright and both maintaining a "close friendship."[15]

Yet, as noted above, Wright became suspect of Caffyn's Christology by 1653–1654. According to Wright, Caffyn later came to believe that the Son of God at the incarnation "did never take our Nature, or any of the Seed of the Woman, or Matter of the Virgin Mary."[16] Caffyn is accused of denying that Jesus had a true human nature as that of Man.[17] Rather, Jesus is

> the Word of God, in the true Nature with the Father and Holy Spirit, did come into the Womb of the Virgin, and was there changed into Flesh, Blood, and Bones, and the likeness of Man, as the Water was changed into Wine . . . so that all the Flesh, Blood, and Bones of Christ, came of his eternal Divine Nature, and were not of any other Matter, or Nature, or Substance originally whatsoever.[18]

Wright seems to suggest that Caffyn held to a form of celestial flesh Christology.

From where and how Caffyn learned or developed celestial flesh Christology is not known. Clint Bass suggests an Anabaptist source. Melchior Hoffman, Caspar Schwenckfeld, and Menno Simmons are possible candidates as all three advocated a form of celestial flesh. Bass rejects Hoffman and Schwenckfeld as the precursors to Caffyn. Hoffman affirmed that Christ had only a divine nature, while Caffyn did not make such an affirmation. Schwenckfeld affirmed two natures in Christ with His human nature being derived from Mary who was sinless. However, Caffyn never affirmed the sinless state of Mary. Bass sees more similarity between Simmons and

---

14. Wright, *Speculum Haereticis*, in Bass, *Caffynite Controversy*, 148 (5).

15. Crosby, *THEB*, 4:333.

16. Wright, *Speculum Haereticis*, in Bass, *Caffynite Controversy*, 148 (5).

17. For clarification, in this discussion the term "Man" when capitalized refers to the joint material and immaterial nature common to all mankind since the first man Adam. This nature is what makes humans distinct from the rest of creation. To not possess the nature of Man is to not be human. This reference to the nature of Man is not a reference to the depravity of Man. A person may be peccable, impeccable, or fallen and still be Man by nature.

18. Wright, *Speculum Haereticis*, in Bass, *Caffynite Controversy*, 148 (5).

Caffyn.[19] Both men never overtly denied the two natures of Christ, but they were never clear as to how the two natures subsisted together in the one person of Christ. Furthermore, both affirmed that Christ received nothing of His human nature from Mary. In Mary's womb God placed the heavenly body, or celestial flesh, of Christ that grew inside of her. Bass may be correct in his conclusion. Anabaptists had a greater presence in southeast England where Caffyn lived. Michael Watts advocates that Caffyn was "attracted to the Christological views of Melchior Hoffman" because "the radicals of southeast England had in the previous century come under the influence of continental Anabaptism."[20] But this influence is not demonstratable. Caffyn, in his writings, does not cite sources for his positions.

Thomas Monck, a General Baptist of Buckinghamshire, joined Wright in accusations against Caffyn's Christology. In 1673, Monck published *A Cure for the Cankering Error of the New Eutychians*. Monck does not call out Caffyn by name in this work, but he does condemn Caffyn's alleged heterodoxy. The new Eutychians are those who assert "that the Divine Nature of Christ which was in the beginning with God, and was God, Joh. 1. 1, 2. compared with the 14 verse was made flesh, viz. by turning his Divine Nature or Godhead into flesh, even as the Water was turned into Wine at Cana, Joh. 2.9. which ceased to be Water and became Wine."[21] The danger here, according to Monck, is twofold. First, if Christ turned His divine nature into flesh, then Christ is no longer God. "God the Creator of Heaven and Earth, ceased from being a Creator, to become a Creatur."[22] And, second, if Christ's flesh is a transformation from His divine nature, then Christ is not a man who can die for Man's sin. "They say in plain words, that our blessed Mediator did not take his flesh of the Virgin Mary, nor of David; and so by Consequence he was not the true Son of David: and if so, how can we be saved?"[23]

---

19. Bass, *Caffynite Controversy*, 95–96. Bass provides a good summary of Anabaptist Christologies in chapter 1.

20. Watts, *From the Reformation*, 299.

21. Monck, *Cure*, A2. Whether Eutychianism is a proper charge against Caffyn is a matter of debate. Caffyn did hold that Christ had only one nature. However, Caffyn did not describe that nature as being the intermingling of divine and human natures becoming one unique nature. Yet, Monck qualified this charge as "new" Eutychianism. Caffyn, in *Envy's Bitterness Corrected*, denied being a Eutychian. Caffyn, *Envy's Bitterness*, 31.

22. Monck, *Cure*, A2.

23. Monck, *Cure*, A2.

Caffyn's Christology

As stated above, few of Caffyn's works are extant. Crosby lists fives works written by Caffyn, stating that one was not published.[24] Of the remaining four, only three are now known to exist today.[25] Of the works listed by Crosby, none of them directly address Caffyn's Christology. One might wonder why Caffyn would not defend himself publicly through writing. Crosby answers this question with Caffyn's own reason. Caffyn did not think the writings by Wright, Monck, and Richard Haines (another accuser of Caffyn) against his alleged Christology necessitated a response by him. Caffyn dismissed Wright's accusations as mere personal attacks, asserting that his claims were unfounded and that his arguments were "the most barren thing he had ever read."[26] Caffyn had little more regard for Monck. Caffyn said Monck's work "was so mysterious, and unintelligible, as to need no confutation."[27] Also, Caffyn asserted that he had already addressed Monck's accusations in his reply to Haines.[28]

When it came to Haines, Caffyn did address his Christology, albeit briefly. Haines and Caffyn shared a long and storied relationship. Haines was a member of the church pastored by Caffyn. The two fell out when Caffyn had Haines excommunicated from the church. The cause for the excommunication was that Haines had filed a patent for a process he invented to clean hop-clover.[29] Caffyn accused Haines of covetousness for filing the patent in order to prevent others from duplicating his invention. In 1674, Haines wrote *New Lords, New Laws*. In it he accused Caffyn of wrongfully excommunicating him from the church, but he also accused Caffyn of heretical Christology.[30] Haines wrote, "The error is his Principle concerning

---

24. Crosby also states that Caffyn had written several "imperfect certain manuscripts on the doctrine of the holy *Trinity*" that were in the possession of Caffyn's friends but they had not yet published the manuscripts at the time of Crosby's writing. Crosby, *THEB*, 4:342.

25. Bass states that Caffyn left behind four written works. Bass, *Caffynite Controversy*, 90. Two of the works were written against Quakers and two works against Haines. However, only three works of Caffyn are listed in the Bibliography of *Caffynite Controversy*: one work against Quakers and the two against Haines.

26. Crosby, *THEB*, 4:338.

27. Crosby, *THEB*, 4:338.

28. Crosby, *THEB*, 4:338.

29. Spivey, "Caffyn, Matthew," para. 4.

30. That Haines accused Caffyn of an unorthodox Christology in this work shows that Haines attempted to defend himself by all means necessary in a church discipline matter. However, it should not be assumed that Haines is untruthful about Caffyn's unorthodoxy. Haines had firsthand knowledge of Caffyn's preaching while he was a member of the church.

our Blessed Lord and Saviour, of whom Caffin saith, That he did not take his flesh of the Virgin Mary, and that he was not made of the Seed of David."[31] That same year Caffyn responded in writing to Haines with *Envy's Bitterness Corrected*. Out of the thirty-three-page response, only three paragraphs near the end are dedicated to Christology. In these paragraphs, Caffyn states what he denies and then what he affirms.

Caffyn first states what he denies. Caffyn denies that Jesus in His incarnation partook of fallen human nature. In response to the accusation Haines and Monck leveled against Caffyn for denying that Christ took His flesh from Mary, Caffyn writes, "And if by his saying, that *I deny Christ took his Flesh of the Virgin Mary*, he means, that the Redemption of Mankind is no more precious then the death, and Blood-shedding of a body of Flesh, in the fallen Estate, under Condemnation for Original sin, and that was in the beginning of the Earth, as the first Man *Adam* was, then do I readily declare my dissent thereunto, and so will (in some respect) the Author of that Book, (Mr. M.) and most others."[32] In this rather elusive statement, Caffyn says that if others thought him to teach that Jesus could partake of a human nature that is fallen and still be a perfect sacrifice for sin, then he readily denies that charge. And not only would he deny such a statement, but so would those who opposed him. Whether this was the intended charge brought against Caffyn by Haines and Monck is debatable. Caffyn either misunderstood their arguments or he intentionally misstated their arguments.

However, in this statement, Caffyn offers some insights into his conception of Jesus' nature. First, Caffyn appears to think that if Jesus did take His human nature from Mary, then Jesus could only have received a fallen human nature like unto hers. That is, it is impossible that an impeccable human could be born even by an immaculate conception.[33] And, second, Caffyn appears to think that even if Jesus could have been born with the original pre-Fall nature of Adam, then He would have received a peccable nature and therefore not a perfect nature suitable to redeem Man.

In the next paragraph Caffyn states what he affirms:

> But this I consent unto, and verily believe, that the true Messiah, whom the Father hath sealed to be the Blessed Saviour of the World, was conceived in the Virgin *Mary*, and there took our Nature and our Form, and so was in all points like unto his

---

31. Haines, *New Lords*, 6.
32. Caffyn, *Envy's Bitterness*, 31.
33. Immaculate conception here is not referring to the Roman Catholicism's belief in the sinless nature of Mary but is referring to the perfect conception of the Son of God in the womb of Mary by the Holy Spirit.

> Brethren, sin excepted; the son of *Abraham*, the son of *David*, confessed to be, while the first Man was of the Earth, Earthey, the second Man the Lord from Heaven, I Cor. 15.47.[34]

As with the previous paragraph, this one is elusive. In the middle of the statement Caffyn affirms that Jesus partook of human nature and yet He was without sin. This is a statement that Caffyn's opponents would affirm. But Caffyn does not intend the same meaning here as would Haines or Monck. Caffyn qualifies this statement with what comes before it and after it. First, Caffyn prequalifies this statement by saying "the true Messiah . . . was *conceived in* the Virgin Mary."[35] Bass points out that traditional language for the immaculate conception was either "conceived *by* the Holy Spirit" or "born *of* the virgin Mary."[36] Caffyn's intention by his unusual phrase is that the Son was placed inside the womb of Mary so that He might become flesh without Mary contributing material or immaterial substance. The post-qualifying statement states what type of flesh Jesus possessed since it was not that of human flesh received from Mary. Caffyn distinguishes between the flesh of the first man, Adam, and the flesh of the second man, Jesus. Adam's flesh was of the earth and therefore peccable and imperfect. The flesh of Jesus was heavenly and therefore impeccable and perfect. For Caffyn there is a distinct difference in the nature of Jesus and that of Man. Jesus' nature was only of a heavenly origin and in no way partook of human nature as possessed by Man.

Crosby, who seems to be sympathetic toward Caffyn, recounts how friends of Caffyn described his Christology. His friends reported that, "He [Caffyn] thought it a little strange and unaccountable, that in respect of the Deity, *one* substance should constitute *three* real persons, and yet, that in Christ, *two* intelligent natures and substances should make but *one* person."[37] Caffyn could not affirm that the person of Jesus could have two natures, one divine and one human, without creating two persons within Him. So, Caffyn only affirmed that within Jesus was a heavenly flesh, a celestial flesh, that descended into the womb of Mary. This flesh was not that of Man's flesh, thus making Jesus of a different nature from Man.

---

34. Caffyn, *Envy's Bitterness*, 32.
35. Caffyn, *Envy's Bitterness*, 32 (emphasis added).
36. Bass, *Caffynite Controversy*, 92 (emphasis added).
37. Crosby, *THEB*, 4:341.

Caffyn's Trinitarianism

So far, the direct discussion has centered around the Christology of Caffyn. Indirectly, this conversation also touches upon the trinitarianism of Caffyn. As already stated above, friends of Caffyn compared his Christology with that of his trinitarianism. Just as Jesus could not have two natures within him and still be one person, neither could "*one* substance . . . constitute *three* real persons."[38] Though Caffyn affirmed that Jesus was divine and had a heavenly, or celestial, flesh, Jesus could not have the same substance as that of the Father.

Crosby again discloses what Caffyn had confided in his friends "with whom he would in conversation freely declare" that

> He could not be reconciled to some of the propositions in the *Athanasian* creed. He could easily understand, and heartily assent to, all that the Scriptures did say, concerning either the Father, the Son, or the Holy Ghost; but he used to complain, that he did not know what to do, when he is told, that he must *perish everlastingly*, unless he believed, that the Son is both co-eternal with the Father, and also begotten of him.[39]

Caffyn thought it contradictory to say the Son is both God and begotten of the Father, who himself also is God. This suggests that the Son and the Father share the same substance, yet Caffyn couldn't fathom how this couldn't inevitably result in a single person. To say that God begot Himself would be illogical.[40] It would not be unfair to say that Caffyn was a rational skeptic regarding the Trinity.[41]

Caffyn appears to hold to a form of subordinationism. In the above quote, Caffyn not only denied that the Son is of co-substance with the Father, but he also denied that the Son is co-eternal with the Father. Turning again to the testimony of Caffyn's friends, Nathaniel Gale, "Besides says Mr. Caffin, as 'tis no where written, so I cannot comprehend, nay, apprehend how Three distinct Persons can be Essentially One; nor how Christ the Son of God, which is a Relative term, and supposeth Subordination, can be

---

38. Crosby, *THEB*, 4:341.

39. Crosby, *THEB*, 4:332.

40. "He could not help running into the express contradiction of *three* eternal almighty persons, and but *one* such person; that each by himself is God, and yet that each by himself is not God, because there are not *three* Gods, and but *One* only." Crosby, *THEB*, 4:332.

41. Taylor claims that Caffyn was a leader of rational skeptics among the General Baptists. Taylor, *HEGB*, 1:464.

coequal, coessential, and coeternal with the Father."[42] Caffyn's trinitarianism is, therefore, closer to Arianism than to orthodox trinitarianism.

Caffyn was a man who sought to be both biblical and rational. He was willing to affirm all that the Scriptures teach about the Son, His incarnation, and the Trinity. However, Caffyn could not rationally explain how three persons can have one substance and thereby constitute only one God, nor could he rationally explain how the Son of God incarnate could be both God and man.

The Response of the General Baptists

As stated previously, accusations of Caffyn's heterodoxy were brought by his opponents to the General Assembly as early as 1653–1656. These accusations would formally resume a few decades later. Between the years 1693 and 1702, the Assembly addressed heretical charges brought against Caffyn. The General Assembly's response on each occasion was to affirm Caffyn as orthodox, condemn the heterodoxy alleged against Caffyn, and usually reaffirm the *Brief Confession or Declaration of Faith* adopted by the Assembly in 1660 and 1691. The *Brief Confessions* will be discussed first and then the assembly meetings.

The Response of the General Baptists in Confessions

The General Baptists formally adopted three confessions. In the General Assembly, they adopted the 1660 *Brief Confession* and the 1691 *Brief Confession*. In the General Association, they adopted the 1703 *Brief Confession*.[43] These confessions will be considered in their chronological order depicting the differences among them regarding the doctrines of Christology and the Trinity.

The 1660 Brief Confession

It's challenging to determine whether the 1660 *Brief Confession* was a direct response by the General Assembly to the accusations leveled against Caffyn's Christology. Certainly by 1660 Wright had made a complaint against

---

42. Bass, *Caffynite Controversy*, 101–2. Bass is citing Nathaniel Gale, *Brief Remarks*, 4–5.

43. The General Association of Baptists was formed in 1697 by General Baptists out of the General Assembly. They split off due to the Assembly's affirmation of Caffyn as orthodox.

Caffyn in an assembly; however, the apparent motive for writing the confession doesn't seem to be a response to heresy. The introduction and the conclusion to the 1660 *Brief Confession* indicate that the confession was written for political purposes and not just for doctrinal purposes.

The year 1660 saw the return of monarchial rule with the restoration of King Charles II to the throne. In such a changing political time, the General Baptists showed their support for the king and for his government. In the introduction, the authors begin by separating themselves from the Anabaptists in the opening paragraph: "Set forth by many of us, who are (falsely) called ANABAPTISTS."[44] Baptists, in general, were frequently confused with the continental Anabaptists based on their common practice of credobaptism by immersion. However, the Anabaptists were usually perceived as being against civil authority. With the inauguration of King Charles II, the General Baptists did not want to suffer persecution because of false identity.[45] In the conclusion, the Assembly recognized that some General Baptists had been accused of anarchy. The Assembly stated such charges as false and wicked lies for they "utterly abhor, and abominate the thoughts thereof, and much more the actions" of anarchy.[46]

Though the impetus for the confession is likely political, that does not suggest that the confession is not also doctrinal.[47] The Assembly sought "to inform all Men (in these days of scandal and reproach) of our innocent Belief and Practice."[48] The confession would become the standard for doctrine and fellowship among General Baptist churches in the Assembly for decades to come.

The minutes for the Assembly of 1660 are not extant. Whitley notes that there was an Assembly held in March 1660 per an endorsement by Thomason, the collector of all printed material at the time, on a manuscript containing the 1660 *Brief Confession*.[49] Then, in 1663, the General Assembly

---

44. Whitley, *MGA*, 1:10.

45. On July 26, 1660, Thomas Grantham and Joseph Wright delivered a one-page printing of the 1660 *Brief Confession* to King Charles II. Along with the confession they delivered a narrative of the General Baptists' sufferings. Taylor, *HEGB*, 1:186.

46. Whitley, *MGA*, 1:21.

47. The introduction and the conclusion would be dropped from reprints of the confession; namely by Thomas Grantham in 1678 (*Christianismus Primitivus*) and the General Assembly's authorized reprinting of the confession, albeit with a change in article 3, in 1691. The conclusion is that the political atmosphere had settled to the point where such statements were no longer necessary. The confession could then stand as a doctrinal statement rather than a political statement.

48. Whitley, *MGA*, 1:10.

49. Whitley, *MGA*, 1:10. Whitley's source is a manuscript held at the Angus Collection at Regent's Park College.

reaffirmed the confession. Again, there are no minutes for this assembly. However, Thomas Grantham in *Christianismus Primitivus* reproduces the confession, with a few alterations, and he gives the date of 1663. Grantham is not referring to a different confession from that of the 1660 for he states that the confession he reproduces was "presented to His Majesty *Charles the Second of England, &c. the King*," which "he courteously received from our hands."[50] Grantham would know this because he, along with Joseph Wright, delivered the copy of the 1660 *Brief Confession* to the king on July 26, 1660.[51]

As presented earlier, Joseph Wright brought charges of unorthodox Christology against Caffyn as late as 1656 in a General Assembly. The 1660 *Brief Confession*, therefore, would be an official statement by the General Baptists concerning Christology soon after such charges. Article 3 of the confession is on the person of Jesus Christ and reads as follows:

> That there is one Lord Jesus Christ, by whom are all things, who is the only begotten Son of God, born of the Virgin Mary, yet as truly *David's* Lord, and *David's* root, as *David's* Son, and *David's* Off-spring, *Luke* 20.44. *Revel.* 22.16. whom God freely *sent into the World* (because of his great love unto the World) who as freely *gave himself a ransome for all,* 1 Tim. 2.5,6. *tasting death for every man,* Heb 2.9. *a propitiation for our sins; and not for ours only, but also for the sins of the whole World,* 1 John 2.2.[52]

The statement contains two parts: the person of Christ and the work of Christ. Neither part is worded in classical confessional language; rather, both are worded in strict scriptural language. In this article, the General Baptists employ the Protestant Principle.[53] Watts asserts that the General Baptists "maintained with Chillingworth that the Bible and the 'Bible only,' is the religion of the Protestants.'"[54] The second part, which affirms general atonement, is far clearer than the first. The person of Christ is stated in vague descriptive terms of Scripture, but not in clear definitive terms of confessions.[55]

---

50. Grantham, *Christianismus Primitivus*, 2:61.

51. Taylor, *HEGB*, 1:186.

52. *Brief Confession*, 3–4.

53. The whole of the 1660 *Brief Confession* is the employment of the Protestant Principle.

54. Watts, *From the Reformation*, 373.

55. William Lumpkin comments on the 1660 *Brief Confession*, "In clarity and definiteness of statement it hardly matches the Particular Baptist Confession of 1644. . . . The Article on Christology is brief, vague, and in the words of Scripture; it was to be a bone for future contention." Lumpkin, *Baptist Confessions*, 221. This is not to imply that the whole of Scripture is vague; it is only to affirm that when *analogia Scripturae* is not utilized, then less perspicuous passages remain so.

The article attempts to affirm both the deity and the humanity of Christ. His deity is affirmed with uniqueness (there is one Lord Jesus Christ), creatorship (by whom are all things), and Sonship (who is the only begotten Son of God). Though not stated in the article, the first two statements of deity probably come from 1 Cor 8:6 (KJV), "But to us there is but one God, the Father, of whom are all things, and we in him; and *one Lord Jesus Christ, by whom are all things*, and we by him" (emphasis added). The third statement on Sonship likely derives from John 3:18 (KJV), "He that believeth on him is not condemned: but he that believeth not is condemned already, because he hath not believed in the name of *the only begotten Son of God*" (emphasis added).[56] The humanity of Christ is affirmed by the incarnation (born of the virgin Mary). This phrase is not found in Scripture, yet the source is perhaps a compilation of Luke 1:27 and 31 (KJV), "And the virgin's name was Mary. . . . And, behold, thou shalt conceive in thy womb, and bring forth a son, and shalt call his name Jesus."[57] Then the article seeks to combine and affirm both Christ's deity and humanity in His relationship with king David and provides Scripture citation. Because Christ is David's Lord and Root, then He is divine. And, because Christ is David's Son and offspring, then He is human.

The article did little to narrow the meaning of Christ's natures and allowed for broader interpretation. Though it is scriptural in its statements, the article did nothing to resolve the accusations Wright brought against Caffyn. Caffyn could and would affirm this article on Christ.[58] Caffyn was not averse to affirm the statements of Scripture, though he was not always able to explain its truth. He was not averse to calling Jesus the Son of God, though he did not believe that meant Jesus possessed the same substance of God the Father. Caffyn admitted Jesus was born of the virgin Mary, though he would typically say Christ was conceived *in* the virgin Mary. And Caffyn had no stated problem in declaring Jesus to be the son of David.

Given the vagueness of article 3 and its lack of clarifying a doctrinal issue that had arisen early in the life of the General Assembly, it is of interest who may have authored the 1660 *Brief Confession*. Both publications of

---

56. Other possibilities include John 1:18; 3:16; 1 John 4:9. However, these verses do not include "of God" after "Son."

57. Another possibility is Matt 1:16 (KJV): "And Jacob begat Joseph the husband of Mary, of whom was born Jesus, who is called Christ." However, this verse does not explicitly state that Mary was a virgin, though 1:18 implies her virginity: "Now the birth of Jesus Christ was on this wise: When as his mother Mary was espoused to Joseph, before they came together, she was found with child of the Holy Ghost."

58. Caffyn was a signatory of the 1660 confession. Whitley, *MGA*, 1:21.

the *Brief Confession* in 1660 were published anonymously.[59] There are two theories for who authored the confession.[60] The first theory, espoused by Taylor and repeated by McGlothlin, is that Grantham authored the confession. Taylor states, "Thomas Grantham, who is supposed to have drawn up this Confession."[61] This theory is not likely for two reasons.[62] First, Taylor himself does not appear confident in its accuracy. This is evident by his statement "who is *supposed*" to have authored the confession. He offers no further support for this claim. Second, Grantham was not a subscriber on the first publication of the *Brief Confession* in March since his name is not included among the forty subscribers; yet his name does appear on the second publication delivered to King Charles II.[63] That Grantham subscribed to the second publication is reasonable since he is one of the messengers who delivered it to the king. But why does his name not appear on the first publication if he was the author, or an author, of the confession?[64] The absence of his name on the first publication suggests that he did not author the *Brief Confession*.

The second theory is that Joseph Wright, Matthew Caffyn, and John Parsons authored the 1660 *Brief Confession*. This theory is argued for by

---

59. The first publication is March 1660. The second publication is July 1660, which was presented to King Charles II.

60. A third theory could be included. Lumpkin suggests that Thomas Monck and Matthew Caffyn "may have made some contribution" to the confession. Lumpkin, *Baptist Confessions*, 220. His theory, though, is not supported and he may not have intended it to be anything but a suggestion. Therefore, it will not be considered.

61. Taylor, *HEGB*, 1:366. McGlothlin quotes Taylor but he gives the wrong page number. McGlothlin, *Baptist Confessions*, 109. McGlothlin cites *HEGB*, 1:466, but it is actually 1:366.

62. A third reason could be given. Lumpkin adds that Grantham "did not become prominent [among the General Baptists] until some years later." Lumpkin, *Baptist Confessions*, 221. However, it is not accurate for Lumpkin to state that Grantham was not prominent at the time of the first publication of the *Brief Confession*. Grantham was selected by the Assembly to be a messenger to deliver the confession to King Charles II. Also, Taylor spoke admirably of Grantham regarding the early history of the General Baptists: "though scarcely twenty-six years of age, was the principal support of the General Baptist cause in the South Marsh of Lincolnshire." Taylor, *HEGB*, 1:186.

63. The March publication has forty signatories. The July publication has forty-one signatories. Grantham is the only new name on the July publication compared to the March publication. Grantham did subscribe to the 1663 publication. His name appears in the first list of names of the 1691 edition. Stephen Holmes argues that "the 1691 list reproduces the signatories of the 1663 Confession (and so, presumably, also reproduces the membership of the 1663 Assembly)." Holmes, "Note," 5.

64. It is possible that his name failed to be included at the time of publication by some oversight, but this cannot be demonstrated.

Stephen Holmes.⁶⁵ Holmes cites an anonymous 1704 document titled *A Vindication of the Antient General Assembly from the False Imputations of the Russelites.*⁶⁶ The key text quoted by Holmes regarding possible authorship of the 1660 *Brief Confession* is:

> And whereas the then present Juncture of National Affairs called, as they thought, for a publick Confession of Faith, 'twas agreed by an Assembly then met, that *Joseph Wright, Matthew Caffen* and *John Parsons* should withdraw themselves some time from the Assembly Affairs, and draw up something of that Nature, withal giving them direction, so to draw up that article wherein they differed, that both Parties might freely subscribe thereunto, which they perform'd to the intire satisfaction of the Assembly.⁶⁷

Three important facts are drawn from this citation. The first is the potential date for the drawing up of a confession of faith. The anonymous author does not give a year for when this confession of faith was authorized to be written. The year, though, seems to be 1660. The "Juncture of National Affairs" that "called . . . for a publick Confession of Faith" fits the political atmosphere of 1660 as described above.⁶⁸ Also, 1660 is the only time the General Assembly authorized the drafting of a confession of faith that included Wright, Caffyn, and Parsons as present.⁶⁹ Second, this citation names these three men as the authors/drafters of the 1660 *Brief Confession*.⁷⁰ The names of these men are included as subscribers on both the March and July publications of the confession.⁷¹ Third, this citation states a reason for these men to write the confession of faith. There was a doctrinal difference between them. Therefore, the three needed to "draw up that article wherein they differed, that both

---

65. Holmes, "Note."

66. At the time of this writing, this document has not been located.

67. Holmes, "Note," 6. The page number of the original citation is 57, as given by Holmes.

68. Holmes, "Note," 6.

69. There is another possibility other than the 1660 *Brief Confession*. In 1691 the Assembly approved the reprinting of the original *Brief Confession* but with article 3 concerning Christology amended per Grantham. Whitley, *MGA*, 1:30–31. All three names of these men appear as subscribers to the 1691 confession. However, this confession is a reprint of a confession of faith and not the drafting of a confession of faith.

70. This is possibly the only extant record indicating the possible authors of the 1660 *Brief Confession*.

71. There are two "John Parsons" listed on both publications. One is Senior and the other is Junior. Which of the two Parsons is referenced in the citation is not known. Holmes believes it is the senior Parsons. Holmes, "Note," 7.

Parties might freely subscribe thereunto."[72] This statement alludes perfectly to the doctrinal difference on Christology between Wright and Caffyn.[73]

If it is true that Wright and Caffyn were co-authors of the 1660 *Brief Confession*, then article 3 on Christology had to have been agreed upon and affirmed by both men. But that article, as demonstrated above, is a vague articulation of Christology. The question is, did both men actually draft the article of the confession from a *shared* understanding of Christ's person, that he is both truly God and truly man, or did they have *different* understandings of Christ's person but they could agree on the shared language of Scripture?

Wright answers this question in his *Speculum Haereticis*. Caffyn would give the latter answer to the question. Wright states, "Yet establishing themselves, that they are and hold, as they did when that Declaration of Faith was subscribed, March 1660."[74] Caffyn, up until 1690, the writing of *Speculum Haereticis*, had been saying the beliefs he held regarding Christ, that he is not truly God nor of the same flesh as man, were the same beliefs he had at the time of the 1660 *Brief Confession*. If this is true, then Caffyn could approve of the vague language of article 3 because he held to a different understanding as to what the language meant. It appears, then, that for Caffyn, article 3 of the 1660 *Brief Confession* affirmed his Christology.

Wright, however, denies that when article 3 of the confession was crafted that it could affirm Caffyn's Christology. Rather, article 3 vindicates Wright's position of Christology. He even goes as far as to say that Caffyn in March 1660 believed the article to affirm Wright's position. He maintains:

> In confutation of which, I writ, in the Year 1690. Animadversions upon five articles in that Declaration,[75] proving it otherwise than they say, and vindicating our Opinion to be both intended and set forth in it: and they well know, that not one of the Forty which set their Hands to it, did then differ about the Divine Nature of Christ, or the Blessed Trinity, as the plain words thereof do hold forth, the Son of God as truly David's Lord and Root, as David's Son and Off-spring, Luke 20.44. Rev.

---

72. Holmes, "Note," 6.

73. How Parsons factors into the debate is uncertain. Since the citation mentions "both parties," Parsons was either on the side of Wright or on the side of Caffyn.

74. Wright, *Speculum Haereticis*, in Bass, *Caffynite Controversy*, 156–57 (13). The "they" is a reference to Caffyn and others within the General Assembly who held to his form of Christology.

75. The year prior to *Speculum Haereticis*, Wright published *Animadversions upon Five Articles in that Declaration*. *Animadversions* was Wright's defense of the 1660 *Brief Confession*, including article 3. Bass, *Caffynite Controversy*, 143.

22.16. most clearly setting forth the Divine and Humane Nature of Christ Jesus.[76]

Wright makes two statements here. First, article 3 clearly demonstrates that Jesus is both divine and human. Wright, it appears, did not think the language to be vague, but certain and precise. Second, none of the forty men who subscribed to the 1660 *Brief Confession* thought article 3 to affirm anything other than that Jesus is both truly God and truly man; and that includes Caffyn who subscribed to the confession. So, for Wright, he believed Caffyn at the time of writing and subscribing to the 1660 *Brief Confession* to have been dissuaded from his previous heresy and convinced of orthodox Christology. The two men, according to Wright, shared the same understanding of Christ's person as reflected in the article.

Who is right? Was Caffyn persuaded to agree with Wright concerning the person of Christ? Or did Caffyn help craft an article that is vague enough to accommodate both his and Wright's Christology? According to Wright's own testimony regarding Caffyn, it would appear that Caffyn affirmed the common language of the article but held to a different interpretation of the article. Wright throughout *Speculum Haereticis* portrays Caffyn as a deceiver and a manipulator. Therefore, if true, Caffyn could affirm article 3 and yet hold, even privately at the time, his own Christology.

And why would Wright agree to use such vague language on a matter that had caused such tension, for him at least, leading up to drafting the confession? Why not be as clear as possible on the topic of Christology? As stated above, Wright thought the article was clear in its language. Nonetheless, Wright could have fought for clearer and more definitive language. Wright may have, out of self-humility or pressure from the Assembly, agreed to language that was not confrontational. Wright recounts an earlier Assembly, prior to 1660, when he and Caffyn were sent away for a week to write out their position on what was the original Christ. Upon returning, the men presented their positions, each publishing about a six or seven-page document. After the presentation, the Assembly feared that if such a debate were made public, it could cause some of their Christian brothers to stumble. The two men agreed and "all Endeavours were used not to divide."[77] Maybe Wright still felt that division should be avoided and, therefore, did not press for firmer Christological language in the 1660 *Brief Confession*. This irenic spirit is commendable but it allowed for differences to pervade within the Assembly for decades.

---

76. Wright, *Speculum Haereticis*, in Bass, *Caffynite Controversy*, 156–57 (13).
77. Wright, *Speculum Haereticis*, in Bass, *Caffynite Controversy*, 153–54 (10).

The 1691 Brief Confession

The General Assembly affirmed the 1660 *Brief Confession* for the next three decades before publishing another confession in 1691.[78] In 1691, the Assembly approved a new edition of the 1660 *Brief Confession* to be published. The Assembly agreed unanimously that the "Confession of ffaith formerly set forth by the General Assembly be owned & acknowledged now which was accordingly Done no man Disalowing with the Explicatition made by Brother Grantham in the 3d. Article."[79] The "explicatition" is Grantham's revision of article 3 in his *Christianismus Primitivus*. By 1691, the General Assembly had been dealing with charges against Caffyn's Christological doctrine for several decades. The Assembly thought Grantham's revision of the article would strengthen and bring more clarity and unity on Christology. Grantham's revision as published by the Assembly in 1691 reads:

> That there is one Lord Jesus Christ, by whom are all things, who is the only begotten Son of God, born of the virgin Mary; Being the true Lord and Root of David, and also his Son and Offspring according to the Flesh; whom God freely sent into the World, because of his great love to the World; who as freely gave himself Ransom for all; tasting Death for every Man; a Propitiation for our Sins; and not for ours only, but also for the Sins of the whole World. Luke 20.24. Rev 22.16. 1 Tim. 2.5,6. 1 John 2.2. Heb. 2.9.[80]

There are two important revisions to the article. The first is the addition of "being the true Lord." The original edition read "truly Davids Lord." The revised language seems to be an effort to reinforce the assertion that Jesus is truly God. Grantham in his explanatory supplement to the article writes Jesus is "secretly God of God his Father" and "God's Son, of God."[81] The supplement reinforces that Jesus' divine substance is that of the same substance as the Father.

---

78. There is the 1663 *Brief Confession*. However, this publication is not a new nor a revised edition, but only a republication of the 1660 edition. Holmes convincingly argues that there was "in fact no 1663 edition of the Confession." Holmes, "Note," 5. So, this confession will not be considered. Another popular General Baptist confession is the 1679 *Orthodox Creed*. This confession will not be considered as it was never affirmed nor published by the General Assembly. However, it should be noted that the *Orthodox Creed* employs orthodox trinitarian terms in reference to the Son of God, "*Coequal, Coessential*, and *Coeternal*, with the Father." *Orthodox Creed*, 5.

79. Whitley, *MGA*, 1:30.

80. *Brief Confession* (1691) art. 3.

81. Grantham, *Christianismus Primitivus*, 2:63.

The second important revision is the addition of the phrase "Off-spring according to the Flesh" in reference to being the son of David. The original reads "Davids Off-spring." The revised language seems to be an effort to reinforce the assertion that Jesus is truly Man. Grantham, in his explanatory supplement to the article, writes that Jesus had taken "on our man."[82] The supplement reinforces that Jesus shared the full humanity of man.

Both revisions would appear to distance the article from Caffyn's Christology as there is less room for a broader interpretation regarding Christ's deity and humanity. Nonetheless, Caffyn was a subscriber to the 1691 *Brief Confession*. Though the Assembly was not trying to distance nor correct Caffyn, the Assembly did attempt to clarify their Christology, which was orthodox. However, the Assembly still employed vague enough language that allowed for unorthodox interpretations.

The 1703 Brief Confession

One other confession needs to be considered—the 1703 *Brief Confession* of the General Association. In 1696 a group of General Baptist churches separated from the General Assembly to form the General Association. The reason for their separation was to preserve the purity of their churches "from that gross heresye."[83] That gross heresy was the unorthodox Christology of Caffyn. After a few years in existence, the Association decided to publish its own confession of faith. That confession was to be an improvement upon the 1660 *Brief Confession*.[84] The articles of the 1703 and the 1660 confessions are approximately the same.[85] The main improvements are found in articles 1 and 3.

While article 1 of the 1660 confession only addresses God the Father, article 1 of the 1703 confession addresses the whole of the godhead: Father, Son, and Holy Spirit. The article reads:

> We believe and are very confident, That there is one, and but one Living and True GOD, who is from Everlasting to Everlasting and changeth not; without Body, parts, or Passions Essentially present in all Places, of Infinite power, wisdom, and goodness, the maker and preserver of all things in Heaven and Earth, visible and Invisible; and in this Divine and Infinite Being, or Unity

---

82. Grantham, *Christianismus Primitivus*, 2:63.
83. Whitley, *MGA*, 1:47.
84. "It was agreed that our Brethern Hook and Wm Smith do take care to make such Improuement upon the sheet Articles of Faith reprinted." Whitley, *MGA*, 1:75.
85. Bass provides a helpful summary of the differences between the two confessions' articles. Bass, *Caffynite Controversy*, 179.

of Godhead, there are three persons, the Father, the Son, and the Holy Ghost, of one Substance, Power, and Eternity; but as for all other Doctrines that are contrary and opposite to this above-said article, we abhor and solemnly protest.[86]

This revised article is significant for three reasons. First, the article is a near restatement of the 1563 *Thirty-Nine Articles of Religion*.[87] The language of the article, therefore, is primarily confessional language rather than purely scriptural language. The Association sought to bring greater clarity to their belief by use of clear, confessional language. Second, the article is on the godhead rather than just on God the Father. Christology cannot be spoken of without treading upon the Trinity. This article clearly affirms that the Son is of the same substance as that of the Father. Third, the Association believed that what they stated in article 1 was so clear that it did deny every doctrine that goes contrary to it; that is, the article does not allow for a broader interpretation.

Article 3 is on Christology and, as stated earlier, it is comprised of two parts. The first part articulates the person of Christ and the second part articulates the work of Christ. The 1703 completely revises the first part and leaves the second part as stated in the 1660 confession. Only the first part will be stated here: "That the second Person of the Trinity is the only Begotten Son of God, who did in the Fulness of Time take to himself of our nature and Substance in the womb of the Blessed Virgin Mary, of whom in respect of the Flesh, he was made; and soe is true God and true Man, our Emanuel."[88] As with article 1, this article employs confessional language. The first part on the person of Christ draws heavily from article 2 in the *Thirty-Nine Articles of Religion*.[89] Since the Son's full deity was already affirmed in the first article, this article addresses the Son's full humanity. The article is clear that the Son took the nature of Man. The General Baptists of

---

86. All quotations of the 1703 *Brief Confession* come from Bass's republication of the confession in *Caffynite Controversy*, 179–86.

87. "There is but one living and true God, everlasting, without body, parts, or passions; of infinite power, wisdom, and goodness; the Maker and Preserver of all things, both visible and invisible. And in unity of this Godhead there be three persons; of one substance, power, and eternity, the Father, the Son, and the Holy Ghost." Dennison, *Reformed Confessions*, 2:754.

88. Bass, *Caffynite Controversy*, 179–80.

89. "The Son, which is the Word of the Father, begotten from everlasting of the Father, the very and eternal God, and of one substance with the Father, took man's nature in the womb of the blessed virgin, of her substance: so that the whole and perfect natures, that is to say, the Godhead and manhood, were joined together in one person, never to be divided, whereof is one Christ, very God and very man." Dennison, *Reformed Confessions*, 2:754.

the Association articulated a confession that Caffyn, and others like him, could not affirm.

The 1703 *Brief Confession*, though all the other articles are similar to the 1660 confession, stands in stark contrast to the 1660 *Brief Confession*. The confession utilized traditional confessional language in the doctrines that the Association sought to distance itself from the Assembly. The language adopted by the Association in article 1 of the 1703 confession from the *Thirty-Nine Articles of Faith* is the language for which the subscribers at Salters' Hall will advocate. However, the General Baptists at Salters' Hall, except for one, rejected this language. A question becomes who were the General Baptists present at Salters' Hall? Were they of the Assembly, the Association, or a mixture of the two? If General Baptists of the Association were present, it is reasonable to assume that more than one would have subscribed to the language proposed at Salters' Hall.

In conclusion, the General Baptists, both the Assembly and the Association, sought to strengthen the language of Christology and the Trinity in their confessions. While the Assembly in 1691 did improve upon the 1660 *Brief Confession*, the language was still vague allowing Caffyn and others to subscribe to it while holding an unorthodox opinion. The Association, on the other hand, employed specific confessional language to articulate an orthodox Christology and Trinity.

The Response of the General Baptists in Assembly

The General Assembly heard no less than four formal complaints against Caffyn in 1693, 1696, 1698, and 1700.[90] The common responses throughout the four assembly responses were either to not address the matter or

---

90. It is commonly supposed that the Assembly addressed an accusation in 1686. The 1686 date of this Assembly is speculation. Whitley's *MGA* does not contain minutes for a 1686 Assembly. In fact, there is a gap in the minutes between 1668 and 1689. The lack of extant minutes for these years is not evidence that the Assembly did not meet. (This gap is not unexpected as it was a time of great persecution against dissenters.) The assumption of a 1686 Assembly in which a charge against Caffyn was discussed is based on Taylor. He says an Assembly met sometime prior to September 1686 because of a statement in the Biddendon Church book dated September 6, 1686. The statement is that the church can have communion with other neighbor congregations "except it be with such persons as standby and justify Joseph Wright in his late accusations, which have been a grief to many." Taylor, *HEGB*, 1:467. The statement appears to be a reference to Wright's accusations against Caffyn. What is in question, however, is whether the statement is a reference to a particular Assembly meeting in 1686 or to an Assembly meeting at all. Up until 1686 the dispute between Wright and Caffyn was not unfamiliar to General Baptist churches. It may be that an Assembly in 1686 addressed a Caffynite accusation; but since it cannot be ascertained, it will not be discussed.

to acquit Caffyn of holding any heretical views regarding Christology or the Trinity. Though the Assembly meetings addressed more than just Caffynite charges, only matters relating to Christology, the Trinity, and charges against Caffyn will be discussed.

The 1693 General Assembly

The Assembly met on June 6, 1693, in Goodman's Fields in London. Caffyn is not listed as a messenger at the Assembly so he may not have been in attendance.[91] At the meeting the "articles of faith being Audible read was Universally ownd."[92] The articles of faith are more than likely the 1691 *Brief Confession*. The reason for the reading and owning of the articles of faith was to declare "all that own it walking suitable thereto" may have communion together.[93] Assuming the minutes as recorded are the order in which the events of the Assembly occurred, this reading and affirmation of the confession occur prior to an accusation brought against Caffyn. By affirming the 1691 *Brief Confession*, the Assembly did not exclude Caffyn nor others of like-mindedness from communion since he and they affirmed the confession.

The Assembly considered a question regarding Christology. This question was posed to the Assembly by the Northern Association.[94] The question was as follows:

> Whether Christ as he was the Word of God John 1,1, Albeit that he was God yet he is not of the Uncreeted Substance of his father But God made him a Creature only And secondly that this Creature was made flesh & Blood & Bones in the Virgins Womb Not by taking flesh of the Virgin Mary but yt ye Matter (viz) the Word was turned into flesh in the Virgins Wombe.[95]

The question has two denials embedded in it. First, it denies Christ's full deity. He is claimed to be the Word of God but with His divine substance being less than that of the Father's—the Father being of uncreated substance and Christ being of created substance. The question also denies Christ's full humanity. He is claimed to be born of flesh, blood, and bone but his

---

91. Caffyn may have been present but not as a messenger and therefore his presence was not recorded.

92. Whitley, *MGA*, 1:39.

93. Whitley, *MGA*, 1:39.

94. Whitley identifies the Northern Association as churches comprised in Buckinghamshire, Essex, and London. Whitley, *MGA*, 1:39.

95. Whitley, *MGA*, 1:39–40.

humanity being different from that of Mary's. Christ did not take his flesh from Mary but was turned into flesh in Mary's womb. These two denials go straight to the heart of the controversy surrounding Caffyn. He was accused as affirming both parts of the question.

The question was audibly read to those in attendance at the Assembly and it was "universally owned to be an error in the Terms aforsed."[96] All those present and voting at the Assembly answered the question in the negative. Of interest is the Assembly's basis for denying the truthfulness of the question. The basis being "in the terms aforesaid." The terms are the terms in which the question was stated. The question utilizes terms that are extrabiblical, yet the terms get to the substance of the Caffynite controversy. The Assembly seems to deny the question based on the extrabiblical terms more than the substance of the question.

The last item of business, according to the order of the minutes, was an accusation brought directly against Caffyn, "Brother Smart charging Caffin wth owning the last aforemenconed Ques."[97] William Smart was from the General Baptist church in Wingrave, part of the Northern Association. He may have been the one, on behalf of the Northern Association, to raise the question to the Assembly. He appears to be in direct opposition to Caffyn. Smart was a signer of the 1679 *Orthodox Creed* primarily authored by Thomas Monck. Since the Assembly answered the question in the negative (at least based on the terms used), Smart accused Caffyn of owning the substance of the question. That is, Caffyn denied that Christ's deity was of the same substance as the Father and Christ's humanity was of the same substance as the virgin Mary. What evidence, if any, presented by Smart is not stated. As discussed above, Caffyn wrote little about Christology and mostly made verbal statements that called his Christology into question; therefore, Smart would have difficulty presenting hard evidence to the Assembly, and most evidence would be hearsay. Also, if Caffyn was not present at the Assembly, as it appears, there would be no way to directly question him. Without any mention of deliberation, "Bror Caffin was acquitted by far the greater part of the Assembly."[98] The vote shows that not all present and voting at the Assembly believed Caffyn to be orthodox; however, there were enough voting who believed he was orthodox.

---

96. Whitley, *MGA*, 1:40.
97. Whitley, *MGA*, 1:40.
98. Whitley, *MGA*, 1:40.

The 1696 General Assembly

The Assembly met on June 3, 1696, in Goswell Street, London. Caffyn was present at the assembly as a messenger.[99] The matter "touching our God & our Lord Jesus Christ" was brought to the Assembly for debate.[100] The matter is a reference to the Trinity and the person of Christ. Caffyn was not directly accused at this assembly; however, the subject matter does pertain to the controversy surrounding him. The matter was brought by the Western Churches via reference to a prayer offered by William Smith.[101] The identity of the Western Churches is not given. It could be a reference to the Western Association of General Baptists located around Taunton in Somerset.[102] William Smith is likely the pastor of a General Baptist church in Welton of Northamptonshire.[103] Bass states Smith "uttered a public prayer in which he stressed the Assembly's need to address heresy within the body."[104] The Assembly's heresy allegedly was that they allowed Caffyn's Christology to be tolerated within the Assembly. The Western Churches sought a vote to be taken on whether the matter of the Trinity and the person of Christ be heard and debated at the Assembly. Whether the Western Churches were supportive of Caffyn and his views is not known.[105] The vote "Carried in the Negative."[106] The Assembly was not willing to address the topic of the Trinity nor of the person of Christ.

This refusal by the Assembly led to the formation of the General Association in 1697. On May 12, 1697, eight General Baptist churches held the first General Association meeting in White's Alley, Moorfields. At this meeting they affirmed their decision to leave the Assembly "because we cannot have communion with any persons at ye Lord's Table, nor admit any to preach amongst vs that are in communion with that General Assembly vntill that assembly purge themselves from ye said heresye for which we made our separation from them."[107]

---

99. His name is spelled "Mathew Cattyn." Whitley, in a footnote, acknowledges this to be "Caffin." Whitley, *MGA*, 1:43.

100. Whitley, *MGA*, 1:43.

101. Whitley, *MGA*, 1:43.

102. See the minutes from the Assembly on June 6, 1693, where the Assembly encourages the Western Association to revive their meetings and to hold their next meeting at Taunton. Whitley, *MGA*, 1:38.

103. Taylor, *HEGB*, 1:233.

104. Bass, *Caffynite Controversy*, 49.

105. See chapter 5 for a discussion of the Western Association's unwillingness to utilize confessional language.

106. Whitley, *MGA*, 1:43.

107. Whitley, *MGA*, 1:45–46.

That same month on May 26 and 27, 1697, the Assembly met in Goswell Street, London. Two matters are of interest. First, the Assembly responded to the churches who separated from the Assembly. The Assembly declared the action of those brethren who separated from them in 1696 as disorderly.[108] The messengers then decided to send letters to the churches of those men to inform them of the Assembly's opinion. The messengers must have feared that more churches considered leaving the Assembly because they also sent the letter to all the General Baptist churches that were not present at the current Assembly.

The second matter of interest is a letter from the West Association that was read at the Assembly.[109] The contents of the letter are not stated in the minutes. The letter raised the same issue as from the 1696 Assembly by the Western Churches—the Trinity and the person of Christ. So, the West Association is more than likely the Western Churches of 1696. The Assembly gave two responses to the letter. The first is that they will maintain their decision from 1696 that it is best to not debate such topics publicly. This response reveals that the Assembly was unwilling, maybe even fearful, to enter a debate that had led several churches to separate.[110] Though the Assembly desired to not debate the Trinity nor the person of Christ, they did recognize that members of churches probably would enter such discussions with one another. Therefore, the second response of the Assembly sought to place perimeters upon such discussions by stating, "And it's further Agreed by this Assembly that if any persons of our Comunity do for time to Come Debate the Controversy respecting the Trinity and the Christ of God whether publickly or privately that they do manage the Controversy in their Debates *in Scripture Words and terms & in no other terms*."[111] Now in a very clear statement the General Baptists publicly uphold the Protestant Principle as their guiding principle regarding the doctrine of the Trinity and of the person of Christ. This is in keeping with article 23 of the 1691 *Brief Confession*, "That the Holy Scripture is the Rule whereby Saints both in matters of Faith, and Conversation, are to be regulated."[112]

---

108. Whitley, *MGA*, 1:50. It appears that the men present at the 1696 Assembly stated their intent to separate while at the Assembly. However, the 1696 minutes do not reflect such action being taken.

109. Whitley, *MGA*, 1:51. This may be a reference to the "Western" Association that was abbreviated as "West."

110. Fearful because the public debate of the Trinity and the person of Christ within the Assembly would only further spread the controversy to more General Baptist churches, potentially causing more fracture.

111. Whitley, *MGA*, 1:51 (emphasis added).

112. *Brief Confession* (1691) art. 23.

The 1698 General Assembly

In 1698, the General Assembly met on June 15. Caffyn is not listed as present at the Assembly. Two separate but related matters were brought before the messengers at the Assembly. The first matter brought was a series of three statements for the Assembly to affirm or deny. The source of the three statements is not given, but it may have been the Western Association of churches who raised similar issues in past Assemblies.[113] The three statements are, "Whether the ffather Distinct or Separate from the Word and the Holy Host is the Most High God. That our Lord Jesus Christ is a God only by Deputation as Magistrates and Judges are. That the Body of our Lord Jesus Christ Consisting of flesh blood and bones is not of the same substance as ours (to Wit) Mankind."[114] The first statement concerns whether the persons of the Triune God are each truly God.[115] The second statement is whether Jesus is God only by declaration, presumably by the Father. And the third statement is whether Jesus is not of the same substance as all of mankind.

The response of the Assembly to the statements was that "all the Members thereof declared that the Sd 3 particulars last above Mentioned and each one of them to be Error."[116] If the recording of the three statements are accurate by the secretary of the Assembly, then the response of the Assembly is peculiar. That the Assembly denied that Jesus was merely deputized as God and that Jesus did not have the same substance as mankind is not surprising. The Assembly was consistent with its previous decisions in 1693 and 1696, but denying the first statement is puzzling. The first statement is not worded like the other two statements. Those statements clearly affirmed that Jesus was not of the same substance as the Father nor of the same substance as mankind. The first statement, however, is more of a question than a statement, appearing to ask whether the Father is distinct from the Word (presumably in substance and not in person) and whether the Holy Spirit is of the same substance as the Father.[117] This statement requires a yes or no

---

113. The beginning of the 1698 minutes state, "An address from the Western Association being read and the particulars therein being largely & Deliberately Debated." Whitley, *MGA*, 1:52. The 1696 Assembly minutes state the Western Churches wanted to discuss and debate the matters of the Trinity and the person of Christ but the Assembly voted to not enter such a discussion. Also, at the 1697 Assembly, the West Association raised the issue of the Trinity and the person of Christ via a letter. The Assembly again voted to not enter such debate. The matter that the Western Churches wanted to bring up in 1696 and 1697 is now being brought up in 1698.

114. Whitley, *MGA*, 1:53. The "Holy Host" is most likely to be read "Holy Ghost."

115. This is the first Assembly to particularly address the deity of the Holy Spirit.

116. Whitley, *MGA*, 1:53.

117. The phrase "Most High God" was a statement that affirmed the Father as being

response. Yet, the Assembly's recorded response is that the statement was found to be in error. What is in error? That the Father is distinct from the Word? If so, then that would be a consistent response by the Assembly as they have affirmed that Jesus is of the same substance as the Father in 1693. But what of the Holy Spirit's status as being truly God? Did the Assembly find it to be in error that the Holy Spirit is the "Most High God" or that the Holy Spirit is not the "Most High God?" The 1691 *Brief Confession of Faith* states in article 7 concerning the Holy Spirit, "There are three that bear record in Heaven, the Father, the Word, and the Holy Spirit, and these are one; 1 John 5:7."[118] Though this statement could be affirmed by both orthodox and nonorthodox persons (i.e., Caffyn), benefit of the doubt ought to be given to the Assembly. The Assembly has sought to be orthodox regarding the deity of the Son, so it may be that the Assembly also sought to be orthodox regarding the deity of the Holy Spirit. If this is true, then the Assembly made a stronger and clearer affirmation regarding the Holy Spirit's deity than the 1691 *Brief Confession*.

The second matter raised at the 1698 Assembly was a letter received from a Brother Garrett written on behalf of the Northamptonshire churches.[119] The letter was in response to the letters sent out by the Assembly in 1697 to churches who separated from the Assembly and who were absent from the Assembly that year. The received letter of 1698 references "a printed paper being produced and the matter therein Menconed to be the opinion of Matthew Caffin."[120] Whether the "printed paper" was actually written by Caffyn or whether it contained alleged teachings of Caffyn is not clear. Either way, the Northamptonshire churches sought the opinion of the Assembly as to whether the Assembly affirmed or denied the opinions of the paper attributed to Caffyn. The opinions were "that the Son of God or the word was not of the Uncreated Nature & substance of the Father neither of the Created Nature & substance of his Mother."[121] In response, the

---

truly God in substance. To attribute this phrase to the Holy Spirit would insinuate the Holy Spirit is truly God in substance as the Father.

118. *Brief Confession* (1691) art. 7.

119. The identity of the writer is not known with certainty. Whitley identifies the man as Thomas Garrett from Northamptonshire. Whitley, *MGA*, 1:53. Whitley also says Taylor believed the writer to be John Garrett of Berkhampstead and cites Taylor at *HEGB* 1:231. Whitley, *MGA*, 1:53. Taylor does mention a John Garrett on that page, but there is no mention of the 1698 letter. Taylor does address the 1698 letter at *HEGB* 1:470–71. However, Taylor gives the man's name only as "Mr. Garrett." Whitley appears to link the John Garrett of p. 231 with the Mr. Garrett of pp. 470–71. Whether Taylor intended the two names to be the same person is not known.

120. Whitley, *MGA*, 1:53.

121. Whitley, *MGA*, 1:53.

"Assembly being Called over by their names it was Owned by all Save one to be Errors."[122] The Assembly, again, is being consistent in their decisions to affirm the full deity and humanity of Jesus. If the letter contained either the actual writing of Caffyn or accurate statements of Caffyn written by others, then the Assembly did vote against the opinion of Caffyn regarding Christ.

The Northamptonshire letter appears to ask for more than just the Assembly's position on the opinions attributed to Caffyn; it seemingly asks for the Assembly to bring Caffyn to trial to determine whether he and the Assembly are in agreement regarding the Trinity and Christology. The Assembly agreed that "Matthew Caffin shall be admitted to a faire Tryall in our Next Assembly."[123] The next Assembly would be held two years later in 1700.

The 1700 General Assembly

The Assembly met May 22–24, 1700, in Horslaydown. Caffyn was present at the Assembly as this was the time for his trial. The minutes do not contain the actual debate that occurred at Caffyn's trial. The minutes record that eight men were selected to "prepare & propose" an expedient to the Assembly, the expedient being on the Trinity and the person of Christ.[124] This committee of eight conferred with Caffyn on the preparation and proposal of the expedient.[125] The men returned to the Assembly and proposed the following:

> That Christ as he was the word is from the Beginning But in Time that words tooke not on him the Nature of Angells but he took on him the Seed of Abraham & as such is Emanuell God with us or God manifest in the flesh & he is the word is one with the ffather & the Holy Ghost & as he was God manifest in the flesh so is he Jesus that Tasted Death for Every Man And further whereas that have been & yet are debates about the most High God wee Conceive he is one Infirmative Unchangable & Eternall Spiritt & Incomprehensable Godhead & doth Subsist in the father ye the word & the Holy Ghost.[126]

---

122. Whitley, *MGA*, 1:54. If all who voted on the three statements also voted on the opinions of the letter, then it is difficult to understand how the one person who did not find the opinions to be in error was able to find all three statements to be in error.

123. Whitley, *MGA*, 1:54.

124. The eight men were Amory, Brown, Miller, Hoshem, Gale, Cooch, Vincent, and Kirby. Taylor states that four of the men were selected from among Caffyn's friends and four of the men from Caffyn's accusers. Taylor, *HEGB*, 1:472.

125. Taylor, *HEGB*, 1:472.

126. Whitley, *MGA*, 1:66–67.

The expedient contains four affirmations. The first affirmation is the humanity of Christ. The statement is not strong as it only states that Christ took on him the "Seed of Abraham" and that he was "God manifest in the flesh." While Christ's humanity is affirmed, it is not clear what is meant by these statements. The committee of eight did not go outside the bounds of scriptural language to articulate Christ's humanity.

The second affirmation Is the deity of Christ. This affirmation, like the first, is not definitive, but simply restates what the 1691 *Brief Confession* already says in article 7—that the Father, Word, and Holy Spirit are one; again, scriptural language only is used. The third affirmation is the general atonement of Christ. This was not a debated point, but regularly found among the General Baptists' statements on Christology. The last affirmation is the triunity of the godhead. This is the most definitive affirmation of the four. The reference to "the most High God" was used specifically in trinitarian discussions of the seventeenth century as a reference to divine substance and attributes; it had little, if no, room for broad interpretation. The expedient declares that the most high God is the godhead that is comprised of the Father, the Word, and the Holy Ghost. Therefore, it assigns divine substance and attributes to all three members of the godhead.

Upon hearing the expedient read audibly several times, the Assembly approved it, but with one restriction. The restriction was:

> That whatever Concepcon any of us might have concerning the Sevall Expressions therein contained Contrary to the Comon Exception thereof yet if any one preaching printing discoursing or otherwise shall publish or Declare such is the Concepcon thereof to the Disturbance of the peace of the Church or Churches of Christ That are of our Comunion such person is by the Assembly declared to be Disorderly & to be accountable therefore Unto the Assembly.[127]

The restriction allowed for churches and members to have different conceptions of the expressions contained in the expedient.[128] And if a person had a different conception, he was not to cause division among other churches or members by declaring his opinion is the opinion of the Assembly.

Since Caffyn participated in the production of the expedient and the Assembly affirmed the expedient, it is not surprising that the Assembly's

---

127. Whitley, *MGA*, 1:67.

128. Taylor's recounting of the restriction clarifies the language of the minutes, "That whatsoever conceptions any of us may have, concerning the several expressions contained in the Expedient, contrary to the common acceptation thereof." Taylor, *HEGB*, 1:474.

trial of Caffyn resulted in Caffyn's acquittal of holding heretical views. Also, the Assembly heard "the Defence Bror Mathew Caffin made in the Assembly and his Acknowledgment was in the satisfaccon of the Assembly."[129] His defense is not conveyed in the minutes. Caffyn could affirm the statements of the expedient as the statement were scripturally vague. The most difficult statement for Caffyn to affirm, most likely, was the fourth statement regarding the Trinity. As stated above, Caffyn held to a form of subordinationism, therefore, he would not have affirmed the full deity of Christ. However, if the Assembly allowed for various, if not private, interpretations of the expedient, then Caffyn could have affirmed the fourth statement holding to his interpretation of the language.

The Assembly tried to walk a middle path between upholding orthodox doctrine regarding the Trinity and the person of Christ and allowing member churches to hold various conceptions of agreed confessions and statements. The reason for this is that the Assembly sought to preserve unity in fellowship by allowing for differing doctrinal views. This response only led to churches separating from the Assembly and allowing questionable doctrine within the Assembly.

Conclusion

The General Assembly sought to remain orthodox regarding the Trinity and the person of Christ. That is, the Assembly wanted to affirm that God exists in three persons—Father, Son, and Holy Spirit—with each person being equally God. Also, the Assembly wanted to uphold that Jesus is both truly God and truly man. But the Assembly, unlike the newly formed Association, was unwilling to utilize classical confessional language to articulate such doctrine. Such language would have clarified what they affirmed. Yet, the Assembly feared subscription to such language would impose another standard of authority outside the scriptural language. Also, the Assembly feared such language would divide the churches on matters that full comprehension is not possible. Therefore, the Assembly sought to be faithful to Scripture and to their conviction by being ambiguous in language and amicable in affiliation.

---

129. Whitley, *MGA*, 1:67.

4

Confessional and Confrontational

How Seventeenth-Century Particular Baptists Responded to Antitrinitarianism

THIS CHAPTER CONTINUES THE subject from the previous chapter but now addresses the Particular Baptists' response to antitrinitarianism. Whereas the General Baptists were ambiguous in their trinitarian language, the Particular Baptists responded with precision in their trinitarian language.

The Trinitarian Dispute with Thomas Collier

The antitrinitarian dispute among the Particular Baptists occurred in the mid to late seventeenth century with Thomas Collier. Collier was an influential Baptist through his writings and his service in the Western Association. His questionable, and at times unorthodox, statements on God and Christ were cause for concern among the Particular Baptists.

The fullest biography of Collier (1613?–1691) is given by Richard D. Land in his 1979 dissertation, "Doctrinal Controversies of English Particular Baptists (1644–1691) as Illustrated by the Career and Writings of Thomas Collier." While Stephen Wright states that nothing is certainly known concerning Collier's birth and early life,[1] Land concludes that Collier was born in the county of Somerset in the year 1613.[2] Collier died in the year 1691.[3]

---

1. Wright, "Collier, Thomas," para. 1.
2. Land, "Doctrinal Controversies," 20.
3. Wright, "Collier, Thomas," para. 1.

How Collier became a Baptist is not known, but he is known to have been a Particular Baptist by the mid to late 1640s. Working from Collier's *A Brief and True NARRATIVE*,[4] Land states that Collier affirmed he had been a member of William Kiffen's church in Devonshire Square, London, before returning to Somerset around 1651.[5] Kiffen left Henry Jessey's church in March 1644 to start his own church based on credobaptism.[6] Also, Collier appears to have had a relationship with Hanserd Knollys, a close friend of Kiffen. Knollys had been a member of Jessey's church, along with Kiffen, until he, too, came to Baptist convictions by 1645. He also left Jessey's church to start his own church based on credobaptism.[7] In 1647, Knollys wrote the preface for Collier's *Exaltation of Christ*. Therefore, Collier would have been a member of Kiffen's church no earlier than March 1644 and possibly no later than 1647.

Collier could have come to Baptist convictions prior to this time. Collier had become infamous in parts of west England where he traveled and taught his convictions. Thomas Edwards took note of Collier in his 1646 *Gangræna*. Edwards reports a Presbyterian minister from west England accusing Collier as among the first to "sow the seeds of Anabaptisme, Antisabbatarianisme, and some Arminianisme."[8] B. R. White reviews Edward's critique of Collier and concludes, "It is clear that, in 1645–46, Collier's own teaching showed close sympathy with the Calvinism, the ecclesiology and the views of the Church and State taught in the 1644 *Confession*."[9] The "1644 *Confession*" referenced by White is the *First London Baptist Confession of Faith*, published in 1644 (1LCF44). If White is correct, then Collier adopted Baptist convictions prior to 1646, the year *Gangræna* was published. Land also notes Collier's agreement with the 1LCF44 by his examination of Collier's earlier writings against Presbyterians and Independents (mid to late 1640s). He, therefore, concludes that Collier came to Particular Baptist convictions soon after 1644.[10]

---

4. Samuel Renihan says that Collier's *A Brief and True NARRATIVE* is "one of the most important sources for understanding the events preceding the publication of the Second London Baptist Confession of Faith, but it has long been unknown because its only surviving copy (to my knowledge) is held in the Congregational Library of London." S. Renihan, *Petty France Church*, 98.

5. Land, "Doctrinal Controversies," 25.

6. Bustin, *Paradox and Perseverance*, 77.

7. Bustin, *Paradox and Perseverance*, 79.

8. Edwards, *Third Part of Gangræna*, 29. By "anabaptisme" is meant the practice of credobaptism.

9. White, "Thomas Collier and Gangræna Edwards," 107.

10. Land, "Doctrinal Controversies," 288. Land admits that the events and means that led Collier to Particular Baptist doctrine are not known by modern-day historians.

Though not as well known in modern day, Collier was a well-known figure in his day. He was known by his published works. Collier wrote or edited thirty-seven works, of which thirty-three are still extant.[11] He was also known by his ministerial activity, primarily in the west of England. Collier was an active evangelist and planter of Baptist churches. Land notes that Collier "had by 1646 already established the pattern of church planting and cultivation which characterized his ministry for four decades after his return to his native Somerset."[12] Upon his return to Somerset in the early 1650s, Collier was able to conduct his ministry of evangelism and church planting through the Western Association. The Association in 1654 ordained Collier "for the performance of that worke that hee hath beene a long tyme exercised in, namely, in gathering and confirming the church."[13] White states that Collier had already been conducting this ministry of evangelism and church planting through the Western Association, but the Association had never formally set Collier apart for the work until this time.[14] Collier's popularity would make it necessary for the Particular Baptists to address his heterodoxy so that they would not be implicated along with him for such views.

Collier's Trinitarianism in Confessions

Collier's antitrinitarianism in his later ministry must be understood in light of what he upheld in his earlier ministry. Two confessions that Collier affirmed provide insight into Collier's trinitarianism in the decades of the 1640s and 1650s. The two confessions are the 1LCF44 and what is generally referred to as the *Somerset Confession* of 1656.

The First London Baptist Confession of Faith

As attested to by White and Land, Collier agreed with the 1LCF44 early in his writings and ministry. The first article of the confession is a general statement on God, but it does include the affirmation "that there is but one God, one Christ, one Spirit."[15] The vagueness of the statement makes it uncertain whether it is an assertion of the Trinity. The statement is from the "one"

---

11. Land, "Doctrinal Controversies," 16. The attestation to the number of works written or edited by Collier are according to Land in 1979.

12. Land, "Doctrinal Controversies," 29.

13. White, *Association Records*, 103. For the dating of Collier's ordination in 1654, see White, *Association Records*, 109n50.

14. White, *Association Records*, 109.

15. *Confession of Faith* (1644), unnumbered page.

statements found in Ephesians 4:4–6, from which the other statements of these verses are given in the first article. If it is trinitarian, then by "God" is to be understood "God the Father." And if that is what the statement is to infer, there are no declarations as to Christ's nor the Spirit's relation with the Father. More likely, the statement is only as intended in the Ephesians passage; that is, the statement articulates what Christians share in common.

The second article of the confession expresses better the Particular Baptist view on the Trinity, which states in part, "In this God-head, there is the Father, the Sonne, and the Spirit; being every one of them one and the same God; and therefore not divided, but distinguished one from another by their severall properties; the Father being from himself, the Sonne of the Father from everlasting, the holy Spirit proceeding from the Father and the Sonne."[16] The statement on the Trinity affirms a classical trinitarianism. Having confessed "that there is but one God" in article 1, it upholds that within the one God there are three distinct persons of the Trinity—the Father, the Son, and the Holy Spirit.[17] The persons are not divided by essence, but each being the same God. What distinguishes each person from the other are their several properties. These several properties are the origins of each person: the Father being eternal, the Son being eternally from the Father, and the Holy Spirit eternally proceeding from the Father and the Son.[18] The trinitarian statement does agree with an Athanasian trinitarianism by neither confusing the persons of the Trinity nor dividing the substance of God.[19]

However, the article is not a strong trinitarian statement. The authors of the 1LCF44 used the 1596 *True Confessions* as a basis for the confession.[20] For reasons unknown, the authors of the confession excluded the words *coeternal, coequal,* and *coessential* from paragraph two of *A True Confession*, which affirm the full deity of each of the persons.[21]

---

16. *Confession of Faith* (1644), unnumbered page.

17. The article does not employ the word "persons" in reference to the Father, Son, or Spirit.

18. The next section will demonstrate that Collier could not have agreed with this statement.

19. J. Renihan, *Vindication of the Truth*, 40.

20. J. Renihan notes that "approximately one-half of the text of the 1LCF44 is drawn from the *True Confessions*." J. Renihan, *Vindication of the Truth*, 13.

21. J. Renihan admits there may have been a form of biblicism among the authors as an explanation for omitting these terms. Citing White's article, "Doctrine of the Church in the Particular Baptist Confession 1644," Renihan agrees with White that these words may not have been considered biblical by the authors and therefore excluded. J. Renihan, *Vindication of the Truth*, 38.

Somerset Confession of Faith

The *Somerset Confession* of 1656 requires an introduction as it relates more directly with Collier. William Lumpkin states that the Western Association approved the confession in its seventh meeting on September 5-6, 1656, and that Collier was the primary author of the confession.[22] Twenty-four messengers representing sixteen churches affiliated with the Western Association did sign the confession.[23] However, regarding the date, White's *Association Records* from the Western Association, which are the reproduction of Collier's own records of the association from 1653 to 1658, do not include the adoption of a confession of faith.[24] In the September meeting a church had posed the question, "What is the saints' duty towards the magistrate at this day in the nation?" The association answered, "We refer those concerned herein for answer to the forty fourth article of the confession of the faith of the churches in these parts."[25] The reference is to the *Somerset Confession* as evidenced by the fact that the forty-fourth article of the confession does address the saints' duty to submit to the civil magistrate as it is an ordinance of God.[26] The association's answer assumes the familiarity by the churches with this confession. Land concludes that the association held a special meeting, for which there are no extant records, between April and August 1656 that approved the confession.[27]

Collier is the assumed author of the *Somerset Confession*. Edward Underhill is perhaps the earliest to attribute possible authorship to Collier. He first cites that Collier authored the "Epistle Dedicatory" as his name appears as such at the end.[28] Underhill then refers to Collier's ordination as a position of authority and leadership within the Western Association. He gives the office to which Collier was ordained as "Office of General Superintendent and Messenger to all the Associated Churches."[29] Although, the records from the association meeting do not use such language in reference to Collier's ordination.[30] Underhill appears to follow the interpretive

---

22. Lumpkin, *Baptist Confessions*, 200.
23. *Confession of the Faith*, unnumbered pages.
24. White, *Association Records*, 53. Collier published the association records in two tracts. One tract is the queries made by churches and addressed by the association. The other tract is the letters from the association to the churches.
25. White, *Association Records*, 66.
26. *Confession of the Faith*, 38-39.
27. Land, "Doctrinal Controversies," 256.
28. Underhill, *Confessions of Faith*, xi.
29. Underhill, *Confessions of Faith*, xi.
30. White, *Association Records*, 103-4.

lead of Ivimey and Fuller before him.[31] Land, following White, disputes this interpretation of Collier's ordination to a position of superintendency.[32] Nonetheless, Collier would not need to hold such a position to author a confession. Whether Collier held the position of superintendent or not, he did play a major role in the association. This is evidenced by the fact that Collier authored and signed many of the association's circular letters and proceedings.[33] Not discounting the role others may have had in the drafting of the *Somerset Confession*, it is not unreasonable to assume Collier's authorship. Regardless, Collier is among the twenty-four messengers who signed the confession. For this reason, the *Somerset Confession* is a much better indicator of Collier's trinitarianism than the 1LCF44.

As stated earlier, Collier agreed in doctrine with the 1LCF44. So, why write a new confession rather than reaffirm the 1LCF44? In the opening paragraph of the "Epistle Dedicatory," Collier states, "That our publishing this narrative of our faith and practice, is not from any dislike we found with the former confession of our beloved brethren, whom we own, and with whom we are one both in faith and practice, neither is there anything in ours contradictory to our brethren, that we know of, that have gone before us."[34] Two points stand out in this opening. The confession was not written for any defect found in the 1LCF44. And, Collier and the Western Association make clear that they are numbered among the other Particular Baptists. So, for Collier, he admits to no change of doctrine or practice from the 1LCF44.

The confession was written due to the spread of false teaching pervading churches within the region of the Western Association. The "Epistle Dedicatory" states, "Being very sensible of the great distractions and divisions that are amongst professing people in this nation, the many ways and wiles of Satan to seduce and deceive souls, the great departing from the faith, and that under glorious notions of spiritualness and holiness, . . . we could not but judge it our bounden duty in this our day to come forth in a renewed Declaration of our faith."[35] The "distractions and divisions" were the effects of the Quakers spread into western England. Based on Collier's writings against the Quakers within western England, Land asserts that Collier led the Western Association to write and publish the *Somerset Confession* to combat and disavow the Quakers.[36] The Quakers were known to have had

31. White, *Association Records*, 109.
32. Land, "Doctrinal Controversies," 49; White, *Association Records*, 109.
33. Underhill, *Confessions of Faith*, xi.
34. "Epistle Dedicatory" in *Confession of the Faith*.
35. "Epistle Dedicatory" in *Confession of the Faith*.
36. Land, "Doctrinal Controversies," 195.

a strong presence in western England. Timothy Dowley notes places of Quaker strongholds in Westmorland, and Cumberland, the southwestern counties of Gloucestershire, Somerset, and Dorset, and particularly in Bristol.[37] In the mid-1650s Broadmead Baptist Church in Bristol experienced its own battle with Quakerism being spread among its people.[38]

Regarding the trinitarianism of the *Somerset Confession*, the first article opens with an affirmation of monotheism, "We believe that there is but one God," and then gives fifteen attributes of God.[39] One would expect that the second article would state a confession of the Trinity, but it does not. In fact, the *Somerset Confession* does not have a specific article, nor even a specific statement, on the Trinity. One has to read through the confession and pull-out statements and inferences to put together the confession's trinitarianism.

Trinitarian implications on God the Son include articles 2 and 13. The second article of the confession is a statement on creation with an implication of God the Son participating in the act of creation. The article affirms that God did "create all things, by, and for Jesus Christ; Who is the Word of God."[40] The article does not assert anything of the Son's relation with the Father, only that God created by him and for him, implying the Son's deity in the work of creation. The thirteenth article addresses the dual nature of Jesus, stating, "We believe that Jesus Christ is Truly God...and truly man."[41] The statement does affirm the deity of the Son but with no further explanation. The *Somerset Confession*'s statements on the Son are statements with which Socinians could affirm.[42]

Trinitarian implications on the Holy Spirit are not to be found in the confession.[43] References to the works of the Spirit are scattered throughout

37. Dowley, "History of the English Baptists," 60. These are regions within the Western Association.

38. See Terrill, *Records* (Hayden), 105–11. The history of Broadmead Baptist Church is given in the next chapter.

39. *Confession of the Faith*, 1–2.

40. *Confession of the Faith*, 2.

41. *Confession of the Faith*, 8. That Jesus is affirmed to be the Son of God is attested to by article 12.

42. This is not to imply that the *Somerset Confession* is Socinian; it is only to suggest that the confession is not making a strong and distinctive statement on the Son. Alan Sell conjectures on the silence of trinitarian doctrine, "but am convinced that there are doctrinal silences at the places specified which could only hinder the objective of demonstrating agreement with the London Confession, and might indicate either inner-Baptist ecumenical concern or doctrinal hesitancy at crucial points, or both." Sell, "Doctrine, Polity, Liberty," in Brackney et al., *Pilgrim Pathways*, 13.

43. By this is not meant that the *Somerset Confession* denied the deity of the Holy

the articles, but the confession says nothing about His deity or relation with the Father or with the Son. The closest trinitarian statement found in the confession is in the twenty-fourth article on baptism. This article declares that those baptized may be baptized in the name of Jesus only or "in the name of the Father, Son and Holy Spirit."[44] While this is a trinitarian formula for baptism, the article makes no further comment.

The 1LCF44 and the *Somerset Confession* represent the trinitarianism of Collier in his early ministry. Neither confession is antitrinitarian; that is, neither confession asserts anything that is contrary to classical trinitarianism. However, neither confession is strongly trinitarian. The 1LCF44 excludes key terms such as "persons" and "coeternal" that would have strengthened its position on the Trinity. And the *Somerset Confession* is weaker on the Trinity than the 1LCF44 since it makes no formal declaration of the Trinity. One can infer from the confession that the Father, Son, and Holy Spirit are God, but nothing is said as to how the three relate. From these confessions, which Collier affirmed both and possibly authored one, one can conclude that Collier's trinitarianism in the 1640s and 1650s was vague at best.

Collier's Trinitarianism in Writings

Tracing Collier's doctrine over his career is not an easy course to follow.[45] Land estimates, based on Collier's known published works, "that there were only relatively brief periods of Collier's career when he was unquestionably orthodox" in comparison to the London Baptist Confessions of Faith in 1644 and 1677.[46] He concludes his dissertation on Collier by dividing Collier's writing career into five periods.[47] Prior to 1646, there is no evidence in Collier's publications that raised theological concern. From 1646 until 1651, some of Collier's writings raised concern among his contemporaries. During the period from 1652 through 1659, Collier is an orthodox Particular Baptist. During the years between 1659 and 1674, little is known of Collier's theology due to the absence of known publications. And, after 1674 until his final publication in 1691, Collier had departed from the doctrinal boundaries of the Particular Baptists.

Spirit; it is only meant that the confession makes no direct, nor indirect, statements on the Holy Spirit as the third Person of the Trinity.

44. *Confession of the Faith*, 20.

45. "Among the Particular Baptists, Thomas Collier (fl. 1634–1691) proved to be a moving target in regard to his orthodoxy." Weaver, "Hercules Collins," 64.

46. Land, "Doctrinal Controversies," 332.

47. Land, "Doctrinal Controversies," 332–33.

Collier's "A General Epistle"

During the early years of concern, Collier wrote "A General Epistle to the Universal Church" in 1649. The purpose of the book was to clear up "much confusion in the knowledge of the things of God" among Christians, as Collier saw it.[48] The book is short, ninety-eight pages, and composed of twenty-three chapters. Collier covers many topics similar to a systematic theological work. In chapter 2, Collier addresses "What God Is Not." The first thing Collier says God is not is that "he is not, first, as some imagine, *Three Persons, yet one God*, or three subsistings, distinguished though not divided."[49] Collier reasons that to distinguish three persons within God would be to divide God into three persons.

In "A General Epistle," Collier did not deny that the Scriptures refer to God as Father, Son, and Holy Spirit. But he did refuse to see the designation of persons as distinction between persons, "yet not three *subsistings* or *persons*, but *one* God made known under *three denominations*."[50] And then, even more explicit, Collier infers that "the *Son* is, *The everlasting Father*; the *Father* is in the *Son*, and so he is the *Son*; the *Spirit* is God, and so he is both the *Father* and the *Son*."[51] By these statements, Collier is closer to modalistic trinitarianism rather than a classical trinitariansim.

When God is referred to as Father, Collier says it is a reference to God as "purely God, of himself and in himself the glory."[52] When God is referred to as Son, Collier offers two options.[53] First, the Son is a reference to God's work in relation to creation, redemption, and the manifestation of love to men. The second option is that the Son is a reference to God taking the body of man at the incarnation. He specifically says, "And so his *body* must be the *body* of God, that is, The *body* that was taken into *union with God*; by which means he bears the denomination of *Son*, so that he is the *Son* by his *union* with man."[54] Since there is no distinction between the Father and

---

48. Collier, "General Epistle," in Collier, *Second Volume*, 2.

49. Collier, "General Epistle," in Collier, *Second Volume*, 4.

50. Collier, "General Epistle," in Collier, *Second Volume*, 7. Collier appears to have held to a form of *modalistic monarchianism*, the blurring of the distinctions between the Father, Son, and Holy Spirit in order to maintain the divine unity of God. See Kelly, *Early Christian Doctrines*, 115–23.

51. Collier, "General Epistle," in Collier, *Second Volume*, 7.

52. Collier, "General Epistle," in Collier, *Second Volume*, 5.

53. Collier, "General Epistle," in Collier, *Second Volume*, 5–6. Collier does not choose one option over the other, thus, he affirmed both options as possible interpretations based on the context of Scripture where God the Son is referenced.

54. Collier, "General Epistle," in Collier, *Second Volume*, 5. Collier seems to affirm *patripassianism*, that the Father suffered on the cross since there is no distinction

Son, Collier denies the eternal generation of the Son. Rather, generation, or begetting, implies that the one who begets is before the one begotten, therefore "the Father is before the *Son*" in time.[55] In respect to God being referred to as Holy Spirit, Collier states that it is a reference to the invisibility of God and His work in the Saints and in the world.[56]

In "A General Epistle" Collier clearly does not affirm classical trinitarianism, but rather a form of modalistic monarchianism.[57] If this true, then is that view of the Trinity consistent with the confessions of 1LCF44 and the *Somerset Confession*?

In regard to the 1LCF44, though the authors of that confession would not have affirmed the position of Collier, Collier's view is not entirely inconsistent with the 1LCF44. As stated earlier, the 1LCF44 has a weak confession on the Trinity though it does not deny classical trinitarianism. Collier's position is consistent with the statement of article 2, "In this God-head, there is the Father, the Sonne, and the Spirit; being every one of them one and the same God."[58] Collier would understand this statement in its literal sense being that there is no designation of persons in the statement.

The following statement, however, would be problematic for Collier as it states, "But distinguished one from another by their severall properties; the Father being from himself, the Sonne of the Father from everlasting, the holy Spirit proceeding from the Father and the Son."[59] This statement, as addressed in the previous section, affirms the eternal origins of each person of the Trinity. The Father is eternal who eternally begets the Son, and the Holy Spirit eternally proceeds from the Father and the Son. The three persons, therefore, are distinct from each other, which Collier denied.

How could Collier affirm the 1LCF44? It is possible that Collier could have interpreted the "severall properties" not literally but according to his understanding of the oneness of the three persons of the Trinity and therefore agree with the 1LCF44. It is possible that Collier affirmed the 1LCF44 prior to the publication of "A General Epistle" in 1649, but then changed

---

between the Father and the Son, "and the *bloud* of Christ, is said to be the, *The bloud* of God, Acts 20." Collier, "General Epistle," in Collier, *Second Volume*, 5.

55. Collier, "General Epistle," in Collier, *Second Volume*, 6. Collier is not articulating a form of Arianism since Arianism affirms the distinction between the Father and the Son both in time and divinity. Collier appears to be saying that God could not be referred to as Son until the time of the incarnation when a human body was united to God.

56. Collier, "General Epistle," in Collier, *Second Volume*, 6–7.

57. Land, "Doctrinal Controversies," 299.

58. *Confession of Faith* (1644), unnumbered pages.

59. *Confession of Faith* (1644), unnumbered pages.

his position contrary to the 1LCF44. Or it may be that White and Land are incorrect in saying that Collier affirmed the 1LCF44. More likely, Collier affirmed the 1646 revised version of the 1LCF44—the *First London Baptist Confession of Faith* (1LCF46). The 1LCF46 states in article 2, "In this divine and infinite being, there is the Father, the Word, and the holy Spirit, each having the whole divine essence, yet the essence undivided; all infinite without any beginning, therefore but one God, who is not to be divided in nature, and being, but distinguished by serverall peculiar relative properties."[60] The 1LCF46 removes language of the eternal origins of the three persons of the Trinity, making it vague enough for Collier to affirm.[61] For this reason, it is more likely that Collier affirmed the 1LCF46 rather than the 1LCF44.

Regarding the *Somerset Confession*, Collier's position on the Trinity in 1649 is consistent with this confession. This is not surprising since Collier is, most likely, the primary author of the *Somerset Confession*. One should note, however, that the *Somerset Confession* does not articulate a modalistic monarchian trinitarianism. Nonetheless, the *Somerset Confession* makes no direct statement on the Trinity, therefore, leaving room for a classical trinitarian and a modalistic trinitarian to affirm the confession.

Why would Collier leave the *Somerset Confession* so vague on the Trinity? Possibly, Collier still held to modalistic monarchianism at the time of writing but did not articulate it in the confession. He would not have stated such a position clearly and directly since the confession was adopted by the churches of the Western Association. It is doubtful that most, if not many, of the churches of the association would have affirmed modalism. Or it may be that Collier softened his modalism prior to 1656 but did not adopt classical trinitarianism at that time. Either option reveals that Collier's trinitarianism is consistent from 1649 to 1656, which demonstrates that his position did not substantively change during that time.[62] This is an argument against Land's assertion that Collier was an orthodox Particular Baptist from 1652 to 1659.

Collier's The Body of Divinity *and* An Additional Word

From the 1650s until the 1670s, Collier's unorthodox trinitarianism did not raise concern as there are no known writings by his contemporary Baptists

60. *Confession of Faith* (1646), unnumbered pages.

61. J. Renihan argues that the 1LCF46, though weak in its trinitarian construction, still affirms a classical confession of the Trinity. See J. Renihan, *Vindication of the Truth*, 39.

62. Another option is that Collier abandoned modalism and adopted classical trinitarianism but wrote the *Somerset Confession* poorly regarding the Trinity.

against him. This could give evidence that during this time Collier was holding to a vague Trinity and not espousing an explicit modalistic Trinity, but this would change with Collier's publication of *The Body of Divinity* in 1674 and then *An Additional Word* in 1676. The reaction of Collier's contemporaries will be considered in the next section.

Body of Divinity might be considered Collier's *magnum opus*. *Body of Divinity* is a systematic theology covering most theological topics ranging from who is God to the second coming of Christ.[63] Collier states in the preface, "And what ever may be found in any other of my Writing that may seem contrary to any thing in this, or is contrary in very deed, either understand it by this, or else let it fall to the ground, for days of Temptation oft-times brings forth effects, which occasions after Repentance."[64] Collier intended *Body of Divinity* to be his final statement on matters of theology. All his previous writings were to be sifted through this work.

The first chapter of *Body of Divinity* is theology proper, "Concerning God." Collier divides the chapter into four sections. The third section, "How He Doth Subsist," articulates Collier's understanding of the Trinity. The section begins with an overall declaration, "So in the Scriptures of Truth, the Father, Son (or Word) and Spirit is declared to be this one God, so that this one God subsistith in three, Father, Son, and holy Spirit, and these there are one, each of the three is God, and yet three is but one God."[65] The section then concludes with this summary statement, "The sum of all this, That God is One, Eternal, Infinite, Substantial Being, distinguished into Father, Son, and holy Spirit, and in all there are Divine and Distinct Relative Properties and Operations, yet in all no one wills, no one acts, without the other."[66] The opening and concluding statements are relatively orthodox.[67] They affirm an Athanasian confession by asserting that in the one God are three: Father, Son, and Holy Spirit; and the three are equally God. The statements affirm that relative properties exist and distinguish among the three. And they affirm divine simplicity by declaring that the three operates and wills as one.

However orthodox the opening and closing bookends of the "subsisting" section appear, Collier raises concerns with what he declared in between

---

63. *Body of Divinity* consists of 31 chapters and spans 606 pages.

64. Preface in Collier, *Body of Divinity*.

65. Collier, *Body of Divinity*, 22. Collier states in the errata that the final clause should read, "and these *three* are one, each of the three is God, and yet *there* is but one God" (emphasis added).

66. Collier, *Body of Divinity*, 44.

67. Land remarks on the second of these statements that "many would probably have considered an acceptable trinitarian doctrine." Land, "Doctrinal Controversies," 299.

the two bookends. One concern regards the term "person" to refer to the Three: Father, Son, and Holy Spirit.[68] Collier states, "That there [are] three Persons in the Divine Essence is a Language I do not yet understand is made use of in the Scriptures; therefore I avoid the terms."[69] That Collier avoided the use of "person" to designate the Three is not substantial evidence that he denied a classical trinitarianism.[70] His main concern is that "person" is not employed in reference to the Three in Scripture.[71] In this sense, Collier employs the Protestant Principle, not willing to use nonscriptural words to express scriptural truth. However, he was not strict in his employment of the Protestant Principle. As demonstrated in the *Somerset Confession* and in a later confession he would write in 1678, Collier employed nonscriptural terms in definitions and descriptions of biblical doctrine. So his apprehension in the use of "person" is more than just it not being a scriptural term.

By avoiding the term "person" Collier does not clearly articulate a distinct three within the Trinity. He acknowledges and articulates that the Three have distinct roles and relative properties, yet he stops short of declaring that each of the Three is not the other.[72] As stated previously, Collier had understood the designations of Father, Son, and Spirit as distinguishing specific roles performed by each and not distinguishing between persons. Though *Body of Divinity* is more substantial than "A General Epistle," Collier did nothing in *Body of Divinity* to retract "yet not three *subsistings* or *persons*, but *one* God made known under *three denominations*."[73]

The next concern raised in this section of "subsisting" regards Collier's understanding of the Son. In a subsection titled "How Christ Is God, and the Son of God" Collier states, "Where-ever the Scripture speaks of Jesus Christ the Son of God, it intends him as in both Natures, not as two, but as one Son . . . it's always in relation to the Union of the two Natures, as

---

68. Since Collier is opposed to the use of "person" to designate the three within the Trinity, the phrase "the Three" will be used in reference to the three of the Trinity (the Father, the Son, and the Holy Spirit) when interacting with Collier's position.

69. Collier, *Body of Divinity*, 43.

70. Collier was not alone in his resistance to the use of "person." Philip Dixon argues that the greatest factor in seventeenth-century trinitarian disputes arose over the use of "person." See Dixon, *Nice and Hot*.

71. Collier admits that "person" is used in reference "to the Son, as God and Man in one Person." Collier, *Body of Divinity*, 43. The focus here, however, is on Jesus as one person with dual natures and not particularly in regard to the Son of God.

72. As previously stated, Collier had affirmed no distinction between the Three. "The *Son* is, *The everlasting Father*; the *Father* is in the *Son*, and so he is the *Son*; the *Spirit* is God, and so he is both the *Father* and the *Son*." Collier, "General Epistle," in Collier, *Second Volume*, 7.

73. Collier, "General Epistle," in Collier, *Second Volume*, 7.

God-Man and Man-God."[74] The two natures referred to by Collier are the divine nature and the human nature. Collier supposed that if the Son of God did not possess both natures in eternity,[75] then there would arise two Sons of God, one by divine nature and the other by human nature at the incarnation.[76] It appears Collier intended that the Son of God manifested a human nature in eternity but did not assume flesh until the incarnation.[77] By asserting that the Son of God must be eternally considered in both natures, Collier sought to uphold God's immutability.[78]

While Collier sought to uphold an orthodox position of God's immutability, his conviction of the eternal union of divine and human natures in the Son of God led him to a questionable position on the eternal generation of the Son. Collier questioned the common position on eternal generation of the Son and its scriptural warrant. He confesses that his understanding "seems to contradict that common notion of Christs being the Son of the Father in the Divine Nature onely, . . . which seems to be an unwarranted expression, and that which the Scripture . . . is unacquainted with, being rightly understood."[79]

For Collier, the Son of God could not be the Son without human nature. Collier writes, "Permitting the sense of its own language, it will appear that all those Scriptures that speak of the begetting of the Son of God, intends him as he was the Christ, the Son of the Father in the Unity of Natures, and not in the Divine Nature onely."[80] That is, the Son could not be spoken of as being begotten of God unless it was in reference to His human nature along with His divine nature. If one held to the eternal generation of the Son in His divine nature alone, then the Son could not be coeternal with the Father.[81] Collier had earlier in his writings held that it is blasphemous to hold forth "a generation in the Godhead, which is proper only to the creature."[82]

---

74. Collier, *Body of Divinity*, 30.

75. "Where-ever Christ is spoken of in the Scripture as the Son of God, and that relating to his Eternity, it is to be understood in his both natures." Collier, *Body of Divinity*, 31.

76. "What doth this less than make him to be two Sons, one in the Divine Nature, and another in the Human Nature, by Grace of Union." Collier, *Body of Divinity*, 30.

77. "The Divine Nature was God eternally, the human considered in the eternal Council as in union." Collier, *Body of Divinity*, 31.

78. "It seems to import that Christ is a Son in differing manner of ways . . . so making things to be various, changable, and new to God." Collier, *Body of Divinity*, 35.

79. Collier, *Body of Divinity*, 36.

80. Collier, *Body of Divinity*, 36.

81. Collier, *Heads and Substance*, 4.

82. Collier, *Heads and Substance* 3.

Not only did Collier have an unorthodox understanding of the eternal generation of the Son, so did he concerning the Son as being the firstborn of all creation. Because Collier could not separate the two natures from the Son, that is, because he could not comprehend the Son as being only divine from eternity prior to the incarnation, Collier put forth that the Son was a creature from eternity. He wrote, "That he was thus considered in his both natures as the Son of God from eternity . . . in this verse [Col. 1:15, 16] and in the verses before, he is spoken of as God and Man; for so he was a Creature, a Son."[83] Collier seems to espouse an Arian heresy that the Son was a creation of the Father and therefore not eternal. However, Collier does not explain, but only asserts, that the Son being both eternally divine and human was a Creature.

Two years after the publication of *Body of Divinity*, Collier published *An Additional Word*. He found it necessary to explain and defend some of the things he had written in *Body of Divinity*.[84] Amongst other topics,[85] some contemporaries had taken offense to what Collier had written about "the Person of the Son of God."[86] Collier begins *An Additional Word* with the chapter "Concerning God." The chapter is no refutation of what Collier wrote in *Body of Divinity* concerning God, but rather a defense of what he already asserted.[87] The chapter consists of eight particular topics concerning God with which Collier's disputants took issue. Only the topics addressed above from *Body of Divinity* will be considered.

First, Collier defends the Son as being only and always considered in both natures. His main defense is that Scripture does not affirm the Son to be the Son of God in His divine nature only.[88] Second, Collier upholds that the Son is a creation. In his explanation of the Son being the firstborn, Collier writes, "The sum of all, is this, That he was the first that was begotten, or born in the Eternal Will and Bosom of the Father, and that as he came forth in time, God and man, the Creator and a Creature, in one Person,

---

83. Collier, *Body of Divinity*, 31.

84. *An Additional Word* consists of nine chapters and is sixty-three pages long. The main topics covered by Collier are God, extent of the atonement, election, will of man, differing dispensations of the standard for salvation and damnation, and eternal judgment.

85. For a more detailed critique of all Collier's positions that raised concern among his contemporaries, see J. Renihan, "Collier's Descent into Error."

86. Preface in Collier, *Additional Word*.

87. "These things (I think) are all stated and cleared in the first Chapter [*Body of Divinity*]. . . . I shall not say much of the ungrounded Arguments against them . . . but what is necessary for the more full confirmation of the things as stated in that Chapter." Collier, *Additional Word*, 1.

88. Collier, *Additional Word*, 1.

him by whom all was made."[89] The Son being eternally divine and human came forth at the incarnation as simultaneously Creator (divine nature) and creature (human nature). And, third, Collier held to his rejection of the term "person" in reference to the Three. On this topic Collier actually clarifies what he asserted, or implied, in *Body of Divinity*. He continues his defense that Scripture nowhere addresses the Three by "person." But Collier goes further in distinction of the Three than he did in *Body of Divinity*: "The Father is not the Son, the Son is not the Spirit, the Spirit is neither the Father nor the Son."[90] This is the most direct statement Collier had made concerning true distinction among the Three. Yet, Collier was far from classical trinitarianism due to his position of the Son being both the eternal Creator and an eternal creature.

This section has viewed Collier's trinitarianism and Christology from three of his writings, "A General Epistle," *The Body of Divinity*, and *An Additional Word*. These writings span from the 1640s to the 1670s. Over this time period, Collier did shift in his trinitarianism from a modalistic monarchianism to a position short of classical trinitarianism. His position is short of classical trinitarianism in two ways. First, Collier refused to designate the Three as "persons," though Collier did assert their distinction. Second, Collier denied a classical understanding of eternal generation. Collier's Christology did not change dramatically over time. In the beginning, Collier denied the distinct person of the Son and his eternal generation. Later, Collier affirmed the distinct person of the Son but still denied His eternal generation. His denial of eternal generation stemmed from his conviction that the Son eternally existed both in His divine nature and human nature. This led Collier to affirm the Son as a creature, albeit an eternal creature.

Conclusion of Thomas Collier

Collier's work in the Western Association and his writings made him an influential person among Particular Baptists in England. His confessions and writings on the Trinity and Christology raise concern as to his orthodoxy on these topics. On the Trinity, Collier ranged from vagueness to heresy to something close to orthodoxy. However, his Christology always suffered throughout his career. He could not affirm an eternal generation of the Son in His divine nature alone. And because he could not separate the human nature from the Son in eternity, he espoused a heterodox Christology. Nehemiah Coxe, a contemporary Particular Baptist with Collier, accused Collier

---

89. Collier, *Additional Word*, 10.

90. Collier, *Additional Word*, 11–12. This is a direct refutation of what he wrote earlier in "General Epistle" (1649).

of treading in the steps of the Pelagians, Jesuits, and Socinians. Coxe's and the Particular Baptists' response to Collier will now be considered.

The Response of the Particular Baptists

The Particular Baptists, like the General Baptists with Matthew Caffyn, had to publicly address Collier, one of their own, for holding and teaching questionable and heretical trinitarian doctrine. Unlike the General Baptists, the Particular Baptists were not organized into a regional general assembly from which they could speak and act. Instead, a small group of pastors from London rose up to counter Collier. And unlike the General Baptists, the Particular Baptists would counter antitrinitarianism with confessional language resulting in the *Second London Baptist Confession of Faith*.

The Response of the Particular Baptists in Writing

As shown above, Collier raised concern with his publication of *Body of Divinity* in 1674. Then, in 1676, Collier's *An Additional Word* did not alleviate the concerns of his contemporaries. So, in 1677, Nehemiah Coxe was selected by Particular Baptist pastors in London to write a response to Collier, *Vindiciæ Veritatis*. Before examining the written response, a brief history of Coxe will be given to demonstrate his credibility and ability to take on this task.

Nehemiah Coxe

Biographical information on Nehemiah Coxe (*bap.* 1649/1650, *d.* 1689) is sparse. Older Baptist historical works include Thomas Crosby and Joseph Ivimey. Crosby gives a short paragraph on Coxe in *The History of the English Baptists*.[91] Ivimey expands Coxe's story to four pages in *A History of the English Baptists*.[92] Modern Baptist historical works on Coxe include James Renihan and Samuel Renihan. J. Renihan wrote an article for the journal *Reformed Baptist Theological Review* in 2007.[93] S. Renihan, in 2019, devotes seven chapters to Coxe in his historical work on the Petty France church.[94] S. Renihan's chapters are the most extensive historical treatment of Coxe's life.

---

91. Crosby, *THEB*, 4:265–66.
92. Ivimey, *AHEB*, 2:403–7.
93. See J. Renihan, "Excellent and Judicious Divine."
94. See chapters 5–11 in S. Renihan, *Petty France*.

Coxe was the son of a first-generation Particular Baptist, Benjamin Coxe.[95] Benjamin, an educated man, earned a Bachelor of Arts degree in 1613 and a Master of Arts degree in 1617 from Broadgates Hall.[96] Benjamin, after graduating, entered the ministry of the Church of England. However, by 1640, he had left the church. Within a few years after this move, Benjamin joined the Bell Alley Baptist Church, pastored by Thomas Lambe, in the winter of 1642/1643.[97] How Benjamin moved from Anglican to Baptist is not known. S. Renihan proposes that it was during Benjamin's advocacy for closed communion between 1640 and 1642.[98] Benjamin would not stay long in Lambe's church. He and Lambe had a disagreement regarding the extent of Christ's atonement. Wright suggests that Lambe affirmed that Christ's death was for the sins of all men, but only had an effectual impact on the elect. Benjamin, who initially agreed with Lambe's position, later changed and asserted that Christ's death was only for the sins of the elect.[99] The disagreement led Benjamin to join one of the seven Particular Baptist churches in London in 1645.[100] Once united with the Particular Baptists, he was quickly endeared to its early leaders, William Kiffen and Hanserd Knollys.[101] Benjamin not only signed the 1LCF46, but he was also selected to write the appendix to the confession.[102]

Nehemiah Coxe was born sometime between 1647 and 1650.[103] Records show that he was paedobaptized on March 22, 1649/1650[104] in

95. Nehemiah Coxe will be referred to as "Coxe" and Benjamin Coxe will be referred to as "Benjamin."

96. S. Renihan, "Benjamin Coxe," in Haykin and Wolever, *British Particular Baptists*, 1:46. For an earlier biographical article of Benjamin Coxe, see Whitley, "Benjamin Cox."

97. Wright, "Cox [Coxe], Benjamin," para. 2.

98. S. Renihan, "Benjamin Coxe," in Haykin and Wolever, *British Particular Baptists*, 1:43.

99. Wright, "Cox [Coxe], Benjamin," para. 2. S. Renihan suggests the disputed matter centered on how to proclaim the gospel to all men. S. Renihan, "Benjamin Coxe," in Haykin and Wolever, *British Particular Baptists*, 1:45.

100. Wright, "Cox [Coxe], Benjamin," para. 3.

101. Benjamin Coxe and Thomas Collier may very well have known of one another due to their common friendship with Kiffen and Knollys. To this author's knowledge, this is nowhere affirmed.

102. Wright, "Cox [Coxe], Benjamin," para. 3.

103. S. Renihan discusses the possible years in which Coxe could have been born. He concludes that Coxe was born post-1647. S. Renihan, *Petty France*, 74–75.

104. S. Renihan gives the year of Coxes paedobaptism as 1650. S. Renihan, *Petty France*, 74. Wright gives the year as 1649. Wright, "Cox [Coxe], Benjamin," para. 4. The difference is most likely due to the use of either a Gregorian calendar (Renihan) or a Julian calendar (Wright).

Bedford.[105] His early years as a child are not known other than tracing the steps of his father. During a time when dissenters were barred from universities, Coxe showed himself to be an intelligent, educated, and well-read man. Having a father who was Oxford educated, Coxe benefited from his father's education. Coxe had a working knowledge of Greek and Hebrew and was able to read and write in Latin.[106] While some historians have thought Coxe earned a doctorate in divinity, he actually earned a medical degree from the University of Utrecht in 1684. He wrote his dissertation, in Latin, on the topic of gout.[107] Upon Coxe's death in 1689, his probate showed that he owned £40 worth of books. S. Renihan calculates that Coxe owned somewhere between eight hundred and one thousand books, about one third of a bookseller's inventory.[108]

Only five publications of Coxe are extant. In 1677, he published *Vindiciæ Veritatis*. This work will be explored later. Four years later, in 1681, Coxe issued what would become his most famous work, *A Discourse of the Covenants*. This work demonstrates how and why Baptists in the seventeenth century held to both covenant theology and credobaptism. Also in 1681, Coxe published a sermon he preached on the occasion of an ordination for an elder and deacons at a London church. The sermon gives insight into seventeenth-century Baptist ecclesiology. One aspect Coxe argues for was the paying of ministers by the church. Knollys will cite portions of Coxe's sermon in his 1689 publication defending the pay of ministers.[109] In 1682, Coxe translated a work, *A Believers Triumph*, from Latin into English that contained dying words from deceased Christians. As the title indicates, Coxe produced the work to comfort Christians in their dying hours. The final publication by Coxe is his previously mentioned dissertation from 1684, "Inaugural Medical Dissertation on Gout."

Coxe is known to have served in two churches. In May 1669, he joined the Bedford church, the town in which he was born.[110] Of interest is that

---

105. Though Benjamin was a credobaptist at this time, he most likely had Nehemiah paedobaptized due to pressure placed upon him by local ministers to confirm his orthodoxy. Wright, "Cox [Coxe], Benjamin," para. 4. This author has not found a record of Nehemiah Coxe being credobaptized.

106. S. Renihan, *Petty France*, 133.

107. For more information on Coxe's medical degree and dissertation, see S. Renihan, *Petty France*, 141–70.

108. S. Renihan, *Petty France*, 135.

109. Knollys, *Gospel Minister's Maintenance Vindicated*, 34. Knollys does not cite Coxe by name. He merely alludes to the author by placing in parenthesis "as one well observes." However, comparison between Knollys's wording and Coxe's wording show he was quoting Coxe.

110. S. Renihan, *Petty France*, 75.

the Bedford church was an open membership church in that members and communion participants were not required to be credobaptized.[111] Then, in December 1671, the Bedford church called Coxe to the office of "gifted brother."[112] The office of "gifted brother" recognized a man as having teaching gifts to be used in the church and for public ministry but did not assign to him pastoral authority. By being a "gifted brother" a man was also marked out as a potential pastor for other congregations.[113] Coxe would later be called as pastor of a Baptist congregation in London, Petty France, which he and his father had been involved in during the 1660s.[114] In September 1675, the Petty France church ordained Coxe and William Collins as pastors of the church.[115] Coxe served as pastor of Petty France, alongside Collins, until his death in May 1689.

The above details of Coxe's life show that he was a man raised as a Baptist, well educated, gifted in teaching, and experienced in ministry. His knowledge and gifting were noticed by six Baptist leaders who wrote the preface to *Vindiciæ Veritatis*.[116] They assert that Coxe did not undertake to write the response to Collier of his own inclination. Rather, "as by joint an earnest persuasion of several of the Elders, and that of elder years, partly because we did judge him meet and of the ability for the work."[117] They selected Collier, a man "inferiority in years," to write on behalf of the London Baptists.[118]

Vindiciæ Veritatis

Vindiciæ Veritatis was not the first response to Collier by London Baptists. S. Renihan states that churches around Collier, as well as members of Collier's church, sent a letter of request prior to October 1676 to London Baptist churches to request help with the matter of Collier.[119] The London Baptists

---

111. J. Renihan, "Judicious Divine," 65.

112. S. Renihan, *Petty France*, 77. At this same meeting, the Bedford church ordained John Bunyan as pastor of the church.

113. S. Renihan, *Petty France*, 77.

114. S. Renihan, *Petty France*, 75.

115. S. Renihan, *Petty France*, 83.

116. The six Baptist leaders who wrote the preface are William Kiffen, Daniel Dyke, Joseph Maisters, James Fitton, Heny Forty, and William Collins.

117. Coxe, *Vindiciæ Veritatis* (Renihan), 16. All citations from *Vindiciæ Veritatis* will come from this reproduction. Per the publisher, the reproduction has only made "minor adjustments in formatting" from the original work.

118. Coxe, *Vindiciæ Veritatis* (Renihan), 16.

119. S. Renihan, *Petty France*, 98. Renihan does not provide a source for this letter

then sent a letter in reply stating their disapproval of Collier's teachings and that they intended to write a book of their own to refute Collier.[120] Prior to the publication of the book, however, a meeting between London Baptists and Collier was arranged for October 1676. Broadmead Baptist Church of Bristol knew of Baptist leaders who traveled from London to Bradford to meet with Collier. The entry on the 26th day of the 8th month, 1676,[121] in the *Records* of Broadmead state, "Five Elders and brethren that were coming down from London, to visit a Neighbouring Church in ye Country about 15 miles off near Bradford or Trowbridge, to settle some disorder there; as ye Pastor thereof, T. C., holding forth some unsound Doctrine, or New Notions, Contrary to ye generall reception of Sound and *Orthodox* Men. Ye names of ye London Brethern were, Br. Kiffin, Br. Deane, Br. Fitten, Br. Cox, and Br. Moreton."[122] The only version of the actual meeting between these five men and Collier is by Collier himself in his *A Brief and True NARRATIVE*. S. Renihan, working from *A Brief and True NARRATIVE*, states that Collier was not pleased with the response of these men, especially with Coxe who "spent the whole time in that rudeness of Debate, as the said T. C. had rarely met with from any sort of People."[123] The results of the meeting were that Collier remained adamant in his position and the London Baptists proceeded with the publication of their response, *Vindiciæ Veritatis*.

The preface to *Vindiciæ Veritatis*, "Christian Reader," states a primary reason why the London Baptists thought a response ought to be published by them. They write, "Because although it be a most unequal judgment, to make the errors of one single person under any profession, to reflect upon the whole of the same."[124] The London Baptists sought to distance themselves as Baptists, and Particular Baptists at that, doctrinally from Collier. As demonstrated earlier, Collier was a popular Baptist, at least in western England. The full title of his recent and controversial work was *The Body of Divinity, Or, A Confession of Faith, Being the Substance of Christianity:*

---

of request. At the time of writing *Body of Divinity* and *Additional Word*, Collier was a licensed teacher at a church in North Bradford, Wiltshire. Wright, "Collier, Thomas." Collier identifies the church as Southwick in his *Brief and True NARRATIVE* (1677).

120. S. Renihan, *Petty France*, 98.

121. The eighth month according to the Julian calendar is October.

122. Terrill, *Records* (Hayden), 185. Broadmead notes the presence of London Baptist pastors so near to Bristol because they desired these men to ordain their pastor, Thomas Hardcastle. Broadmead sent men from Bristol to Trowbridge to make the request. The London pastors denied the request because they needed to return to London due to "personall concerns at home." Terrill, *Records* (Hayden), 186.

123. S. Renihan, *Petty France*, 98. Renihan is quoting Collier from *Brief and True NARRATIVE*.

124. Coxe, *Vindiciæ Veritatis* (Renihan), 15.

Containing the Most Material Things Relating to Matters Both of Faith and Practise. Having included the phrase "Confession of Faith" in the title, the work could be construed by others, especially non-Baptists, that *Body of Divinity* was the confession of faith for all Baptists. Opponents of Baptists could potentially use *Body of Divinity* as a way to smear Baptists. The London Baptists believed they couldn't prevent such people from spreading slander about Baptists or "silencing the mouth of malice." However, they did want to clear their names in the minds of those "who are not biased by evil affections" toward Baptists.[125]

In the introduction to *Vindiciæ Veritatis*, Coxe states his reasons for writing against Collier. Coxe warned those "of weak souls" who might be led into the false and dangerous teachings of Collier that "eat as doth a canker."[126] The false and dangerous teachings Coxe charged Collier with include Pelagianism and Socinianism.[127] Coxe also sounded an alarm to awaken those already unorthodox in their beliefs and would defend their positions by deferring to Collier, those who "rest in peace on those pillows he [Collier] has prepared for them."[128]

While Coxe is familiar with Collier's *Body of Divinity* and will cite it in *Vindiciæ Veritatis*, he primarily addresses and cites what Collier wrote in *An Additional Word*. Coxe focuses attention on *An Additional Word* because it was Collier's response to the critics of his *Body of Divinity*. Instead of retracting or revising what he previously wrote, Coxe charges Collier with repeating the same errors with "new confidence" and adding "more dangerous" doctrines in it.[129] Coxe lists twenty "gross errors" that he provides chapter and page numbers for as found in *An Additional Word*.[130] He covers these errors under seven topics in the seven chapters of *Vindiciæ Veritatis*. The topics are the divine nature and three subsistences (chapter 1), election (chapter 2), extent of the atonement (chapter 3), original sin and the moral power of man (chapter 4), the perseverance of the saints (chapter 5), justification (chapter 6), and final judgment and everlasting punishment (chapter 7). Only the first chapter will be considered here as it relates to the Trinity.

Chapter 1 is headed by Coxe as "Concerning God; The Distinct Subsistencies in the Divine Nature: And More Especially, the Person of the Son."

125. Coxe, *Vindiciæ Veritatis* (Renihan), 15.

126. Coxe, *Vindiciæ Veritatis* (Renihan), 20. Coxe will later say that this group of people is "for whose sake this work was undertaken." Coxe, *Vindiciæ Veritatis* (Renihan), 38.

127. Coxe, *Vindiciæ Veritatis* (Renihan), 20.

128. Coxe, *Vindiciæ Veritatis* (Renihan), 20.

129. Coxe, *Vindiciæ Veritatis* (Renihan), 27.

130. Coxe, *Vindiciæ Veritatis* (Renihan), 25.

He devotes the matter of this chapter to the first chapter of *An Additional Word*, which is also titled "Concerning God." Coxe calls attention to four questionable teachings espoused by Collier: omnipresence, uncreated heavens, subsistence, and the Son of God. The four topics will be addressed in the order they appear, as they all hold significant value in Coxe's refutation of Collier's perspective on the Trinity.

Coxe begins with the charge that Collier does not apply all the attributes of God to each of the persons of the Trinity. As evidence of the charge, Coxe presents Collier's denial that the Father is not omnipresent but the Holy Spirit is. Collier wrote in *An Additional Word*, "As to the Omnipresence of God the Father, I say what the Scripture saith, which directeth us to the Father as in Heaven; and that by his Spirit he is present in all places."[131] Coxe takes issue that Collier is applying omnipresence to the Spirit and not to the Father. For Coxe, essential properties of God are essential properties of all three persons of the Trinity for all three are coequally God, "It is all one therefore whether we speak of the omnipresence of the Father, or of the Son, or the Holy Spirit, these three being that one incomprehensible and infinite Jehovah."[132] To deny essential properties of God to any of the three persons is to be in alignment with Socinians.[133]

Coxe next highlights Collier's notion of the uncreated heavens. The charge by Coxe is that Collier implies that either God is dependent or that God is limited. Collier wrote, "As for the Increated Heavens: Though in the term of Increated, it be not express, yet there is enough in Scripture to prove the truth thereof. . . . For the Eternal God must have some Eternal Habitation, and its called, [in] Isa. 57.15. the high and holy place."[134] Based on Isaiah 57:15, Collier concluded that the eternal God could not exist apart from an eternal place in which to exist. To answer Collier, Coxe offers three different uses of "eternal" in the Scriptures.[135] The Scripture employs "eternal" in its absolute sense, without beginning or end, which is only proper of God. "Eternal" may refer to that which has a beginning but will have no end, as with man and creation. The last sense of "eternal" is that which has a beginning and will have an end, as with time. Heaven is referred to as eternal in the second sense. Regarding the absolute sense, to apply that use to anything other than God is to remove the Creator and creature distinction.[136]

---

131. Collier, *Additional Word*, 12. See also Coxe, *Vindiciæ Veritatis* (Renihan), 28.
132. Coxe, *Vindiciæ Veritatis* (Renihan), 28.
133. Coxe, *Vindiciæ Veritatis* (Renihan), 28.
134. Collier, *Additional Word*, 12. See also Coxe, *Vindiciæ Veritatis* (Renihan), 30.
135. Coxe, *Vindiciæ Veritatis* (Renihan), 33–34.
136. Coxe, *Vindiciæ Veritatis* (Renihan), 29.

Thereby, it makes God as either dependent upon something outside of Himself for His existence, or it imagines God is limited to a particular space and denies His immensity.[137]

Coxe then turns his attention to subsistence within the godhead. Coxe appeals to the relative properties of the Three as affirmed by the Athanasian Creed.[138] The Father begets. The Son is begotten. And the Holy Spirit proceeds from the Father and the Son. While Collier affirmed the relative properties, he was unwilling to employ the term "person" to speak of the Three. For Coxe, however, the relative properties consequentially affirm the Three as "persons." "Therefore as considered in him [God] they [relative properties] do infer personality, because a personal subsistence, is the most perfect manner of being in the whole reasonable nature."[139] Collier's refusal to use the term "person," in Coxe's opinion, is that he really disowns what is intended by the term. "But it is commonly seen, that men have been offended with apt terms, because the things expressed by them have been displeasing to them."[140] Coxe is right to make the charge. Collier did deny the distinction of persons, or subsistences, in *Body of Divinity*, "although in this one God there is a plurality of Titles, and varieties of discoveries, properties, and operations; yet I dare not say of persons, or distinct subsistings . . . yet to us there is no other God but one."[141]

Coxe last takes up Collier's Christology. Collier held to a form of Chalcedonian Christology that maintained that the two natures were distinct in the one person of the Son. However, he concluded that the Son could only be considered the Son in both His natures, divine and human, eternally.[142] Coxe charged Collier with an over-realized understanding of God's decrees concerning the prophecy of Christ's coming in the flesh. Such Scriptures that prophecy the coming of the Christ were, in part, the basis of Collier's position. "Because it was from eternity decreed that the Son of God should become Immanuel, he [Collier] concludes, that he is to be considered as being actually God-man from everlasting; and because it was foretold what

---

137. Coxe, *Vindiciæ Veritatis* (Renihan), 32–33.

138. Coxe, *Vindiciæ Veritatis* (Renihan), 34–35. Coxe does not cite from the Athanasian Creed, however, the expressions he employs are Athanasian.

139. Coxe, *Vindiciæ Veritatis* (Renihan), 35.

140. Coxe, *Vindiciæ Veritatis* (Renihan), 35.

141. Collier, *Body of Divinity*, 7; cf. 25. Collier's apprehension is that distinct subsistences, or persons, entailed three Gods.

142. As stated earlier, Collier believed that if Christ was God in eternity past and then took on human nature only at His incarnation, then there are two Sons of God, not one. Collier, *Body of Divinity*, 30.

he should be, therefore he always was such an one."[143] Coxe maintains that Christ subsisted only in the divine nature prior to His incarnation, and only then did He take on human nature.[144] This also is in accordance with the Athanasian Creed, "He is God from the Father's substance, begotten before time; and he is man from his mother's substance, born in time."

To deliver from what Coxe called "that strange confusion," he offers two standards for understanding Christology.[145] First, the incarnation caused no change in the Son of God. The Son has but one subsistence that is to be considered in a twofold manner, His eternal divine nature and then His manifestation in the flesh. The incarnation was a relation that the Son took with humanity, but he remained what he was, truly God. Second, there is personal communication of properties in the person of Jesus. Each nature worked in "concurrence of both natures unto the same operation" in accordance with its own property.[146] Thought at times, certain actions must be referred to as his divine nature or human nature only in regard to immediate principle.

From these two standards Coxe offers three interpretive guidelines.[147] First, Scripture at times speaks of what is proper only to one nature of Christ regarding certain acts. That Christ suffered and died are in regard to His humanity only. And that Christ created all things regards His divinity only. This distinction of properties in action, however, is no division in the person of Christ. Second, Scripture at times speaks of what is proper only to one nature as being done by the other nature. For example, Acts 20:28 speaks of God shedding His blood. Such instances emphasize that Christ is one person, divine and human, who cannot be separated. And third, Scripture at times speaks of what is proper to the person of Christ in attribution to only one nature. For example, 1 Timothy 2:5 speaks of the man Christ Jesus as being the one Mediator between God and men. Such instances demonstrate that Christ never acts in His divine nature or His human nature alone.

Collier posed a public problem for the Particular Baptists. Both his *Body of Divinity* and *An Additional Word* raised doctrinal concerns, especially in the areas of the Trinity and Christology. Collier's teachings could well be taken by others as the doctrine of the Particular Baptists since he had been identified with them. London Particular Baptist ministers took the lead to address Collier publicly by calling upon Coxe to write a response

---

143. Coxe, *Vindiciæ Veritatis* (Renihan), 46.
144. Coxe, *Vindiciæ Veritatis* (Renihan), 46.
145. Coxe, *Vindiciæ Veritatis* (Renihan), 38. For Coxe's interpretive rules, see p. 37.
146. Coxe, *Vindiciæ Veritatis* (Renihan), 37.
147. Coxe, *Vindiciæ Veritatis* (Renihan), 37–38.

on their behalf. Coxe did so in *Vindiciæ Veritatis*. His first chapter refuted Collier's doctrine of God and its implication in Christology. Coxe achieved this by appealing to the truth of past confessions and by implementing appropriate guidelines for interpreting Scripture.

The Response of the Particular Baptists in Confession

Vindiciæ Veritatis was not the only response to Collier by the Particular Baptists. In 1677, the same year *Vindiciæ Veritatis* came out, a confession of faith was produced, *A Confession of Faith Put Forth by the Elders and Brethren of Many Congregations of Christians (Baptized upon Profession of Their Faith) in London and the Country*. The second edition of this confession, published in 1688, was endorsed by the 1689 General Baptist Assembly for all Particular Baptist churches, stating that it encapsulates the core beliefs and practices of their faith.[148] Ever since the Assembly's recommendation, the confession has been referred to as the 1689 London Baptist Confession of Faith. However, the confession goes back to the 1677 edition. The confession will be referred to as the *Second London Baptist Confession of Faith* (2LCF). The origin of the confession in relation to the Particular Baptists' response to Collier will be considered first and then the confession's articulation of the Trinity and Christology.

Origin of the 2LCF and Connection with the Collier Event

The origin of the 2LCF is most likely the Petty France church of London. The reason for lack of certainty is that the first publication of the confession does not give an author(s) or publisher.[149] A reason for the anonymity is that the confession was written during the era of persecution under King Charles II.[150] The first to attribute origin and authorship of the 2LCF is Ivimey, "The authority for attributing this work [the 2LCF] to these ministers [William Collins and Nehemiah Coxe] rests upon the following minute in the records of the church in Petty France, August 26, 1677, 'It was agreed, that a Confession of Faith, with the Appendix thereunto, having been read and considered by the brethren, should be published.'"[151] Historians today accept Ivimey's deduction that the 2LCF originated at the Petty France

---

148. J. Renihan, *Faith and Life*, 42.

149. Subsequent editions (1688 and 1699) give a publisher but no author(s).

150. The 1688 publication probably stated the publisher with the installation of King William in 1688, and the 1689 General Assembly could openly endorse the 2LCF with the passage of the Act of Toleration in 1689.

151. Ivimey, *AHEB*, 3:332.

church and that Coxe and Collins are the authors of the confession.[152] It should be said that though Coxe and Collins are likely the authors of the 2LCF, they probably did not act alone in composing the confession. The title of the confession asserts that it was put forth by "many Congregations of Christians." The Petty France church, then, was not the only church that affirmed the 2LCF from its inception. Since Coxe had worked closely with other Particular Baptist pastors in dealing with Collier, these churches may also have been involved in composing and adopting the 2LCF.

The date of the acceptance and decision to publish a confession of faith by Petty France is certainly close in time with the Particular Baptists' dispute with Collier. But there is another link between the two events. That the 2LCF is linked to the Collier disputation is implied in the introduction to and the appendix of the confession. In the introduction, "To the Judicious and Impartial Reader," it states, "wherein our faith and doctrine is the same with theirs, and this we did, the more abundantly, to manifest our consent with both, in all the *fundamental articles of the Christian Religion*, as also with many others, whose orthodox confessions have been published to the world."[153] The statement is in regard to the 2LCF being an adaptive edition of the Presbyterians' *Westminster Confession* and the Congregationalists' *Savoy Declaration*. The authors of the 2LCF sought to demonstrate that they, and the churches who accept the 2LCF, were in doctrinal alignment with the wider Reformed Christian community. The phrase "fundamental articles of the Christian Religion," however, is significant. Similar wording is found twice in the Appendix: "Fundamental articles of Christianity" and "fundamental articles of the Christian faith."[154] S. Renihan deduces that this wording is related to a letter written by a gathering of Particular Baptists, Coxe included, on August 2, 1677, in Bristol. The letter was sent to Collier's church at Southwick. The letter states that they, the signers of the letter, had investigated the matter with Collier and found him to be a heretic. The letter defines a heretic as one "that chooseth an Opinion by which some *fundamental article of the Christian Religion* is subverted."[155]

Another link from the 2LCF with the Collier event is in the Appendix. The second paragraph of the Appendix reads, "This we have done, That those who are desirous to know the principles of Religion which we hold and practise, may take an estimate from our selves (who jointly concur in

152. R. Oliver, "Baptist Confession Making"; Haykin, *Kiffin, Knollys, and Keach*, 115; J. Renihan, "Judicious Divine," 73–74.

153. *Confession of Faith* (1677), unnumbered page (emphasis added).

154. *Confession of Faith* (1677), 109, 139.

155. A copy of the letter is found in S. Renihan, *Petty France*, 100–102 (emphasis added).

this work) and may not be misguided, either by undue reports; or by the ignorance or errors of *particular persons, who going under the same name with our selves*, may give an occasion of scandalizing the truth we profess."[156] As already stated, the Particular Baptists worried that other Christian churches might take Collier's *Body of Divinity* and assume it was the position of Particular Baptists as a whole. It may well be, then, that Collier is the "particular person" who goes by the same name, Particular Baptist, and scandalizes the truth held by the Particular Baptists.

The Trinitarianism and Christology of the 2LCF

The 2LCF has broader implications than just with the Collier disputation. However, when read in light of the Particular Baptists' dispute with Collier, certain terms and statements stand out as significant. Portions of two chapters from the 2LCF will be examined. Both will demonstrate that Coxe and the Particular Baptists affirmed Nicaean and Chalcedonian theology in the confession and, therefore, rejected Collier's antitrinitarianism.

Chapter 2 of the 2LCF is "Of God and of the Holy Trinity." The third paragraph of the chapter states the Particular Baptists' articulation of the Trinity.

> In this divine and infinite Being there are three subsistences, the Father the Word (or Son) and Holy Spirit, of one substance, power, and Eternity, each having the whole Divine Essence, yet the Essence undivided, the Father is of none neither begotten nor proceeding, the Son is Eternally begotten of the Father, the holy Spirit proceeding from the Father and the Son, all infinite, without beginning, therefore but one God, who is not to be divided in nature and Being; but distinguished by several peculiar, relative properties, and personal relations; which doctrine of the Trinity is the foundation of all our Communion with God, and comfortable dependance on him.[157]

The statement on the Trinity is a clear affirmation of Nicaean and Chalcedonian trinitarianism.[158]

Coxe used the *Westminster Confession* (*WCF*) and the *Savoy Declaration* (*SD*) as the basis of the 2LCF. He modified the confessions in regard to Baptist ecclesiology where necessary. However, there are other places throughout the confession that Coxe made modifications to the *WCF* and

156. *Confession of Faith* (1677), 109–10 (emphasis added).
157. *Confession of Faith* (1677), 12.
158. Weaver, "Three Subsistences," 14.

CONFESSIONAL AND CONFRONTATIONAL   89

SD not in relation to Baptist ecclesiology. The opening statement of 2LCF 2.3 is one of those places.

Both the *WCF* and the *SD* open the statement with, "In the unity of the Godhead there be *three persons*" (emphasis added). Coxe opened the statement with *three subsistences*. The change of wording, though not in meaning from the other confessions, is likely due to the dispute with Collier.[159] Collier was not hesitant to use "subsistence" in regard to God. He stated in *Body of Divinity*, "So in the Scriptures of Truth, the Father, Son (or Word) and Spirit is declared to be this one God, so that this one God subsisteth in three."[160] However, he refused to designate the Three as three subsistences, "yet I dare not say of persons, or distinct subsistings."[161] Coxe's opening almost parallels Collier's statement. Both affirm that the Father, Son (or Word), and the Holy Spirit are the one God. Yet, Coxe declares the Three to be "three subsistences." The change from "persons" in the *WCF* and the *SD* to "subsistences" demonstrates that Coxe sought to counter Collier.

Chapter 8 of the 2LCF is "Of Christ the Mediator." Paragraph two addresses the incarnation. It opens as follows: "The *Son* of *God*, the second Person in the *Holy Trinity*, being very and eternal *God*, the brightness of the Fathers glory, of one substance and equal with *him*: who made the World, who upholdeth and governeth all things he hath made: did when the fullness of time was come take unto him mans nature."[162] Coxe alters the *WCF* and the *SD* by adding the phrases in regard to creating the world. It seems out of place, though not wrong, to include such phrases. However, Coxe might be alluding back to Collier. Collier in *Body of Divinity* refused to acknowledge the Son as being divine in eternity past and then human at a particular point in time because that would lead to two Sons of God.[163] Collier then says, "Whereas the Scripture presents us with one onely Son of the Father, God and Man, *by whom he made the worlds, and by whom it all consists*."[164] Coxe's addition of creation language amidst a statement on the incarnation, therefore, harkens back to Collier.[165] Coxe in 2LCF 8.2 affirms

---

159. J. Renihan offers explanation as to how "person" and "subsistence" essentially convey the same meaning. However, the Particular Baptists sought to use a more technical word that was in alignment with past creeds, and it also avoided the charge of tritheism that Socinians brought against the term "person" during the seventeenth century. See J. Renihan, *Judicious and Impartial Reader*, 94.

160. Collier, *Body of Divinity*, 22.

161. Collier, *Body of Divinity*, 7.

162. *Confession of Faith* (1677), 28–29.

163. Collier, *Body of Divinity*, 35.

164. Collier, *Body of Divinity*, 35 (emphasis added).

165. The additional wording in the 2LCF 8.2, when compared with the WCF 8.2

that the Son of God, who made the world and upholds and governs it, is the very one who took human nature upon Him at a later point in time after creation. The Son possessed only the divine nature in eternity past and then took human nature at the incarnation.

The end of 2LCF 8.2 states, "So that two whole, perfect, and distinct natures, were inseparably joined together in one *Person*: without *conversion*, *composition*, or *confusion*: which *Person* is very *God*, and very *Man*; yet one *Christ*, the only *Mediator* between *God* and *Man*."[166] This statement affirms, contra Collier, that the union of the human nature with the divine Son at a point in time did not result in two Sons nor two persons. He remained one in the hypostatic union. Coxe continues to affirm Chalcedonian Christology.

In response to Collier's confession of faith, *Body of Divinity*, the Particular Baptists composed and published a confession of their own, the 2LCF. They acted to preempt others from associating Collier with them and their beliefs. The confession, being based on orthodox confessions by the Presbyterians and the Congregationalists, demonstrated that the Particular Baptists agreed in orthodox matters with the wider Christian community, and the language of the confession demonstrated that the Particular Baptists stood in the orthodox heritage of the early church through affirmation of the creeds, especially Nicaea and Chalcedon.

Conclusion

The Particular Baptists, like the General Baptists, had to address one of their own, Thomas Collier, in the matter of unorthodox trinitarianism and Christology. Yet, the Particular Baptists addressed the matter differently than did the General Baptists. The General Baptists would not go beyond the bounds of scriptural language to discuss and define the Trinity and Christ. The Particular Baptists, however, not only affirmed the scriptural language but also used confessional language and even the writing of a confession to address Collier's unorthodox teaching. As will be discussed in a later chapter, this confession, the 2LCF, anchored and guided Particular Baptists into and through the eighteenth century.

---

and SD 8.2, comes from the 1LCF46, chapter 9. The wording is "the brightness of His glory, by whom He made the world; who upholdeth and governeth all things that He hath made."

166. *Confession of Faith* (1677), 29.

5

An Orthodox Heritage

History of Broadmead Church, Bristol Academy, and the Salters' Hall Debates

THE DEBATES OF SALTERS' Hall influenced the discussion of churches for years after the debates had ended. The debates brought to the forefront how churches would address doctrinal differences within and among churches. Would churches and organizations require agreement with confessional statements or allow leeway in the use of Scripture-only language? The histories of Broadmead Baptist Church, Bristol Baptist Academy, and the Salters' Hall Debates will now be considered to determine how the church and the academy would respond to the outcome of the debates.

The History of Broadmead Baptist Church

The origins of Broadmead reach back to the rise of separatist churches in early seventeenth-century England. Broadmead's history is primarily known today by the labors of Edward Terrill. Terrill joined Broadmead in 1658 and served as a ruling elder from 1664 until his death in 1684(5). Around 1672, Terrill assumed responsibility to transcribe and record the church's minutes into a church book titled *The Records of a Church of Christ*.[1] Terrill, later in 1675, employed the assistance of two other Broadmead members, Robert Bodenham and Henry Davis, to help him in the transcribing of the church's

---

1. Terrill, *Records* (Hayden), 109.

minutes and events.² Sometime after 1720, Bernard Foskett, a later pastor of Broadmead, resumed the efforts of Terrill, Bodenham, and Davis. Foskett transcribed material from the church's "wastebook" that included church minutes and events up to 1687.³ Though the *Records* are a reliable history of Broadmead, Hayden cautions the reader to not assume that Terrill's recounting of the early history of Broadmead is entirely accurate prior to the year 1658, the year Terrill joined Broadmead.⁴

Other than the original *Records*, there have been three later editions published. Edward Bean Underhill produced an edition in 1847 for the Hanserd Knollys Society. The second edition, published by the Bunyan Library, came in 1865 by a pastor of Broadmead, Nathanial Haycroft. The Bristol Record Society published an edition in 1974 edited by Roger Hayden. Underhill's edition places within the text information that was consigned in the back of the *Records* after Terrill's death but not recorded by him. Haycroft sought to give a more accurate edition of the *Records* by transcribing only what Terrill wrote. Also, Haycroft brought the history of Broadmead up to date from 1688 to his present time with the inclusion of "A Continuation of the Records."⁵ Hayden mostly followed Haycroft's text but at times would give a different transcription of Terrill's original text.⁶ All three editions introduce the *Records* with a history of Broadmead along with inclusion of contextual notes.

Few histories have been written on Broadmead Church. The first comes from J. G. Fuller in 1840, *The Rise and Progress of Dissent in Bristol; Chiefly in Relation to the Broadmead Church*. Fuller relied heavily on Terrill's *Records* and other seventeenth-century documents to tell the story of Broadmead. Then, in 1927, Sir John Swaish wrote a brief history of Broadmead up to 1923, *Chronicles of Broadmead Church, Bristol, 1640–1923*. Swaish was a lifelong member of Broadmead. He walks through the tenure of each Broadmead pastor giving both highs and lows of the ministry. A valuable contribution in the book are the photographs of how the church appeared prior to major renovations in the 1960s. Robert L. Child and C. E. Shipley's *Broadmead Origins: An Account of the Rise of Puritanism in England and of the Early Days of Broadmead Baptist Church, Bristol, Issued for*

2. Terrill, *Records* (Hayden), 173. Hayden comments on the change in handwriting from that of Terrill's to that of "an unknown hand" for the year 1680 but only for seven pages. Terrill, "Introduction," 12.

3. Terrill, "Introduction," 12.

4. Terrill, "Introduction," 11.

5. Terrill, *Records* (Haycroft), 296–323.

6. Hayden's edition of the *Records* will be used throughout this chapter unless otherwise noted.

the Tercentenary, 1940 appeared in 1940. Child served as Broadmead's pastor from 1934 to 1942. The authors solely focus on Broadmead's history in the seventeenth century. Their purpose was to show how the church began as a Puritan nonconformist church that suffered persecution after the English Restoration of 1660. In 1991, C. Sidney Hall and Harry Mowvley wrote *Tradition and Challenge: The Story of Broadmead Baptist Church, Bristol from 1685 to 1991*. Both men were former administrative staff of Bristol Baptist College. The book picks up where Child and Shipley left off to bring the history of Broadmead up to the close of the twentieth century. The authors provide brief summaries of Broadmead's pastors along with historical context within which the church existed in the three-century span. Though not an official history, Roger Hayden wrote an article for the *Baptist Quarterly* in 1970 titled "Broadmead, Bristol in the Seventeenth Century." Hayden primarily relied on the *Records* but offered critique of Terrill's historical narrative of Broadmead.

Reformed Separatist Origin of Broadmead Church

Broadmead Church originated in the first four decades of the seventeenth century as a separatist gathering in the heritage of the English Reformation. Terrill's chief concern at the beginning of the *Records* is not only to present the historical setting of Broadmead but also to offer the reason for Broadmead's origination.[7] Those who would form Broadmead's first membership developed contrary convictions concerning beliefs and practices of the Church of England, especially in regard to the style and manner of worship. What Terrill says of Dorothy Hazzard, a founding member of Broadmead, can be applied to all the original members, that they "practiced that truth of ye Lord (which was then hated and Odious), namely, *Separation*."[8]

Terrill opens the *Records* with twofold praise to God.[9] He first praises God for England's separation from the Roman Catholic Church in the days of King Henry VIII. Terrill then praises God for the reformation of worship in the Church of England during the reigns of King Edward VI and of Queen Elizabeth. However, Terrill laments the reigns of King James I and King Charles I for those kings did not bring further reform to the Church of England. Instead, the church traveled a path of "Papall Hierarchy" that was "directly opposite to ye holy Scripture, and Rule of True Worship."[10]

---

7. The first seventeen pages of the *Records* are Terrill's historical narrative of Broadmead leading up to its formation in 1640.
8. Terrill, *Records* (Hayden), 85.
9. Terrill, *Records* (Hayden), 81.
10. Terrill, *Records* (Hayden), 82.

Terrill introduces the first two ministerial leaders of what would become Broadmead Church, Robert Yeamans and Matthew Hazzard.[11] Robert Yeamans became the first leader of a separatist group in Bristol.[12] He was vicar at St. Philip's in Bristol from around 1604 to 1633. Though Yeamans "did observe According ye time" certain practices of the Church of England, he "would not suffer his hearers to use any blind devotion" to other church practices such as bowing at the name of Jesus.[13] Because of his desire for pure practice of worship in church, Yeamans attracted to him "awakened souls" for the next twenty years until his death in 1633.[14] Then, in 1639, some who gathered around Yeamans began to meet with Matthew Hazzard, the new vicar at St. Ewins in Bristol who served there until his death in 1671. Hazzard was a man of the same spirit with Yeamans. He "could not close with ye grossenesse of those times" and was of a "Puritanicall spirit, preaching against ye Debauchery of ye people and priests."[15]

After nearly thirty years of informal meetings, Broadmead began as an official church in the year 1640. Five persons from Hazzard's group made a "holy Resolution to Separate from ye Worship of ye World and times they lived in, and that they would goe no more to it" and would "worship ye Lord more purely."[16] These five persons were Goodman Atkins, Goodman Cole, Richard Moone, Mr. Bacon, and Dorothy Hazzard.[17] Terrill emphasizes their separatist disposition when he says, "Then it pleased ye Lord to stir up some few of ye professors of this Citty, to begin to lead ye way out of Babilon, (ye Corrupt Worship, and to Separate from them, and not as much as come near any of their Superstitions)."[18] On the Lord's Day these five would not attend the common prayer during the church service but would enter the church afterwards to hear Mr. Hazzard deliver the sermon. In the afternoon they normally met at Mr. Hazzard's house for further edification. During the week the members gathered for times of prayer and teaching.

Though Broadmead started in 1640, it reconstituted in 1645. In between these years, Broadmead relocated from Bristol to London due to the

---

11. These two men were never officially ordained as pastors of Broadmead.
12. Terrill, *Records* (Hayden), 84.
13. Terrill, *Records* (Hayden), 84.
14. Among those awakened souls was a Mr. Anthony Kelly whose widow, Dorothy, would become a founding member of Broadmead.
15. Terrill, *Records* (Hayden), 85.
16. Terrill, *Records* (Hayden), 90.
17. Dorothy Hazzard was the widow of Anthony Kelly who gathered with Mr. Yeamans. Dorothy married Matthew Hazzard in 1640.
18. Terrill, *Records* (Hayden), 88.

Royal army taking control of Bristol in 1643.[19] Broadmead returned when the Parliament army regained control of Bristol in September 1645.

Upon its return, the church was weakened by "a Chaos of Confusion" so that most meetings were "filled with Disputes and debates" primarily in regard to the practice of the ordinances.[20] Terrill does not give great detail surrounding these spirited discussions within the church. While in London the members decided to refrain from partaking of communion together.[21] Upon return to Bristol, some members were "against the Ordinances, as having gott above them."[22] Why some were against the ordinances is not revealed.

There may have been debate over who is qualified to partake of communion, whether only credobaptists are qualified or whether paedobaptists may also partake.[23] During Broadmead's interval in London, the members divided in attendance between two existing churches. One church was All Hallows pastored by Henry Jessey. All Hallows practiced open communion whereby paedobaptists and credobaptists could both partake of communion together. The other church was Devonshire Square pastored by William Kiffen. Terrill notes that "those professors that were Baptized before they went up, they did sitt downe with Mr. Kiffen and his Church in London, being likewise Baptized."[24] Kiffen's church practiced closed communion whereby only credobaptized believers may partake of communion.

---

19. Broadmead, as a separatist church, opposed the national church and therefore supported the Parliamentary party. The church's support for the Parliament may have been the minority position in Bristol. Winston Churchill says at the time of the civil war, "on the whole [Bristol's] inhabitants were Royalists." Churchill, *New World*, 240.

20. Terrill, *Records* (Hayden), 98.

21. Terrill, *Records* (Hayden), 98.

22. Terrill, *Records* (Hayden), 98.

23. Hayden questions whether Broadmead had discussions this early regarding the mode of baptism and its qualification for communion. He states the discussion did not occur until the early 1650s. Hayden, "Broadmead," 351. From this point forward "credobaptism" will signify baptism by immersion in water upon a person's confession of saving faith in Christ, which is in accordance with articles 39 and 40 of *Confession of Faith of Seven Congregations*, published in 1646. "Paedobaptism" will signify baptism of infants by sprinkling with water as practiced by the Church of England, Presbyterians, and Congregationalists.

24. Terrill, *Records* (Hayden), 98. The baptized professors were those credobaptized prior to going to London. While it is not known whether Broadmead had administrated credobaptism prior to 1643, the practice was unlikely. The reason is that Terrill states later in the *Records* that in 1653 Broadmead sent a member to London to be credobaptized by Jessey rather than baptizing him at Broadmead. The "professors that were Baptized before they went up" may have been members from the Welch church in Llanvaches that traveled with Broadmead to London.

Broadmead appears to have had open membership whereby both paedobaptists and credobaptists were members. Also, Broadmead practiced open communion based upon its open membership.

Terrill does disclose how the dispute over ordinances was resolved. The church decided "to New Modell themselves."[25] This meant those who wanted to remain members of Broadmead would sign a church covenant stating:

> *That they would in ye Strength of Christ, keepe close ye Holy Scriptures, ye word of God; and ye plaine truths and ordinances of ye Gospell, of Church fellowship, breaking bread, and Prayers; And to subject to one another, according to ye Discipline and admonition by ye Rules of Christ, in ye New Testament, or ye Scriptures.*[26]

Not all the former members signed the covenant, but many did.[27] If the covenant was intended to resolve the ordinance debate, the debate revolved around how certain individuals disregarded the fundamental principles of the Scriptures in relation to the ordinances. The covenant emphasizes what the members of Broadmead held since 1640, that the church is to conform to the clear teaching of Scripture regarding the practices of the church.

Reformed Baptist Development of Broadmead Church

Broadmead was not a Baptist church at its formation.[28] Terrill titled the church book he kept as *The Records of a Church of Christ* with no further designation. As it has been shown, Broadmead originated as a separatist church within the English Reformation. The church's concern was to conduct worship in accordance with the clear teaching of Scripture. Over the decades, Broadmead became a Baptist church within the Particular association of Baptists.[29] The process by which Broadmead became a Particular

---

25. Terrill, *Records* (Hayden), 99.

26. Terrill, *Records* (Hayden), 99.

27. Terrill, *Records* (Hayden), 99. Terrill does not say how many members actually signed the new church covenant. Prior to the retreat of Broadmead to London the church had one hundred sixty members. Terrill, *Records* (Hayden), 97.

28. "The originally Independent congregation meeting in Broadmead, Bristol, was an early example of one which moved from being predominantly Independent to being predominantly Baptist." White, *English Baptists*, 10.

29. By Particular Baptist is meant those Baptist churches that held to credobaptism by immersion and affirmed Reformed doctrine. Both of these distinctions are used by such Baptist churches to distinguish themselves from those who held contrary beliefs. The General Assembly of Baptist Churches held in London in 1689 designated the churches who attended as "*Baptized Churches* . . . Owning the Doctrine of Personal Election, and Final Perseverance." Renihan, *Faith and Life*, 25. The ministers and messengers who attended the assembly recommended *Confession of Faith Put Forth by the*

Baptist church is first in the practice of credobaptism by immersion and then in the doctrine of Particular Baptists.

Broadmead Church and Baptist Practice

As stated previously, Broadmead had strong debates in the mid-1640s regarding the ordinances of baptism and communion. The covenant signing to renew membership in the church appears to have resolved that debate. However, the matter of credobaptism did not go away. Terrill records that in 1651, "in those Halcyon days of prosperity, liberty, and peace, it pleased the Lord to break forth more primitive light and purity in reformation of worship, to bring the church to a more exact keeping to the holy scripture; so that some of the members began to question what rule they had for sprinkling of children; and upon examination, finding no bottom for it, but men's inventions and tradition."[30] No recorded action was taken by the church nor by members until the following year of 1652. One member, Thomas Munday, was given leave by Broadmead to join another church in Bristol "that were all Baptized."[31] Since no mention is made of Munday's baptism, he was probably credobaptized sometime in the past. The other church, meeting at the Fryers and pastored by Henry Hynam, required credobaptism for membership.[32]

Munday, however, was not the only member to hold such convictions. In 1653, Timothy Cattle became "convinced of ye ordinance of Baptism, that none ought to be partakers thereof but such as professe faith in our Lord Jesus Christ."[33] The difference between Munday and Cattle is that Cattle was not yet credobaptized for "he had declared his desires of enjoying that ordinance."[34] Since Thomas Ewins, the teaching minister at Broadmead,[35] was not as yet credobaptized, Cattle was sent to London

---

Elders and Brethren (1688). The title of the confession designates those who wrote it as "baptized upon profession of their faith." In recommending this confession, the ministers and messengers described themselves as those "denying *Arminianism.*" Renihan, *Faith and Life*, 42.

30. Terrill, *Records* (Hayden), 103. It is of note that Terrill sees the matter of credobaptism raised by these members as not being an issue of dissent as it was five years earlier but being a work of the Lord.

31. Terrill, *Records* (Hayden), 105.

32. The church would later be pastored by Andrew Gifford Sr. and move from the Fryers location to the Pithay. Strivens, "Andrew Gifford, Sr.," in Haykin and Wolever, *British Particular Baptists*, 1:298, 307.

33. Terrill, *Records* (Hayden), 105.

34. Terrill, *Records* (Hayden), 105.

35. Ewins was officially ordained as pastor of Broadmead in 1662.

with a letter addressed to Jessey of All Hallows church requesting him to credobaptize Cattle.[36] After his baptism, Cattle returned to Broadmead and remained a member.

Following Cattle's baptism, Broadmead faced yet another internal disputation. The matter chiefly concerned the member and ruling elder Dennis Hollister. Hollister had accepted Quakerism and began to spread it among other members of Broadmead.[37] Nearly a fourth of the members left Broadmead to become Quakers.[38] After the matter settled, Broadmead reflected on why the Lord would allow such a difficulty within the church. They concluded the reason was "because they had not walked faithfull to their light in ye ordinances of God . . . and that they had not kept Close to ye holy Scriptures for ye Rule of worship."[39] What the church had not walk faithfully unto is the ordinance of baptism. That baptism, specifically credobaptism, was the issue is evidenced by the actions of Broadmead's two leaders—Thomas Ewins, their teaching minister, and Robert Purnell, their ruling elder. At the time of the dispute with Hollister, neither man had been credobaptized. In 1654, both men traveled to London and were baptized by Jessey.[40] Upon Ewins and Purnell's return to Broadmead, is the possible time that "divers others of ye Church were Baptized, according to Scripture Example, in a River."[41] Hayden declares this to be the time that Broadmead becomes an open communion Baptist church.[42] A majority of Broadmead's members would be credobaptized by 1670 when Ewins died.[43]

---

36. Why would Broadmead send Cattle to London to be credobaptized and not to the church meeting at the Fryers? The reason is that Broadmead had more in common regarding practice with All Hallows than with the Fryers church. Fryers practiced closed membership and All Hallows practiced open membership. Also, Broadmead had already formed a relationship with Jessey during its two-year stay in London. During that time, Broadmead witnessed Jessey adopt the practice of credobaptism for himself. When Broadmead arrived in London in 1643, Jessey had not yet undergone credobaptism. Prior to Broadmead returning to Bristol in September 1645, Jessey was credobaptized by Hanserd Knollys in June 1645. Terrill describes Jessey as a "Baptized minister." Terrill, *Records* (Hayden), 105.

37. Terrill devotes six pages to this matter. Terrill, *Records* (Hayden), 105–10.

38. Terrill, *Records* (Hayden), 110. Terrill records that eighteen or nineteen members left Broadmead, leaving near sixty members in the church.

39. Terrill, *Records* (Hayden), 111.

40. Terrill, *Records* (Hayden), 111.

41. Terrill, *Records* (Hayden), 105.

42. Terrill, *Records* (Hayden), 105n26.

43. Terrill, "Introduction," 47.

Broadmead Church and Particular Baptist Doctrine

By 1654 Broadmead was a Baptist church in practice. Over the next three decades Broadmead would become associated with Particular Baptist churches in doctrine. Broadmead had no known doctrinal statement for its first fifty years of existence. The only indication of a possible doctrinal statement for the church is found in the April 7, 1682, entry in the *Records*. The entry states that Mr. Whinnell sought membership at Broadmead since the church at which he had been a former member dissolved.[44] In addition to declaring his salvation, Whinnell professed "to believe ye principles contained in ye *Baptist Confession of Faith*, 1667."[45] Hayden notes that Terrill probably refers to the Particular Baptist Confession of 1677.[46] James Renihan states Whinnell was required to express his agreement with the *Baptist Confession of Faith* for membership.[47] There is no indication, however, in the entry that Whinnell was *required* to do this for membership, nor any other person admitted for membership at Broadmead during this time.[48] As the entry states, and Renihan acknowledges, Whinnell's church that had dissolved held to the free will of man, most likely being a General Baptist church. Broadmead being a reformed Baptist church would have questioned Whinnell's beliefs. Whinnell uses the *Baptist Confession of Faith* as a measure and expression of what he believed at the time of joining, which then had to be the belief and doctrine of Broadmead.[49] Whether the *Baptist Confession of Faith* was the actual doctrinal statement of the church is uncertain. Broadmead could agree with the confession without having it as its own doctrinal standard.

Broadmead Church's doctrine from its beginning is generally characterized as the doctrine of the reformation, excepting that of baptism. This is primarily witnessed to by the writings of Purnell and Terrill, ruling elders

---

44. An entry from February 8, 1681, in the *Records* states the former church was Christ-Church in Dorsetshire pastored by Captain Kitchen. See Terrill, *Records* (Hayden), 225. From this entry Whinnell had been seeking membership at Broadmead for over a year.

45. Terrill, *Records* (Hayden), 241.

46. Terrill, *Records* (Hayden), 241n65. This confession of faith is the *Second London Baptist Confession of Faith* produced in 1677 by Nehemiah Coxe and William Collins of the Petty France Church in London in response to Thomas Collier. See chapter 4 for the context of this confession.

47. J. Renihan, "Ingeneous Unfolding," in Ascol and Finn, *Ministry by His Grace*, 261.

48. In February 1681, when Whinnell had sought membership at Broadmead, there is no indication that he was required to give assent to a confession of faith.

49. Whinnell either never held to free will while at his previous church or he changed his belief prior to coming to Broadmead.

of Broadmead. Purnell wrote *The Way to Heaven Discovered* in 1655.[50] He upholds such doctrines as divine election, sovereign grace, and regeneration by the Spirit prior to saving faith. Also, Terrill's *Records* demonstrate that Broadmead held reformational doctrine. This is evidenced by Terrill distinguishing Broadmead, a credobaptist church, as distinct from Anabaptists, who also practiced credobaptism. The difference was that Broadmead rejected the Anabaptists' denial of original sin and their affirmation of free will.[51] He goes on to say that those who hold to believers' baptism may also "hold, with that sound truth [believers' baptism], all other Sound Principles of Christian Religion equally with the Godly, called Presbyterians and Independents."[52] Terrill is adamant to demonstrate that Broadmead, though Baptist, is among the doctrinally reformed company of Presbyterians and Congregationalists. Broadmead's reformational doctrine is further testified to by Thomas Hardcastle who served as pastor from 1671 to 1678. Underhill notes in his edition of the *Records* that Hardcastle commenced a series of thirty-five lectures on the Westminster Assembly's catechism.[53]

With Broadmead's reformational doctrine and practice of credobaptism, it is not surprising that the church would officially endorse and adopt Particular Baptist doctrine in 1689. This is the year that a General Assembly of "Baptized churches . . . owning the Doctrine of Personal Election, and final perseverance" met from September 3–12 in London.[54] During this assembly, the pastors and messengers recommended to all other such likeminded churches *A Confession of Faith Put Forth by the Elders and Brethren of Many Congregations of Christians (Baptized upon Profession of their Faith)*. The confession of faith is generally referred to as the *Second London Baptist Confession of Faith* of 1689 (2LCF), though written in 1677.[55] Among the pastors who attended this assembly and signed on to the recommendation of this confession of faith was Thomas Vaux, pastor

---

50. Terrill read Purnell's book and testifies that it was significant in his own conversion. "Sometime after this (five or six weeks), reading in a book of Mr. Purnell's, called The Way to Heaven Discovered, I met with those words, Isa. xxx .21, which when I found I was more confirmed that it was of God, because it was scripture, as the Spirit of God doth usually work according to the written word." Terrill, *Records* (Underhill), 61.

51. Terrill, *Records* (Hayden), 92.

52. Terrill, *Records* (Hayden), 92.

53. Terrill, *Records* (Underhill), 164.

54. This description of the churches attending the General Assembly of 1689 is found on the title page of the General Assembly's Narrative of Proceedings. J. Renihan, *Faith and Life*, 25.

55. The circumstances that led to the writing of the 2LCF is discussed in chapter 4. For background of the 2LCF, see Oliver, "Baptist Confession Making."

of Broadmead (1687–1693). From this time and for nearly 150 years after, Broadmead's doctrine was the 2LCF.[56]

Broadmead Church began as a separatist church holding to reformational doctrine in 1640. After several discussions and disputes, Broadmead adopted credobaptism in 1654. Since it was not mandated for all members to undergo credobaptism, Broadmead was a Baptist church with open membership. Broadmead then joined the ranks of the Particular Baptists in 1689 when Vaux, pastor of Broadmead, attended the Baptist General Assembly and signed the endorsement of the 2LCF. Both of these factors will contribute to the forming of the Bristol Baptist Academy.

Broadmead Church and the Founding of Bristol Baptist Academy

By the late seventeenth century, dissenting churches needed academies to give theological and ministerial training to the upcoming generation of church leaders. Earlier in the century, dissenting churches were led by men who had received university training while they were Anglican before they separated from the Church of England. During the interregnum (1649–1660), dissenting ministers were allowed to attend universities. However, with the restoration of the monarch along with a Parliament biased toward the Church of England, dissenting ministers were excluded from universities after 1660. The Clarendon Code Acts imposed restrictions upon dissenters requiring them to give subscription to the Thirty-Nine Articles and to the Book of Common Prayer in order to attend university.[57]

During this time, Baptists had come to know of their need not just for academies but for Baptist academies.[58] In the eighth month of 1675, London Baptist pastors sent a letter to Baptist churches throughout England and Wales inviting them "to meet the following May in the metropolis with a view to form a plan for the providing an orderly standing ministry in the church, who might give themselves to reading and study, and so become able ministers of the new testament."[59] Whether this meeting occurred or not is unknown.[60] However, the request demonstrates that there was broad interest to form Baptist academies in order to train Baptist ministers.

It is likely that Broadmead received the 1675 letter. One of the senders of the letter was William Kiffen who had interactions with Broadmead

---

56. Hayden, "Bristol Baptist Academy."
57. See Watts, *From the Reformation*, 218–27.
58. This is the estimation of John Rippon in 1795 as he reflected back on the state of Baptist education in the seventeenth century. See Rippon, *Brief Essay*, 7–8.
59. Ivimey, *AHEB*, 1:416.
60. Ivimey, *AHEB*, 1:416.

over the past three decades. Whether this letter was the stimulus or not for Broadmead to consider starting an academy cannot be determined. It is known that Broadmead had sat under the teaching of educated ministers. By 1679, five of the six leaders of Broadmead were university educated.[61] From this, Harry Foreman concludes that Broadmead "had a preference for an educated ministry and was likely to be sympathetic towards any suggestions for its provision within the Baptist denomination."[62]

Terrill was convinced that Baptist educated ministers were needed for the future of Baptist churches. On June 3, 1679, Terrill drafted a deed of gift to provide money after his death for the funding of an academy.[63] The deed of gift instructed his trustees:

> To devote the proceeds of his estates to the maintenance of "a holy learned man, well skilled in the tongues, viz., Greek and Hebrew, and doth own and practise the truth of believers' baptism, as a pastor or teacher to the congregation." Three half days in the week is the tutor to employ in the instruction of some young men, not exceeding twelve, members of any baptized congregation in or about Bristol, for two years at the most. Ten pounds yearly, to the amount of forty pounds, may be granted to any student, whose friends are unable to support him; if none such appear, to be lent to members of the congregation. From a reserved portion of his property, he further directs the trustees to pay £100 yearly to the pastor thus engaged, and £13 yearly to each of four students; the surplus to be for the benefit of the poor of the congregation.[64]

Terrill, by his deed of gift, accomplished two key factors for the academy. First, he provided the financial means for an academy. The principal and students would receive the necessary funds to devote time to an education. Second, he established directions for the academy. A pastor of Broadmead was to be the principal of the academy, as long as he met the

---

61. The five university educated leaders were Robert Yeamans (1612–1633), Matthew Hazzard (1640–1645), Nathanael Ingello (1645–1650), Thomas Hardcastle (1671–1678), and George Fownes Sr. (1679–1685). The only man not university educated during this time was Thomas Ewins (1651–1670), who served the longest tenure.

62. Foreman, "Baptist Provision," 359.

63. Terrill was a man of wealth in seventeenth-century Bristol. He had married the daughter of a wealthy businessman and Terrill had a successful business in the sugar trade. See Hayden, "Broadmead, Bristol," 314–15. The date of Terrill's death is unknown. His will was read in April 1685. Hall and Mowvley, *Tradition and Challenge*, 3. The funds for an academy would not be available, however, until after the death of his widow, Dorothy, in 1697.

64. Underhill, "Historical Introduction," xcii–xciii.

qualifications, and he was to devote one and-a-half days per week to the instruction of students.

Of greater importance, this deed of gift conveys two convictions of Terrill concerning the academy.[65] The first conviction is that of an educated ministry. To qualify for the principalship of the academy, the pastor of Broadmead had to have knowledge of the original biblical languages, thereby, be educated himself. From this it is implied that the students would then also learn the languages. Therefore, Terrill desired to have educated men who would enter the ministry of the local church. The second conviction is that of a Baptist ministry. For the pastor of Broadmead to qualify as principal of the academy, he had to be a man who was credobaptized and practiced credobaptism. Also, for students to qualify for financial assistance, they had to come from churches that also held to credobaptism. Terrill understood that Baptist churches needed ministers who were not just educated but educated in a Baptist academy.

Terrill died by early 1685. His widow, Dorothy, died twelve years later. The academy would not begin until the early eighteenth century.

That Broadmead Church affirmed and adopted the 2LCF is significant. As has been shown, Broadmead was a church that sought to conduct itself according to Scripture alone. However, Broadmead was not against stating its beliefs in other than scriptural terms. This places Broadmead among churches willing to express doctrine via confessions. Bristol Academy, originating from Broadmead, will adopt a similar approach to confessions when discussing doctrines like the Trinity and Christology.

The History of Bristol Baptist Academy

Seven books have chronicled the story of Bristol Academy.[66] The earliest narrator of Bristol Academy's story is John Rippon in 1796. At the August 1795 Bristol Education Society meeting, Rippon, a former student, gave a history of the academy, *A Brief Essay towards an History of the Baptist Academy at Bristol*. The print edition of the lecture reads more as a memorial than an historical account of the academy.[67] Rippon focuses on the three previous principals of Bristol Academy then deceased: Bernard Foskett,

---

65. See Clements, "Significance of 1679," 2–6.

66. These are the recommended books as given by Gouldbourne and Cross, including their own. Gouldbourne and Cross, *Story*, 211.

67. In print, the essay is forty-eight pages in length. The print edition includes nearly six pages devoted to James Newton, a former tutor of the academy, that did not appear in Rippon's original address.

Hugh Evans, and Caleb Evans. Rippon praises them for their academic instruction and godly character.

Stephen Albert Swaine, also an alumnus of Bristol Academy, wrote *Faithful Men: Or, Memorials of Bristol Baptist College* in 1884. Swaine gives a full account (being 345 pages in length) of the academy from its beginning up to the year 1868, the year he entered the academy as a student. As the title indicates, Swaine focuses on the lives of faculty and students who were involved in the life of the academy. Of historical value, Swaine recounts the forming of the Bristol Education Society (BES) by Caleb Evans and his father Hugh. *Faithful Men* may be the only surviving resource that contains the founding documents of the BES.

In 1929, Bristol Academy published a commemorative 250th anniversary of the academy, *Bristol Baptist College: 250 Years, 1679–1929*. The account is brief, being only sixty pages in length with about every other page dedicated to pictures. The commemoration pays tribute to key persons and times in Bristol Academy's history. Other than carrying forward in time some of the academy's history from that of Swaine, not much new is learned when compared to Swaine's account.

Norman S. Moon, L. G. Champion, and Harry Mowvley recognized the bicentenary anniversary of the BES with the publication of *The Bristol Education Society 1770–1970*. The BES was started in 1770 by Hugh and Caleb Evans to engage more Baptist churches in the financial assistance of training students at Bristol Academy. The authors tell how the BES came to be started and also how it helped shape the direction of Bristol Academy from the eighteenth century to the twentieth century.

The tercentenary anniversary of the academy would not go unnoticed. Norman S. Moon in 1979 wrote *Education for Ministry: Bristol Baptist College, 1679–1979*. Moon at the time was both a tutor and the librarian of the academy. Moon offers a sufficient history of the academy by bringing together the best of Swaine and Bristol Academy's edition. Moon's primary focus was to demonstrate how Bristol Academy theologically and practically prepared students for ministry in local churches.

In 2006, Roger Hayden wrote a restricted history of Bristol Academy to demonstrate its influence in seventeenth-century England. The book is a published form of his dissertation from 1991, *Continuity and Change: Evangelical Calvinism Among Eighteenth-Century Baptist Ministers Trained at Bristol Academy, 1690–1791*. Hayden argues that Particular Baptists in eighteenth-century England held to evangelical Calvinism because of the influence of Bristol Academy; namely, its principals, Bernard Foskett, Hugh Evans, and Caleb Evans. A bonus of *Continuity and Change* is the list of students at Bristol Academy between 1720 and 1790. Prior to 1770, the academy did not keep official student records. Through Hayden's research, he gives an annotated alumni list of 189 students.

The most recent account of Bristol Academy, published in 2022, is *The Story of Bristol Baptist College: Three Hundred Years of Ministerial Formation*. The authors, Ruth Gouldbourne and Anthony Cross, faculty at Bristol College, use 1720, the year Foskett became principal, as the official start of the academy, which differs from the academy's commemorative edition and Moon. Gouldbourne describes the book as more of a "family history" of the school for those who have been part of the Bristol family, therefore, the chronicling is less academic and more popular.[68] A theme of Gouldbourne and Cross is how the academy adapted to the changing times and, therefore, is a viable college today and into the future.

The Start of Bristol Baptist Academy

As indicated by some of the academy's history books, there is not an officially recognized start for Bristol Academy. The academy's origins can be traced back to June 1679 when Terrill drafted his deed of gift, which provided detailed instructions and financial support for its establishment. However, since the funds would not be available until after his death and the death of his widow, Bristol Academy could not officially begin until the close of the seventeenth century.

The unofficial start of Bristol Academy is no later than 1714.[69] The pastor of Broadmead at this time is Peter Kitterell (1707–1727). Being untrained in the original languages as Terrill's deed of gift required, he did not serve as principal of the academy.[70] The church turned its attention to a promis-

---

68. Gouldbourne and Cross, *Story of Bristol*, xi. The reason for the format is that Anthony Cross had been researching an extensive history of Bristol Academy that would have been three volumes in print form. However, Cross died in 2021 during his research and writing. Gouldbourne, in agreement with Cross before his death, shortened his work and omitted his footnotes. Gouldbourne states well that Cross's death "is a loss not only to the family to whom he was devoted . . . but to the field of Baptist research in so many ways." Gouldbourne and Cross, *Story of Bristol*, xii.

69. Ivimey gives 1714 as the start of Caleb Jope's ministry at Broadmead and, therefore, as principal of Bristol Academy. Ivimey, *AHEB*, 4:262. However, Swaine believes Jope's beginning at Broadmead would have been a few years earlier. Swaine, *Faithful Men*, 31.

70. Ivimey, *AHEB*, 4:262. It is interesting that Broadmead had not acquired a pastor who was also qualified to serve as principal of Bristol Academy. That Broadmead sought after Jope to be an assistant pastor at the church and to be principal of the academy demonstrates the church's desire to fulfill Terrill's vision. That Broadmead provided funds for Jope's continued education so that he might be qualified to serve as Bristol Academy's principal demonstrates there may not have been an adequate number of

ing young man, Caleb Jope.[71] Hall and Mowvley cite Isaac James, a tutor at Bristol Academy (1796–1825), as witnessing a letter written by Caleb Evans, tutor and later principal of the academy (1758–1791), stating that Jope had been called by Broadmead to assist Kitterell and to educate young men.[72]

In 1707, the Western Association had to give an opinion regarding two churches attempting to acquire Jope, the Baptist church of Plymouth and Broadmead. Plymouth had already extended an invitation for Jope to be their pastor. At some point after that invitation, Robert Bodenham, a member of Broadmead and a trustee of the Terrill estate, on behalf of Broadmead offered Jope the associate pastor position along with the principalship of Bristol Academy. The association judged that Jope ought to keep his original commitment to Plymouth and that Broadmead ought to cease its pursuit of him. Jope and Broadmead ignored their judgment.

At the time of the offer, Jope did not possess the training necessary to fulfill the principalship requirements. From 1707 to 1709, Broadmead paid tuition expenses in the amount of £129 for Jope to receive further training at an academy in London.[73] The funds more than likely came from Terrill's deed of gift.[74] Jope then moved to Broadmead sometime between 1710 and 1712.[75] Jope's tenure at Broadmead and Bristol Academy was a disappointment. Caleb Evans is reported to have written that Jope "did not adorn his character while in Bristol, and in the latter part of his life became quite infamous."[76] Jope removed himself from Broadmead in 1719. There are no existing records to indicate whether Jope educated any students.[77]

Though Broadmead intended to start Bristol Academy under Jope's principalship, it was an unofficial start since Jope failed to actually train students. But 1720 would prove to be the official start of the academy with Bernard Foskett taking the principalship in October of that year.[78] The exact

---

Baptist educated pastors at the time. If so, it also demonstrates the need for Bristol Academy.

71. For a brief account of Jope's life and ministry, see Ivimey, *AHEB*, 4:263–66.

72. Hall and Mowvley, *Tradition and Challenge*, 6.

73. Hall and Mowvley, *Tradition and Challenge*, 6. Jope was at an academy in Trowbridge. With Broadmead's assistance, he then transferred to an academy at Tewkesbury and then to London.

74. Hayden, "Bristol Baptist College," 27.

75. Hall and Mowvley, *Tradition and Challenge*, 6.

76. Fuller, *Rise and Progress*, 180; Hall and Mowvley, *Tradition and Challenge*, 6.

77. Hayden, *Continuity and Change*, 24.

78. For an account of Foskett's life see Strivens, "Bernard Foskett (1685–1758)," in Haykin and Wolever, *British Particular Baptists*, 4:87–103; Hayden, "Contribution of Bernard Foskett," in Brackney et al., *Pilgrim Pathways*, 189–206.

education of Foskett is unknown, but he must have had knowledge of Hebrew and Greek in order to fulfill Terrill's requirements.[79] The only objection to Foskett being paid from Terrill's trust was by a trustee. His objection was that Foskett was not the pastor of Broadmead as Terrill's deed of gift stated but was only the associate pastor of the church.[80] The other trustees, however, decided Foskett did qualify and paid him £18 from the Terrill fund.[81]

With an approved principal in place, Bristol Academy was ready to enroll students. In November 1720, Thomas Rogers was admitted as the first student of the academy. Ten months later, in August 1721, John Phillips was admitted. However, due to an interpretation of Terrill's deed of gift by the trustees that "only gifted persons" be admitted as students, no other students were enrolled for several years.[82] For this reason, the third student at Bristol Academy, Daniel Garnon, would not be registered until 1727.[83] Though the student enrollment was low in the first seven years, Foskett ultimately trained seventy-three students in his tenure as principal of Bristol Academy from 1720 to 1758.[84]

Confessional Doctrine of Bristol Academy

Bristol Academy is not known to have had a stated confession of faith from its inception. Since Broadmead had, by its pastor Vaux, signed and endorsed the 2LCF, the academy, being a ministry extension of Broadmead, would have held the 2LCF as its confession.[85] This section will explore Bristol

79. It is believed that Foskett had training to be a physician. "And though he [Foskett] had spent a considerable time in qualifying himself to do good to the bodies of men, he rather chose now to serve them in a more important way, by doing good to their souls; preferring the character of an able Minister to that of a skilful Physician." Evans, *Elisha's Exclamation*, 23.

80. Swaine, *Faithful Men*, 38. Due to Kitterell's poor health, Foskett accepted Broadmead's call to the pastorate in March of 1725. Hall and Mowvley, *Tradition and Challenge*, 13. Foskett assumed the pastorate solely in 1727 upon the death of Kitterell.

81. Strivens, "Bernard Foskett," in Haykin and Wolever, *British Particular Baptists*, 4:92.

82. Hayden, *Continuity and Change*, 68. The trustees interpreted "gifted" to mean students who already knew Hebrew and Greek and could apply such knowledge in further education at the academy.

83. Hayden believes that young men at Broadmead who were gifted to preach were informally trained by Foskett between 1721 and 1727. Hayden, *Continuity and Change*, 68.

84. Hayden, *Continuity and Change*, 70.

85. "The academy and Church both accepted the 1689 Baptist Confession of Faith as their doctrinal standard until 1832, when the basis of the Baptist Union changed to admit ministers and churches who 'agree in the sentiments usually denominated evangelical.'" Hayden, "Bristol Baptist Academy."

Academy's affirmation of confessions to express doctrinal beliefs. To do this, two of the academy's principals will be considered. The first is Foskett and his use of the 2LCF as a means of doctrinal unity. The second is Caleb Evans's defense of the use of confessions as a means of doctrinal clarity.

The Confessionalism of Bernard Foskett

Foskett was not opposed to the use of confessions to express one's understanding of doctrine. He not only didn't oppose confessions, but he encouraged churches to use confessions to ensure doctrinal unity among themselves. Foskett's use and encouragement of confessions is witnessed by the *Alcester Confession* and the 2LCF.

Prior to the Salters' Hall Debates, Foskett stood in the company of Particular Baptists who confessed the faith through subscription to traditional confessions. Before his pastorship at Broadmead, Foskett served as assistant pastor at the Henley-in-Arden church in Warwickshire from 1711 to 1720. The church was affiliated with the Baptist church in Alcester pastored by John Beddome.[86] At the time, the church did not have a confession of faith. In 1712, both Foskett and Beddome worked together to write a confession for the church, *A Short and Compendius Confession of Faith Held by the Church of Christ Meeting at Aulcester in the County of Warwick* (*Alcester Confession*).[87] The confession has thirty-two paragraphs.[88] The *Alcester Confession* is trinitarian and Calvinistic.[89] The trinitarian affirmations are that of classical trinitarianism. Whether or not Foskett based the confession on another written confession is not known. The *Alcester Confession* is in doctrinal agreement with the 2LCF and shares common terminology. There are also similarities with the *Baptist Catechism A Brief Instruction in the Principles of Christian Religion* (1695).[90]

The first three articles of the *Alcester Confession* address the doctrine of God and the Trinity. Foskett began with an affirmation of monotheism,

---

86. The Alcester church met in three locations that included Henley-in-Arden.

87. A copy of the confession is found in Hayden, *Continuity and Change*, 212–16. Though both Foskett and Beddome are the authors of this confession, only Foskett will be named from henceforth since he is the subject of this section.

88. The original confession is neither numbered nor given subject titles. The numbers and subjects used here are supplied by this writer.

89. Strivens, "Bernard Foskett," in Haykin and Wolever, *British Particular Baptists*, 4:89.

90. This catechism is typically referred to as the *Baptist Catechism*. It may be that Foskett and Beddome used the *Baptist Catechism* as a reference. The catechism is historically attributed to both William Collins and Benjamin Keach. Prior to Alcester, Beddome was at Horsleydown in Southwark pastored by Keach.

"That there is one God who is Infinite, Eternal, Unchangeable, Omnipotent, Immense Spirit; who beyond measure is full of Holiness, Justice, Goodness & Truth."[91] Then the next two paragraphs state how the one God exists in three persons. Paragraph 2 distinguishes and designates the persons within the godhead, "We believe that this god subsists in three distinct personalities and yet these three are one undivided essence and have distinguished themselves by the names or titles of Fath, Son & Spirit."[92] The third paragraph upholds the unity and equality of the three persons of the godhead, "We believe that the Father is God, the Son of God,[93] and the Holy Spirit is God; all equal in power, authority and glory & we believe this God is the only object of Divine worship and Adoration."[94] The opening paragraphs of the *Alcester Confession* place it firmly in classical trinitarianism.

Paragraph 15 is the longest paragraph in the *Alcester Confession*. This paragraph addresses the great mystery of the two natures of Jesus, His deity and humanity. The opening of the paragraph reads, "We believe that the glorious person of our Redeemer was not only God over all, God blessed for evermore, the only begotten & brightness of the Father's Glory; but also that He was the Essential & Eternal Word—was made flesh & dwelt among us."[95] Though this statement upholds the two natures of Christ, it does not delve into how the natures dwelled in the person of Jesus. The focus of the paragraph is on the necessity of Jesus' human nature to accomplish redemption. Nevertheless, Foskett upholds the full deity of Jesus as that equal to the Father.

---

91. Hayden, *Continuity and Change*, 212. All quotations of the *Alcester Confession* are from Hayden, *Continuity and Change*. This language is similar to question 7, "What is God?" in the *Baptist Catechism*: "God is a Spirit, Infinite, Eternal, and Unchangeable, in His Being, Wisdom, Power, Holiness, Justice, Goodness, and Truth."

92. Hayden, *Continuity and Change*, 212. Question 9 of the *Baptist Catechism* asks, "How many Persons are there in the Godhead? There are three Persons in the Godhead, the Father, the Son, and the Holy Spirit; and these Three are One God, the same in Essence, equal in Power and Glory."

93. The phrase "the Son of God" appears out of place. Just prior to this phrase the confession predicates "God" to the Father and then just after it the confession predicates "God" to the Holy Spirit. It may be that the phrase is meant to say "the Son *is* God" which would predicate "God" to the Son. If this is a typed error, this writer does not know whether the error is original to Foskett or to Hayden in his copy or possibly somewhere in between the two men.

94. Hayden, *Continuity and Change*, 212. Paragraph 3 also has similarities to question 9 of the *Baptist Catechism*.

95. Hayden, *Continuity and Change*, 214. The wording and structure of paragraph 15 in the *Alcester Confession* are similar to chapter 8, section 2, "Of Christ the Mediator," in the 2LCF.

The *Alcester Confession* demonstrates that Foskett affirmed classical trinitarianism and that he affirmed subscription to traditional confessions within the church. Whether Foskett used the 2LCF and/or the *Baptist Catechism* to compose the *Alcester Confession*, he undoubtedly affirmed the practice of and adherence to the 2LCF upon his arrival at Broadmead. By 1720, the 2LCF had been the confession of Broadmead for at least three decades given that Vaux subscribed to the 2LCF at the 1689 Baptist General Assembly.

In 1720, when Foskett assumed leadership of Bristol Academy, just over a year had passed since the Salters' Hall Debates. That short time had not diminished the effects of the debates. The question of whether to use and subscribe to confessions was still a concern to those on both sides of the issue. The Western Association, to which Broadmead belonged, had been involved in the debates. John Sharpe, a member of the Particular Baptist church in Frome, attended the debates as a messenger from the Western Association and then reported back to the association.[96] Sharpe and others in the association sided with the subscribers at Salters' Hall. However, other churches within the association were not in agreement.

Broadmead determined that the issue needed to be addressed. Fuller reports that in May 1723, Broadmead requested Foskett to write a letter on behalf of the church to the Western Association. The letter recommended the following:

> That seeing many errors have been broached, and ancient heresies revived, of late, in the world, no messenger [of the Western Association] shall be received from any church whose letter don't every year express, either in the preamble or body of it, that they of the church do approve the Confession of Faith put forth by above a hundred baptist churches, (edit. 3d, AD 1699,) and do maintain the principles contained therein; such letter being signed at a church-meeting, in the name and by the consent of the whole church.[97]

Foskett and Broadmead feared the presence of "ancient heresies," Arianism in the form of Socinianism, within the association. To assure that all churches in the Western Association affirmed classical trinitarianism, Foskett proposed that all churches subscribe to the 2LCF in order be a member of the association.[98] The majority of the messengers at the 1723 associational

---

96. Sharpe is listed among the subscribers in *True Relation*, 7, 10.

97. Fuller, *Rise and Progress*, 181.

98. After the Western Association agreed to the confessional standard of the 2LCF in 1733, Foskett wrote another letter in 1734 to encourage the association to stand by

meeting denied Foskett's proposal. Whether the messengers rejected classical trinitarianism outright or merely subscribing to confessions, Foskett found both suspect. Undeterred by initial defeat, he persistently presented this proposal before the association. After certain events, the proposal was finally adopted ten years later in 1733.

Foskett's actions to promote the 2LCF were primarily aimed at encouraging subscriptions from Broadmead and churches within the Western Association. Although not directly related to Bristol Academy, these actions indirectly suggest Foskett's approach to incorporating the confession within the Academy.

The Confessionalism of Caleb Evans

Foskett's involvement in the reformation of the Western Association demonstrates that he viewed subscription to traditional confessions that espoused classical trinitarianism as a means of establishing unity among various churches. Caleb Evans, the third principal of Bristol Academy, shared the same views as Foskett. Evans served as tutor from 1758 to 1781 and then as principal from 1781 to 1791 of Bristol Academy.[99] The confessional conviction of Evans, therefore, will illustrate well Bristol Academy's conviction regarding subscription to confessions.

After eight years of service in Broadmead, the church ordained Evans in 1767 as an elder, his father Hugh Evans being the pastor.[100] Though the church was familiar with Evans's service and doctrine, Broadmead requested that he draw up a personal confession of faith so as to state publicly and clearly what he professed to believe.[101] Prior to reading his confession before the church, Evans gave his opinion as to confessions in general. He was aware that in his day many recoiled at confessions. "I am very sensible it is become now quite fashionable, zealously and indiscriminately to decry all creeds and systematic confessions of faith, and vehemently to inveigh against them, as invading the liberty where with CHRIST hath made us free."[102] Evans remarked that those who denounce confessions are not

---

its decision. See the letter at Hayden, *Continuity and Change*, 219–21.

99. All uses of "Evans" will designate Caleb Evans. If Hugh Evans is referenced, he will be cited as H. Evans.

100. Caleb served at Broadmead as assistant pastor to his father from 1758 to 1781. He would assume the pastorate of Broadmead upon his father's death in 1781 and serve in that position until his own death in 1791.

101. Evans et al., *Charge and Sermon*, 17. Swaish says, "Some fears were expressed concerning the son's [Caleb's] orthodoxy." Swaish, *Chronicles*, 35.

102. Evans et al., *Charge and Sermon*, 16.

against confessions. Rather, "the grand rock of offence" with them "is that particular system of faith which has long been and still is the bulwark and glory of the reformation, which is the object of their aversion, and to destroy which they seem determined to leave no artifice untried."[103] Evans surmised that most nonsubscribers were against the content of confessions, not the form of confessions.

Nevertheless, Evans defended the right of Christians to believe in their convictions, upholding their freedom and liberty. The opening sentence of his introduction reads, "The right of private judgment, especially in matters of religion, I apprehend is the undoubted and unalienable privilege of every rational intelligent creature."[104] Although Christians have the right to form their own opinions about doctrine, Evans did not conclude that written confessions infringed upon this freedom. "Nor can I think this privilege is in any measure infringed by the request now made on the behalf of this society [Broadmead], that I would give a free confession of my faith upon this occasion."[105] Rather, Evans concluded that writing a confession is "a necessary consequence" of one's personal freedom to believe what one thinks is right.[106] It is a necessary consequence because those who labor together in the gospel, especially a church calling a man to be their elder, have a right to know what the other confesses to be true. A church determines what doctrines they hold essential to the gospel and therefore "it is certainly incumbent upon them to be well satisfied that the person they chose to minister to them is well acquainted with these doctrines, and established in the belief of them for how can two walk together except they be agreed?"[107] Confessions for Evans were an necessary means to determine doctrinal agreement and ministerial alignment.

For two persons to walk together in doctrinal unity, confessions ought to be written with specifics and ascribed to with integrity. As to specifics,

---

103. Evans et al., *Charge and Sermon*, 17. Evans makes the same conclusion as Coxe regarding those who oppose confessional terms. See Coxe, *Vindiciæ Veritatis* (Renihan), 35.

104. Evans et al., *Charge and Sermon*, 13.

105. Evans et al., *Charge and Sermon*, 13.

106. Evans et al., *Charge and Sermon*, 17.

107. Evans et al., *Charge and Sermon*, 13–14. Caleb's point is witnessed in the life of Broadmead. Just over three decades earlier Broadmead had experienced that two cannot walk together in disagreement. In 1731, the church called Edward Harrison to assist Foskett. Within two years of his service, Harrison left because he disagreed with some of the church's confessed doctrine. Fuller says the issue was Arminianism. Fuller, *Rise and Progress*, 185. Harrison may have hidden his views upon coming to Broadmead. "Harrison simply admitted that he held an interpretation of the faith which caused disquiet to some in the Church." Hall and Mowvley, *Tradition and Challenge*, 14.

Evans said, "Nor is it by any means sufficient that a minister declare his belief of the bible in general, since this is a declaration which a papist will make as well as a protestant, the greatest enemy to the doctrines of the gospel, as well as the most zealous friend of them."[108] Evans did not abide by the Protestant Principle. Evans understood that confessions that use general scriptural terminology were no indication as to agreement in doctrine. The reason is that papists and enemies of the gospel could use scriptural terminology and yet intend differently than what another intends by the same words. This is not a matter of deception but of obscurity. For this reason, Evans exhorted that those who write and ascribe to confessions should do so with integrity. He warns, "And though, after the fullest confession of faith it is possible . . . for a minister to impose upon a people and to declare he believes what he really does not believe."[109] The caution here is that a person might give verbal agreement to even the fullest of confessions and yet not actually believe what is said, or have a different interpretation. Evans knew confessions were not fully adequate and could be abused; nonetheless, he defended the use of confessions, "yet still there is no more reason upon this account to abolish the custom of a minister's giving a confession of his faith previous to his ordination."[110]

Bristol Academy would, post-Salters' Hall Debates, affirm the use of and subscription to traditional confessions. This has been evidenced by the origin of Bristol Academy out of Broadmead, and also by its leaders. Foskett wrote an orthodox confession and he argued for the use of the 2LCF among the Western Association churches. Evans affirmed that though Christians have a right to religious liberty, it is no impingement upon their liberty to affirm confessions.

The History of the Salters' Hall Debates

Among the first of the Baptist historians to reference the Salters' Hall Debates are Thomas Crosby and Joseph Ivimey. Crosby's reference is brief. He introduces the debates by means of demonstrating how the dissenters, like the Church of England, had mistreated those who held a different position regarding the doctrine of the Trinity. He describes the events leading up to the debates at Salters' Hall as "furious measures taken by some ministers in the *west country*, against their reverend and learned brethren Mr. *Peirce*,

---

108. Evans et al., *Charge and Sermon*, 15.
109. Evans et al., *Charge and Sermon*, 15.
110. Evans et al., *Charge and Sermon*, 15.

Mr. *Withers*, and Mr. *Hallet*."[111] Crosby's only comment regarding Baptists at Salters' Hall is that ministers of other denominations had maligned the Baptists who refused subscription. From Crosby's comments regarding the Salters' Hall Debates, it appears he allowed for wide trinitarian differences within denominations and affirmed nonsubscription.

Ivimey does not come to the same conclusion. He devotes eight pages to the debates, including an initial list of Baptists who either subscribed or refused to subscribe.[112] At the end of his account, Ivimey, though he understood the religious freedom argument by nonsubscribing Baptists, concluded that their position was vulnerable to trinitarian heresy.[113] In his estimation, the General Baptist churches pastored by nonsubscribing ministers mostly died out during the eighteenth century, while the Particular Baptist churches pastored by subscribing ministers flourished due to their orthodox stance.[114]

The *Baptist Magazine* published a nineteen-page article, "History of the Conference at Salters' Hall on the Doctrine of the Trinity, in 1719," on the centurial anniversary of the Salters' Hall Debates. The article provides good historical background to the debates as well as the proceedings of the debates. The author's purpose for drawing attention to Salters' Hall was to exhort modern-day orthodox Protestant Dissenters "to contend earnestly for the faith once delivered to the saints."[115] By this he means orthodox Protestants ought to hold to trinitarian doctrine as expressed in classical confessions. He perceived a weakness in the nonsubscribers' position as they "unconsciously introduced principles which have 'eaten like gangrene'" among their congregations.[116] The principle was primarily that nonsubscription to confessions leaves churches vulnerable to heterodox beliefs.

Two articles appeared in the early twentieth century that provide critical assessment of the Salters' Hall Debates. In 1916, *Transactions of the Congregational Historical Society* published Powicke's article "The Salters' Hall Controversy." His intent was to determine whether churches pastored by

---

111. Crosby, *THEB*, 3:293.

112. Ivimey, *AHEB*, 3:162–63. This list would later be corrected in 1916 by Powicke, "Salters' Hall," and in 1917 by Whitley, "Salters' Hall."

113. Ivimey, *AHEB*, 3:166.

114. Ivimey, *AHEB*, 3:166. Both Powicke and Whitley disagree with Ivimey. Powicke states that when the lists of represented churches are compared, it disposes "of the notion that more churches of the nonsubscribers became extinct than of subscribers, owing to the 'Arian blight.'" Powicke, "Salters' Hall," 123–24. Whitley concurs that there is "no connection between non-subscription and death." Whitley, "Salters' Hall," 180.

115. "History of the Conference," 110.

116. "History of the Conference," 110.

subscribing or nonsubscribing ministers "yielded to the advancing tide of Arianism and Unitarianism; or forsook the cause of Nonconformity."[117] He thereby researched the names of the ministers present at the debates and the churches they served at the time. His list is an update and correction to that offered by Ivimey.[118] Powicke concluded that most of the nonsubscribing ministers were orthodox and that, contra common opinion, nonsubscribing churches became no more extinct than subscribing churches.[119]

In 1917, *Transactions of the Baptist Historical Society* published Whitley's article "Salters' Hall 1719 and the Baptists." Whitley's focus on the Baptists at Salters' Hall was, first, to demonstrate that Baptists "asserted a right to meet with the Two Denominations."[120] Also, he sought to prove that there were more Baptists, General and Particular, present at the debates than reported by previous authors. His list is an update to that of Powicke's.[121] Whitley has fifteen subscribing Baptists to Powicke's twelve,[122] and he has sixteen nonsubscribing Baptists to Powicke's fourteen.[123]

A century would pass after Powicke and Whitley before critical considerations of Salters' Hall Debates would appear again. Stephen Copson, in 2020, edited a volume in Centre for Baptist Studies in Oxford Publications, *Trinity, Creed, and Confussion: The Salters' Hall Debates of 1719*. The book primarily focuses on the Baptists present at the debates to demonstrate that the debate among them was not about orthodoxy versus heterodoxy, as most all the Baptists present were classical trinitarians. Instead, the issue was religious freedom to not subscribe to confessions in order to demonstrate one's orthodoxy.[124]

Jesse Owens in 2021 completed his dissertation, "The Salters' Hall Controversy of 1719." The dissertation provides historical, political, and theological context to the events before and surrounding the debates. Owens's thesis is similar to that of *Trinity, Creed and Confusion*. He argues that while there were antitrinitarians present at the debates and they were counted among the nonsubscribers, the vast number of the nonsubscribers

---

117. Powicke, "Salters' Hall," 111.

118. Powicke provides the denominational affiliation of the ministers, even distinguishing between General and Particular Baptists where known.

119. Powicke, "Salters' Hall," 123–24.

120. Whitley, "Salters' Hall," 178. The "two denominations" were the Presbyterians and the Congregationalists.

121. Whitley, "Salters' Hall," 189.

122. Fourteen were Particular Baptists and one was a General Baptist.

123. Fourteen were General Baptists and two were Particular Baptists.

124. Copson, *Trinity, Creed and Confusion*, 2–3.

were not antitrinitarians.[125] Again, the issue of Salters' Hall was primarily freedom to not subscribe.

From these summaries of authors' assessments of the Salters' Hall Debates, it is apparent there is a wide difference of opinion as to the material issue of the debates.[126] Was it orthodoxy versus heterodoxy or a matter of religious liberty among orthodox trinitarians? Crosby seemingly believed there was a trinitarian difference, but it was not significant enough to rise to the level of debate. Ivimey also believed the issue was of a difference in trinitarianism and those who did not subscribe showed themselves to be unorthodox. The author of the *Baptist Magazine*, more in line with Crosby, feared churches in his day would deny confessing the Trinity via confessions and would become unorthodox. Copson et al. and Owens do not take the tolerant view of Crosby nor the bleak view of Ivimey and the *Baptist Magazine*. They understand the issue as religious freedom that would not impose orthodox tests upon ministers and churches.

Each of the authors above have warrant for their estimation of Salters' Hall. The situation at Exeter among Presbyterian ministers that led to the debates clearly centered on a difference of trinitarian understanding between orthodoxy and heterodoxy. But when the issue was brought before the ministers of the Three Denominations in London, the discussion shifted from the right of churches to hold their ministers accountable for their doctrine to the need for ministers to affirm their doctrine via confessional statements.[127] A brief history of the events leading to Salters' Hall will first be explored to understand that orthodox trinitarianism was being denied by certain persons in Exeter that then led to the debates. Then a brief account of the debates will be given to appreciate the position of both subscribers and nonsubscribers.

The Origin of the Salters' Hall Debates

The origin of the debates was in the town of Exeter, in western England. Among the Presbyterian churches there were primarily two ministers who came to deny confessional trinitarianism. They were James Peirce and

---

125. Owens, "Salters' Hall Controversy," 14–15. Owens identifies only four men who were antitrinitarian among all the nonsubscribers. They were Nathaniel Lardner, Benjamin Avery, Jeremiah Hunt, and Samuel Chandler. Owens, "Salters' Hall," 121. Joseph Burroughs, a General Baptist who did not subscribe, is sometimes named among the antitrinitarians. Owens defends him against such charges. Owens, "Salters' Hall," 120.

126. It can said that the material cause of the debates is orthodoxy verses heterodoxy and the formal cause of the debates is freedom to subscribe or not subscribe.

127. The three denominations were Presbyterians, Congregationalists, and Baptists.

Joseph Hallett who ran an academy in Exeter. While both men were involved in the trinitarian debate in Exeter, only Peirce will be considered as representative of the two men.

James Peirce and Antitrinitarianism

Prior to 1713, Peirce held to classical trinitarianism. Peirce, after his departure from classical trinitarianism, stated his former belief as "a scheme, of which I can now make nothing else but *Sabellianism*; and a set of unscriptural expressions had been inculcated upon me from my youth, which I had a great veneration for."[128] His departure from classical trinitarianism came as a result of his reading the early church fathers and two modern authors of his day. As to the early church fathers, Peirce found the ante-Nicene fathers to not hold the common opinion of his day and that post-Nicene fathers tended to teach a form of tritheism.[129] As to the modern-day authors, Peirce was greatly influenced by the writings of Samuel Clarke and William Whiston, who both came to deny classical trinitarianism and to speak of the Trinity in only scriptural terms.[130] Upon his study of the church fathers and Clarke and Whiston, Peirce stated, "I was soon convinc'd the common opinion could not reasonably be esteem'd a fundamental article of the christian faith, as I had been too apt before to take it to be."[131] Peirce then resolved to refer to the Father, Son, and Holy Spirit only in scriptural terms and not in common confessional terms.[132] A primary reason for Peirce's Scripture-only position was that inferences of reason from Scripture, or consequences of Scripture of which confessional trinitarianism utilizes, were not to be believed above the "plain assertions" of Scripture.[133]

Peirce's change in trinitarian belief was a major shift from the common confessional orthodoxy of his day. Peirce's opponents in Exeter accused him of being an Arian; an accusation he denied.[134] Peirce denied being an Arian because he could not affirm that the Son was a creation of the Father; yet

---

128. Peirce, *Western Inquisition*, 5. Whether Peirce was actually taught some form of modalism is not known. After Peirce came to deny classical trinitarianism, he would describe it as either tritheism or modalism.

129. Peirce, *Western Inquisition*, 6.

130. Peirce, *Western Inquisition*, 8.

131. Peirce, *Western Inquisition*, 9. The "common opinion" was classical trinitarianism.

132. Peirce, *Western Inquisition*, 9.

133. Peirce, *Plain Christianity Defended*, 29.

134. Peirce, *Evil and Cure*, 25.

at the same time he could not affirm that the Son was the supreme God.[135] Peirce concluded "that there is but one GOD the Father, because the Scriptures are express in saying so; but we cannot be so certain that the Father, Son, and Holy Ghost are one GOD, because the Scripture never so much as *once* says so."[136] Peirce confessed that this was the primary difference between himself and his opponents: "Here begins our Difference, our Adversaries asserting, that not the Father alone, but that He and the Son and Holy Ghost are together the One God."[137]

Response by the Committee of Thirteen in Exeter

Concerned about the spread of Arianism in Exeter by men like Peirce and Hallett, a committee of thirteen lay trustees who managed the affairs of the Exeter dissenters met to address the issue.[138] In November 1718, the Committee of Thirteen requested the ministers of Exeter to state their confession of the Trinity in one of three ways: the first article of the Church of England, the answer to the sixth question of the Westminster Catechism, or to the agreed upon Assembly's statement from September 1718.[139] Peirce and other ministers refused to state their position on the Trinity in any of the three ways. They claimed it was a test imposed upon them in unscriptural terms and without scriptural warrant.

Unwilling to act against Peirce and others at that time, the committee reached out to London ministers for advice. The London ministers advised the committee to gather seven ministers from the surrounding area of Exeter to address the matter.[140] The committee followed the advice. On March 4, 1719, the seven ministers, after surmising the situation in Exeter, concluded that the doctrine of the Trinity was of such importance that the denial of the Son as "one God with the Father" should be rejected, therefore ministers ought "to give reasonable Satisfaction to the People of their Soundness in the Faith" regarding the Trinity.[141] The next day the Committee of Thirteen called the ministers of Exeter to give satisfaction of their trinitarian doctrine in one of three ways as before stated in November 1718 or by stating

---

135. Peirce, *Western Inquisition*, 14–15. Peirce's position is close to Socininianism.

136. Peirce, *Plain Christianity Defended*, 29.

137. Peirce, *Propositions*, 5.

138. Wykes, "Peirce, James," para. 7.

139. *Account of the Reasons*, 8. The Assembly's 1718 statement read, "There is but One God; and that the Father, Word, and the Holy Spirit, is that One God."

140. *Account of the Reasons*, 9–10.

141. *Account of the Reasons*, 10.

"that the Son of God was one God with the Father." Both Peirce and Hallett refused, again, to state their beliefs according to such standards. The committee this time acted against the two men by ejecting them as ministers of the church.[142]

The Inclusion of the Three Denominations in London

While the Committee of Thirteen was in contact with the London ministers and during the investigation of the seven ministers, Peirce had reached out to a friend in London, and a member of Parliament, John Shute Barrington. Barrington was a Dissenter himself and fought for the right of Dissenters in Parliament. Even without Peirce's contact with Barrington, the disturbance in Exeter had already made it to the floor of Parliament in December 1718 causing anti-Dissenters to question the orthodoxy of the Dissenters.[143] Barrington wanted to quell such concerns, so he reached out to the Committee of the General Body of the Three Denominations in London. On February 5, 1719, Barrington provided the committee with his own list of advices for how the situation at Exeter ought to be handled.[144] Included in his advices was that there ought to be no doctrinal test regarding the Trinity except for statement of the Trinity in scriptural terms only.[145] Barrington's advice was based more on political resolution than doctrinal resolution. The committee agreed with Barrington's advices but thought it best to consult and get the agreement of the whole of the Body of the Three Denominations. This then led to the Salters' Hall Debates.

The origin of the Salters' Hall Debates shows two issues occurring simultaneously. The first issue is that there was great concern among many that the classical doctrine of the Trinity was being denied by some in Exeter, such as Peirce and Hallett. As evidenced above, Peirce himself admitted his doctrine of the Trinity had changed. Ministers gathered at Salters' Hall had a legitimate reason to believe the doctrine of the Trinity was of primary interest at the debates. The second issue in the origin of the debates is that of imposed doctrinal tests regarding the Trinity. Peirce and Hallett were not so much opposed to tests if the wording of such tests were only scriptural in language. Ministers at Salters' Hall who saw this as the only issue to debate had warrant for their position.

142. *Account of the Reasons*, 11. It should be noted that the Committee of Thirteen already took action against Peirce and Hallett before receiving advices from the General Assembly of the Three Denominations.

143. Wykes, "Peirce, James," para. 8.

144. Wykes, "1719 Salters' Hall Debate," 40.

145. Wykes, "1719 Salters' Hall Debate," 40.

The Debates at Salters' Hall

The debates at Salters' Hall occurred over the span of four weeks. The first meeting was held on Thursday, February 19, 1719. The remaining three meetings were held on the three subsequent Tuesdays—February 24, March 3, and March 10.[146]

The First Meeting, February 19

On February 19, the General Body of the Three Denominations was called together to consider a paper, *Advices for Promoting Peace*.[147] The paper contained the advices given by Barrington to the Committee of the Three Denominations. The meeting concluded peaceably with the approval of all present to consider the advices paragraph by paragraph at the next meeting.

The Second Meeting, February 24

The second meeting on February 24 proved to be contentious. During the meeting, some of the ministers proposed the question whether a declaration of the Trinity ought to be placed within the advices though no particular declaration was suggested.[148] The debate lasted for several hours and concluded with the majority voting to not include a declaration of the Trinity in the advices.[149] The vote was fifty-three in favor and fifty-seven not in favor of including a declaration on the Trinity.[150]

The Third Meeting, March 3

The third meeting, March 3, increased the level of tensity at the debates. The nonsubscribing ministers said the subscribing ministers broke order by resuming the debate of a declaration of the Trinity that had already been

---

146. The days of the weeks are according to the Julian calendar. The authors of *True Relation* use the Julian calendar, stating the meeting on March 3 occurred on a Tuesday in the year 1718/1719. The authors of *Authentick Account* also used the Julian calendar. *Authentick Account*, 7. If a Gregorian calendar is used, the first meeting occurred on a Sunday and the other meetings on the subsequent Fridays.

147. *Authentick Account*, 17–18.

148. *Vindication*, 22. This pamphlet is the subscribers' response to the nonsubscribers' *Authentick Account*. The nonsubscribers responded to *Vindication* with *Reply to the Subscribing Ministers*. The proposal to include confessional trinitarian standards in the advices went directly against Barrington's advice.

149. *Authentick Account*, 18–19.

150. Barrington, *Account of the Late Proceedings*, 10.

settled at the previous meeting.[151] The subscribing ministers argued they raised a different question. The question this time was whether they should make a declaration of their trinitarian belief for their own vindication and not to be included in the advices to the Exeter churches.[152]

The recommended declaration of the Trinity included both the first article of the Church of England and the fifth and sixth questions of the *Westminster Catechism*.[153] Debate lasted for several hours with the result being separation between the nonsubscribing ministers and the subscribing ministers. Those who wished to subscribe their names to the confessional declarations of the Trinity departed and those who wished to not subscribe remained in the room. If the count of those who departed and those who remained were considered to be a vote, sixty voted in favor of subscribing to a declaration and "around fifty" voted to not subscribe.[154]

The subscribers on that same day, March 3, wrote out their own set of advices to the churches in Exeter.[155] They acknowledged that certain doctrinal errors were so grievous that church members ought to withdraw from their minister should he hold such a position. To help the members of churches know how to proceed in these matters, the subscribing ministers gave five advices. The first advice was that members ought not separate from their minister over matters of opinion but only over true doctrinal division.[156] Next, churches who suspect their minister to hold erroneous doctrine ought to include unbiased ministers from their region to help determine the matter.[157]

151. *Authentick Account*, 16.

152. *Vindication*, 22.

153. *Authentick Account*, 16; *Vindication*, 24.

154. *Vindication*, 25. The usual numbers given for subscribers is seventy-eight and seventy-three for nonsubscribers. The number seventy-eight comes from *True Relation* written by subscribers for those in Exeter. *True Relation*, 9–10. Seventy-eight ministers subscribed their names to the statement, "There is but One only, the living and true God. There are three Persons in the Godhead; the Father, the Son, and the Holy Ghost: And these three are One God, the same in Substance, equal in Power and Glory." *True Relation*, 8. It then gives the names of seventy-eight men who subscribed their names to the first article of the Church of England and the fifth and sixth questions of the Westminster Catechism. The number seventy-three for nonsubscribers comes from *Authentick Account* written by nonsubscribers for those in Exeter. *Authentick Account*, 11–12. It gives the names of seventy-three men who refused to subscribe and who also approved of the advices sent by them.

155. *True Relation*, 11–16. Broadmead's request of Caleb Evans to give an account of his doctrinal beliefs via a written expression, as stated earlier in this chapter, closely follows the advice given by the subscribers.

156. *True Relation*, 12–13.

157. *True Relation*, 12.

Their third advice addressed the issue of declaration of doctrine. It is quoted here in full:

> If any minister is suspected by his hearers to hold dangerous Errors, and the People in a serious and respectful Manner desire him to be plain with them, and let them know what his real Belief is, that they may not by Mistake either wrong him or their own Souls; we think it reasonable he should comply with their Desire, and be ready to give an Account of the Hope that is in him with Meekness and Fear, that the People may have no Ground to charge him with Pride or Prevarication, sacrificing his own Peace and theirs too, to a Stiffness of Humour, or Punctilio of Honour.[158]

This advice counters those who would only state their doctrine in scriptural terms only. Such scriptural statements could remain vague and allow heretics to hide behind scriptural words. To only repeat words of Scripture is not to explain one's sense and understanding of what Scripture declares.[159] The use of other expressions of doctrine, as found in confessions, is necessary for people to determine and assess what another believes or denies.[160] Therefore, the subscribers advised those in Exeter to require a suspected minister to declare his belief clearly in other than Scripture-only words. It is worth noting that the subscribers did not advise what declaration the churches ought to employ. Along with these advices, the subscribers included statements they had subscribed to regarding the Trinity.[161] These declarations would have served as an example for the Exeter churches. Nonetheless, the subscribers left it to the churches to decide what declarations ought to be used.

The fourth advice encourages members to extend grace to a minister who is found to not be in disagreement with the church in doctrine.[162] Should the minister be found by the members to be in disagreement, or should the minister find himself in disagreement with the church, the last advice encourages the minister and the church to part from one another for the sake of unity and peace.[163] Should such departure occur, it should be conducted in such a manner that none judge the other as to their "eternal

---

158. *True Relation*, 13–14.
159. *Vindication*, 6.
160. *Vindication*, 6.
161. *True Relation*, 5–6, 8.
162. *True Relation*, 14–15.
163. *True Relation*, 15–16.

state."[164] This is important to note—though the subscribers thought it right to impose a doctrinal test by way of declaration to determine one's position on the Trinity, they did not see it as a test of one's salvation.

The Fourth Meeting, March 10

The nonsubscribing ministers also began work on their set of advices on March 3 but would not complete them until March 10.[165] They sent a letter with eight advices to the Exeter churches.

The letter includes a strong statement by the nonsubscribing ministers as to their disavowal of the doctrine of Arianism and their affirmation of the Trinity. The statement is here in full:

> And freely declare, that we utterly disown the Arian Doctrine, and Sincerely believe the Doctrine of the Blessed Trinity, and the proper Divinity of our Lord Jesus Christ, which we apprehend to be clearly revealed in the Holy Scriptures; But are far from condemning any who appear to be with us in the Main, tho' they should chuse not to declare themselves in other than Scripture-Terms, or not in Ours.[166]

The nonsubscribing ministers, though not averse to confessions, thought the Scriptures sufficiently and clearly affirmed the full divinity of the Son as also affirmed in trinitarian confessional statements. Also, they denounce Arianism as a false doctrine of the Trinity and divinity of the Son because it does not adhere to the plain statements of Scripture.

The introduction to the advices begins with an affirmation that churches have a right to determine what doctrine they hold as essential and a duty to part with ministers who hold contrary doctrine as determined by them.[167] The first three advices give caution to churches to not act rashly or publicly when a minister is first suspected of erroneous doctrine. If a minister states his disagreement with the church's "Sense of Scripture" on a particular doctrine, the sixth advice encourages the minister to "quietly withdraw" from the church in order to maintain peace within the church.[168] The seventh advice then encourages churches to maintain a spirit of love with those who disagree over doctrines with which Christians may differ.[169]

164. *True Relation*, 16.
165. *Authentick Account*, 7–8.
166. *Authentick Account*, 15–16.
167. *Authentick Account*, 5–6.
168. *Authentick Account*, 9–10.
169. *Authentick Account*, 10.

The final advice gives churches in Exeter freedom to not follow these advices but exhorts them to "preserve Charity and Communion" with those churches who chose to follow these advices.[170] This is most likely a reference to the difference of opinion regarding whether churches ought to require ministers to state their doctrine in confessional words or Scripture-only words. Advices four and five address this matter.

The nonsubscribing ministers appealed specifically to the Protestant Principle in advice four, this principle being "that *the Bible is the only and the perfect Rule of Faith*, obliges those who have the Case before them, not to condemn any Man upon the Authority of Humane Decisions, or because he consents not to Human Forms or Phrases."[171] Since the Bible is the only rule of faith for Christians, no minister ought to be ejected for either refusing to own or to state his belief in confessional terms. However, if a minister contradicts or refuses to own the "express Declarations of Holy Scripture" regarding matters of faith necessary for salvation, then the church ought to censure him.[172] Of interest in this advice is that the nonsubscribing ministers allowed for ministers to disagree with confessional statements, such as statements regarding the Trinity, and yet he may still be considered orthodox because he affirms scriptural terms. Also, the advice does not clarify what matters of faith are necessary for salvation.

The fifth advice addresses two key elements in this discussion—confessions and consequences of Scripture. The nonsubscribing ministers did see a role for confessions and catechisms in the discussion of doctrine as they may be "great Helps to understand the Mind of God in the Scriptures."[173] But confessions are only to be used with the common consent of all in the discussion and only as personal expression of one's sense of Scripture. Regarding Scripture consequence, the nonsubscribing ministers accepted that the statements of Scripture could logically lead to further assertions or conclusions. Such assertions or conclusions may either agree with or contradict commonly accepted doctrine. Should the minister's logical consequence lead to a contradiction of commonly accepted doctrine, he should not be "charged with holding those Consequences of his Opinion, which he expressly disclaims."[174]

170. *Authentick Account*, 10–11.
171. *Authentick Account*, 8.
172. *Authentick Account*, 8–9.
173. *Authentick Account*, 9.

174. *Authentick Account*, 9. An example of this is James Peirce. Peirce denied that the Son is one God with the Father because the Scriptures never expressly state this affirmation. Peirce's opponents charged him with Arianism because the logical consequence of his position contradicted classical confessions of the Trinity. However, Peirce always denied Arianism and that he was himself an Arian.

From this survey of the debates, the Salters' Hall debates were less about orthodox trinitarian doctrine and more about how one ought to expect others to state trinitarian doctrine. The nonsubscribing ministers concluded that Scripture is sufficient to declare one's orthodoxy, while the subscribing ministers concluded that confessional statements accurately express one's understanding of Scripture. This survey also reveals that the subscribing ministers affirmed confessional statements as logical consequences of Scripture and therefore necessary to determine one's trinitarian position. While the nonsubscribing ministers did not deny the logical consequences of Scripture, they did deny such consequences as necessary.

Conclusion

Prior to the Salters' Hall Debates, Broadmead Church had already demonstrated that it was a church that utilized an orthodox traditional confession by way of the 2LCF. The church's position would naturally be imbedded in that of Bristol Academy. The Salters' Hall Debates foisted the issue of whether ministers and churches ought to subscribe to confessions or rely on scriptural terms only to express the Trinity. Foskett came to Broadmead and Bristol Academy post-Salters' Hall. He stood with the subscribers in his advocacy of the 2LCF among Western Association churches. Evans, the third principal of the Academy, gave by personal example and exhortation that affirmation of confessions was no infringement on personal religious liberty. Rather, such affirmation was necessary to determine doctrinal agreement.

6

"Teach What Accords with Sound Doctrine"

Trinitarian Teaching at Bristol Baptist Academy

SEVENTEENTH-CENTURY ENGLISH CHURCHES FACED two issues that merged into one. The two issues were the Trinity and Scripture. Antitrinitarians became more vocal in the seventeenth century, particularly with the emergence of Socinianism in England. The antitrinitarians did not deny the teaching of Scripture. They affirmed the scriptural teaching about God insofar as their reason of Scripture would allow them to believe. This became known as the Protestant Principle, the affirmation of scriptural language alone. The Protestant Principle, therefore, would not allow one to confess the Trinity in confessional terms.

While the Protestant Principle was employed by antitrinitarians, it was also utilized by trinitarians who were uncomfortable with confessional terms to explain the Trinity. For instance, the nonsubscribers at the Salters' Hall Debates were predominantly trinitarians who were hesitant to demand confessional language as a prerequisite for affirming their trinitarian beliefs. Similarly, the General Baptists in the seventeenth century were also reluctant to use and require confessional language regarding the Trinity. On the other hand, the Particular Baptists were not hesitant. They wrote, affirmed, and recommended confessions that aligned with orthodox trinitarianism. At Salters' Hall, most all Particular Baptists subscribed to the Westminster Catechism questions five and six, as well as the first article of the Church of England.

Bristol Baptist Academy formally started one year after Salters' Hall. The principals of Bristol Academy were aware of the debates and differences between subscribers and nonsubscribers. Bristol Academy was born in the tradition of the Particular Baptists by Broadmead Baptist Church. So, how would Bristol Academy teach the Trinity to its students? This chapter explores the question and will conclude that Bristol Academy affirmed and taught orthodox trinitarianism as evidenced by its library, curriculum, and staff.

The Trinitarian Library of Bristol Baptist Academy

The library of a school is not a sole determining factor for what a school may or may not teach. Schools will have books that affirm its doctrinal standards. Schools may also have books that deny its doctrinal standards for educational and research purposes. Nonetheless, libraries can give insight into what a school may use and recommend to its students for teaching certain subjects. This is particularly true when the school's doctrinal standard is known, allowing for a comparative analysis of library resources.

1722 and 1795 Catalogues of Bristol Academy

Two years after coming to Broadmead Church as an assistant pastor and to Bristol Academy as its principal, Bernard Foskett undertook an inventory of the books held by the church and the academy. Thirty-eight years had elapsed since an inventory had been conducted.[1] The previous catalogue of books from 1685 specified that the church held 195 books. Henton Davies suggests that these books were those bestowed to the church and for the future academy by Edward Terrill's deed of gift that provided the finances for the academy.[2] The books had been held in the homes of three different members of the church. The inventory in 1722 found that forty-three of the 195 books were missing.[3] The other books were accounted for and then deposited in Broadmead's vestry from the members' homes.[4] Among the collection were thirty-four copies of the *Second London Baptist Confession of Faith* (2LCF). Copies of the 2LCF accounted for the most numerous of all the books.[5] Books on doctrine included John Calvin's *Institutes of the Christian Religion*. The presence of these resources within Bristol Academy's

---

1. Hayden, *Continuity and Change*, 67.
2. Davies, "Bristol Baptist College," 15.
3. Hayden, *Continuity and Change*, 67.
4. Hayden states a list of the books deposited with Broadmead in 1722 is located at the library of Bristol Baptist College. Hayden, *Continuity and Change*, 67.
5. Hayden, *Continuity and Change*, 67.

library indicates that the academy from its beginning recommended and used confessions of faith and books that upheld orthodox trinitarianism.[6]

Just as Foskett inventoried the academy's library upon his appointment as principal, John Ryland Jr. also did the same when he assumed the role of the fourth principal in 1793. In 1795, he comprised a catalogue of all the books held by the Bristol Education Society (BES).[7] The BES was formed in 1770 by Hugh and Caleb Evans to help expand the reach and service of Bristol Academy.[8] In 1772, the BES began to raise funds to expand the library of Bristol Academy.[9] These efforts led to Andrew Gifford Jr. and Thomas Llewellyn, a former student of Bristol Academy, to bestow their libraries to the academy in 1784 upon their deaths. James Newton, a former classical tutor of the academy (1770–1790), also bestowed his library upon his death in 1790.[10] The catalogue lists over 3,700 titles available to the students.[11] Whelan observes that the catalogue was not a daily working catalogue for checking out books, but rather it was a permanent list of Bristol Academy's library holdings.[12]

Competing Authors on the Trinity Among the Library Catalogues

Bristol Academy's catalog is noteworthy for including books written by authors who held varying opinions on the Trinity. One example is Thomas Ridgley and John Gill. The catalogue lists "Ridgley's Body of Divinity, folio" and "Gill's Body of Divinity, 4to."[13] Ridgley was hesitant to utilize classical

---

6. By "beginning of Bristol Academy" is both meant when Terrill provided for the academy through his deed of gift and leading up to its formal start with Foskett. Though Caleb Jope appears not to have educated any students at the academy, he had access to these materials.

7. See *Alphabetical Catalogue*. That Ryland served as the compiler of the catalogue, see Whelan, "Glance," 36.

8. For more information on the Bristol Education Society, see Moon et al., *Bristol Education Society*. See also Moon, "Caleb Evans." The aims of the BES were to supply churches with educated ministers, financially assist students at Bristol Academy, involve churches in the selection of suitable candidates for ministry, and support missionaries and itinerant preachers. The BES became the main organization to raise and receive money for these and other purposes.

9. Moon et al., *Bristol Education Society*, 10.

10. Whelan, "1795 Catalogue," 37. Whelan lists Newton's death in 1789. Moon lists Newton's death in 1790. Moon, *Education for Ministry*, 13, 115, 140.

11. "Though numerous catalogues of private libraries exist from the eighteenth century, few if any *actual* college catalogues of this period—ones used by the librarian and students themselves—exist today." Whelan, "1795 Catalogue," 35.

12. Whelan, "1795 Catalogue," 37.

13. *Alphabetical Catalogue*, 36, 18.

expressions of the Son's eternal generation as he thought such expressions confused the truth.[14] Gill argued against Ridgley that without affirmation of the Son's eternal generation there could be no distinction between the Father and the Son.[15] Both of these works will be considered later as both were used as textbooks by the academy.

Another example is Isaac Watts and Abraham Taylor. The catalogue lists "Watts's (Dr. Isaac) Works, 4to" and "Taylor (Abraham) on the Trinity, 8vo."[16] Watts wrote *The Christian Doctrine of the Trinity* in 1722. His reason for writing was due to the "late Controversies of the important doctrine of the Trinity," by which he means the Salters' Hall Debates of 1719.[17] Watts believed that the discussion of the Trinity had necessitated too much assent from Christians in explaining the mystery of the Trinity, specifically the eternal generation of the Son and the eternal spiration of the Holy Spirit.[18] He, therefore, set out to explain in twenty-two propositions what Christians must believe about the Trinity. Watt's conclusion is that a Christian need only affirm that each of the three Persons of the Trinity have sufficient divine power to carry out their office and duties as stated in Scripture.[19] Taylor took offence at Watt's method and conclusion in his *Scripture Doctrine of the Trinity Vindicated*. Taylor accused Watts of employing too much reason in his method of explaining the Trinity in order to appease others in such an "enlightened age."[20] Watts's reliance on reason, according to Taylor, led him to conclude that the Son and the Holy Spirit are merely two divine powers through whom the Father operates, thereby negating the Son and the Holy Spirit as distinct entities within the Trinity.[21] Whether Taylor's assessment of Watts is accurate or not, there was genuine disagreement between the two authors.[22]

---

14. Ridgley, *Body of Divinity*, iii.
15. Gill, *Complete Body*, 210.
16. *Alphabetical Catalogue*, 45, 54.
17. Watts, *Christian Doctrine*, iii. Though Watts was not present at the Salters' Hall Debates, Powicke lists Watts as "Neutral" in the debate. Powicke, "Salters' Hall," 123.
18. Watts, *Christian Doctrine*, vii.
19. Watts, *Christian Doctrine*, 12.
20. Taylor, *Scripture Doctrine*, xviii.
21. Taylor, *Scripture Doctrine*, 33–34.
22. Evans, in his *Scripture Doctrine*, twice recommends Watts's *Christian Doctrine of the Trinity*. See Evans, *Scripture Doctrine*, 16, 26.

An Antitrinitarian Among the Library Catalogues

The catalogue also lists "Clark on the Trinity, 8vo."[23] Clark's first name is not mentioned, making it difficult to ascertain who he is. The author is most likely Samuel Clarke, who denied orthodox trinitarianism, and the book is likely *Scripture-Doctrine of the Trinity*. An argument against this being Samuel Clarke is that the author's name is spelled in the catalogue listing without an "e" at the end. However, there are five other references directly under this listing with the name "Clarke." Two of those five references suggest that "Clark" is Samuel Clarke. One of the two references is "Clarke on the Attributes, 8vo."[24] Samuel Clarke wrote *Demonstration of the Being and Attributes of God* in 1705. The second of the two references, however, indicates more explicitly that "Clark" is Samuel Clarke. The catalogue lists "Clarke's and Leibnitz's Letters 8vo."[25] Leibniz accused Isaac Newton of downgrading natural religion by his affirmation of God's existence. Newton sought the help of Clarke to defend him against such a charge. Clarke then entered into a letter correspondence with Leibniz in which he defended Newton.[26] Therefore, it appears the catalogue misspells Clarke as "Clark."[27]

Three conclusions may be drawn from this survey of some of the books held by Bristol Academy's library. First, the academy did have authors who affirmed orthodox trinitarianism by inclusion of Gill and Calvin. Second, the academy had authors who disagreed with another regarding the explanation of the Trinity but were trinitarian as evidenced by Ridgley and Watts. And third, the academy had an author who denied orthodox trinitarianism as evidenced by Clarke. From this it appears that the academy sought to keep students informed of modern trinitarian discussions and debates.

The Trinitarian Curriculum of Bristol Baptist Academy

The library catalogues provide valuable information about the resources available to students for study and research. However, it's important to note that not all the resources in the library are textbooks used by the students. It is possible to know the authors studied by the students for their Trinity-related

23. *Alphabetical Catalogue*, 66.

24. *Alphabetical Catalogue*, 66.

25. *Alphabetical Catalogue*, 66. The catalogue misspells "Leibniz" as "Leibnitz."

26. Gascoigne, "Clarke, Samuel," para. 20.

27. Evans, in his *Scripture Doctrine*, cites Samuel Clarke twice. Neither citation is affirmative of Clarke's antitrinitarianism. See Evans, *Scripture Doctrine*, 39, 66–67.

readings, as three students recorded their assigned readings for different subjects. From these testimonies, we will explore the three authors used by the academy to gain insights into how the academy taught the Trinity.

Bristol Academy Students' Records of Studies

John Collett Ryland (1723–1792) studied at Bristol Academy from 1744 to 1746 under the instruction of Foskett.[28] During his tenure at the academy, Ryland kept a diary.[29] In the earliest diary, Ryland records the studies he undertook during his first year at Bristol Academy.[30] This account by Ryland of his studies is the earliest known curriculum of the academy. Ryland divides the subjects of study into three categories: Languages, Sciences, and Divinity. Under the category of Divinity, Ryland studied Vincent's *Explicatory Catechism* and Ridgley's *Body of Divinity*.[31] In the next entry, Ryland includes the *Baptist Catechism* and the *Second London Baptist Confession of Faith* (2LCF) as part of his studies.[32] Ryland's divinity studies for his first year were centered around reformed catechisms, aside from the 2LCF. The *Baptist Catechism* is an edited version of the Westminster *Shorter Catechism* to conform it to Baptist faith and practices.[33] Thomas Vincent's *Explicatory Catechism* is an explanation of the shorter catechism, and Thomas Ridgley's *Body of Divinity* is an explanation of the Westminster *Larger Catechism*.

Another student, Thomas Dunscombe (1748–1811), has left a record of his studies at Bristol Academy. Dunscombe studied at Bristol Academy from 1770 to 1773.[34] He submitted a report to the BES of studies he un-

28. Naylor, "John Collett Ryland," in Haykin and Wolever, *British Particular Baptists*, 4:292–93. Ryland's son, John Ryland Jr., would become the fourth principal of Bristol Academy, from 1793 to 1825.

29. The complete diary consists of nine notebooks and is held at the Angus Library, Regent's Park College, Oxford. See Naylor, "John Collett Ryland," 292n4.

30. For this entry, see Ryland, "Student's Programme." For further commentary on Ryland's diary entries, see Wheeler, "Baptist Student."

31. Ryland, "Student's Programme," 249.

32. Ryland, "Student's Programme," 251.

33. The General Assemblies of Particular Baptists held in London in the years 1693 and 1694 requested William Collins, pastor of the Petty France church in London, to draw up a catechism for use by Baptist churches and families. J. Renihan, *Faith and Life*, 134, 136. Whether Collins is the actual author of the catechism or not is unknown as the early extant editions of the catechism never assigned an author on the title page. The "Advertisement to the Reader" of the fifth edition of the catechism states: "And do now put forth a short Account of *Christian Principles*, for the Instruction of our Families, in most things agreeing with the *Shorter Catechism* of the *Assembly*." *Brief Instruction*, unnumbered page.

34. Hayden, *Continuity and Change*, 230.

dertook in his first year, 1770–1771. Among other subjects, Dunscombe reports he had read the first volume of John Gill's *Body of Divinity*.[35] John Sutcliff (1752–1814) confirms the same course of study. He studied at Bristol Academy from 1772 to 1774.[36] Sutcliff reported to the BES of his studies in his final year, 1773–1774. Weekly Sutcliff drew up an abridgement of sections from Gill's *Body of Divinity*.[37]

These three authors—Vincent, Ridgley, and Gill—will now be considered to observe the trinitarian teaching of Bristol Academy.

Thomas Vincent, An Explicatory Catechism

Thomas Vincent (1634–1678) was a Presbyterian minister in London. In 1673, he wrote *An Explicatory Catechism: Or an Explanation of the Assembly's Shorter Catechism*. Among other names in the "Epistle to the Reader," both John Owen and Thomas Watson recommended this work.[38] Vincent dedicates the work to the families of his congregation at the Hand-Alley church in London.[39] His purpose is to explain the *Shorter Catechism* of the Assembly "as plainly and familiarly" as he could so that it is "more intelligible and useful unto such as either learn or read it."[40] The format Vincent uses is that of Question and Answer under each question and answer of the catechism. Only Vincent's explanations of questions 6 and 21 of the *Shorter Catechism* will be considered.

Question 6 of the *Shorter Catechism* asks, "How many Persons are there in the God-head," to which it answers, "There are three Persons in the Godhead; the Father, the Son, and the Holy Ghost; and these Three are One God, the same in Substance, equal in Power and Glory."[41] Vincent begins by affirming the unity and oneness of the God-head. He defines the "Godhead" as the divine nature or essence of God. Thereby, there are not three Gods but one God because the three Persons equally share in the divine nature or essence.[42] The equality of nature of the three Persons is evidenced by each Person being described in Scripture as partaking of divine works

---

35. McLachlan, *English Education*, 94.
36. Hayden, *Continuity and Change*, 246.
37. Haykin, *One Heart*, 54.
38. Vincent, *Explicatory Catechism*, unnumbered page.
39. Vincent, *Explicatory Catechism*, unnumbered page. For Hand-Alley Church, see Wilson, *History and Antiquities*, 1:399.
40. Vincent, *Explicatory Catechism*, unnumbered page.
41. Vincent, *Explicatory Catechism*, 28.
42. Vincent, *Explicatory Catechism*, 28.

and holding the divine name.[43] For Vincent, the equality of essence is what grounds the unity of the godhead.

He then affirms the distinction of the three Persons of the godhead. He defines "Persons" as three ways of subsisting and each having distinct personal properties. Vincent upholds the affirmations of the Constantinople Creed in regard to the personal properties.[44] The Father eternally begets the Son, the Son is eternally begotten by the Father, and the Holy Spirit proceeds from the Father and the Son. These relations are what make the three Persons distinct.[45] Those who deny the three distinct Persons in the godhead are judged by Vincent as being blasphemers and heretics. He gives by way of example Socinians and Quakers who deny this truth.[46]

Question 21 of the catechism asks, "Who is the Redeemer of God's Elect," to which it answers, "The only Redeemer of God's Elect is the Lord Jesus Christ, who being the eternal Son of God, became Man, and so was, and continueth to be God and Man, in two distinct Natures, and One person for ever."[47] From this answer, Vincent goes on to affirm the full deity and humanity of Jesus. He then upholds the Chalcedonian Definition of Christ's two natures in the hypostatic union, "both Natures, divine and humane, remaining distinct, without Composition or Confusion, in one and the Same Person."[48] He affirms that the eternal generation of the Son by the Father is what makes him distinct from any creatures identified as "sons of God" (i.e, angels and men).[49]

Thomas Ridgley, A Body of Divinity

Thomas Ridgley (1667–1734) was an Independent minister of the church Three Cranes, Fruiterers' Alley, Thames Street, in London. He was also a tutor of theology at the Congregational Fund's academy in Tenter Alley, Moorfields.[50] Ridgley attended the Salters' Hall Debates and he sided with the subscribers.[51] In 1731, he published *A Body of Divinity: Wherein the*

---

43. Vincent, *Explicatory Catechism*, 29–30.
44. Vincent, *Explicatory Catechism*, 29.
45. Vincent, *Explicatory Catechism*, 31.
46. Vincent, *Explicatory Catechism*, 31–32.
47. Vincent, *Explicatory Catechism*, 63.
48. Vincent, *Explicatory Catechism*, 66.
49. Vincent, *Explicatory Catechism*, 64–65.
50. Gordon and Ruston, "Ridgley, Thomas," para. 1.
51. Powicke, "Salters' Hall," 113.

Doctrines of the Christian Religion, Are Explained and Defended. This book is based on his lectures on the Assembly's *Larger Catechism*.

In his review of the 1993 reprint of *Body of Divinity*, Richard Muller states that "Ridgley is thoroughly orthodox and quite representative of the forms and arguments of late seventeenth-century Puritan and Reformed teaching of which his theology the direct descendant."[52] Specifically regarding Ridgley's trinitarianism, Muller goes on to say that "Ridgley confesses the full divinity of Father, Son, and Spirit and, indeed, argues pointedly the Reformed doctrine of the aseity of the Son and Spirit."[53] Therefore, it will be assumed that Ridgley was an orthodox trinitarian. What will be shown is how Ridgley differed from some of his contemporaries regarding the language used to describe the Trinity and his understanding of the term "Son" in regard to the second Person of the Trinity.[54] The conclusion is that Ridgley held to a confessional trinitarianism but not to a classical trinitarianism.

Ridgley's address of the Trinity begins with questions 9–11.[55] He acknowledges that the doctrine of the Trinity was a much-contested doctrine in his day. Although Ridgley doesn't explicitly mention how the Trinity was contested, he seems to refer to Arianism and Socinianism. In *Body of Divinity*, he mentions Arianism over eighty times and Socinianism just over fifty times. In contrast, he mentions Sabellianism fewer than ten times.[56]

Ridgley asserts that the doctrine of the Trinity is a matter of "pure revelation" and that it cannot be learned from the "light of nature."[57] This does not place Ridgley squarely among those of the Protestant Principle for he does not discount the use of reason in understanding doctrine.[58] Ridgley is, however, skeptical of philosophical language to articulate the Trinity.[59]

52. Muller, "Review," 608.

53. Muller, "Review," 608.

54. Muller acknowledged this variance of Ridgley. He writes, "There are certain peculiarities, arising from the context of debate with Arians and Socinians, in Ridgley's trinitarian language." Muller, "Review," 608.

55. Ridgley, *Body of Divinity*, 60–61. The questions are: 9. How many persons are there in the Godhead? 10. What are the personal properties of the three Persons of the Godhead? 11. How doth it appear that the Son and the Holy Ghost are God equal with the Father?

56. These calculations are based on the number of times these specific titles appear in the third edition of Ridgley, *Body of Divinity*.

57. Ridgley, *Body of Divinity*, 61, 67.

58. "Thus revelation discovers what doctrines we are to believe, and demands our assent to them, reason offers a convincing proof that we are under an indispensable obligation to give it—it proves the doctrine to be true and such as is worthy of God, as it is derived from him, the fountain of truth and wisdom." Ridgley, *Body of Divinity*, 66.

59. Muller comments that a philosophical explanation of the Trinity was common

He specifically is skeptical of those, especially the church fathers, who revert to Platonic reasoning. Ridgley is suspect of those who have cited Plato in defense of the Trinity for two reasons. First, though some divines utilized Plato in their trinitarian defense, they did so at the cost of a clear teaching of the Trinity. Platonic philosophy only made the doctrine of the Trinity unintelligible to most people.[60] Most importantly, and secondly, the use of Plato had been detrimental to the doctrine of the Trinity. The detriment is that some antitrinitarians suspected the Trinity as nothing more than Platonism and not as scriptural.[61] Not only that, but some antitrinitarians laid claim to church fathers who had used Platonic philosophy as a way to affirm their own antitrinitarianism.[62]

Ridgley not only had concern with a philosophical explanation of the Trinity, he was also concerned about "commonly received sentiments" from the early church in explanation of the Trinity, especially as to the eternal generation of the Son.[63] The concern is that Arians assumed, though wrongly, that such language affirmed their own position that the Son had a beginning.[64] Ridgley advised the expression that the Son was eternally generated "had better be laid aside, lest it should be thought that we conclude the Son not equally necessary, and, from all eternity, co-existent with the Father."[65] Ridgley's advice stems from the fact that eternal sonship can be interpreted in two ways. On the one hand, it can be understood as conveying the Son's eternal coexistence and consubstantiality with the Father. On the other hand, it can be misinterpreted as implying that the Son acquired His divine essence from the Father.[66]

After discussing Scripture that supports the eternal generation of the Son, Ridgley concludes that such verses are better understood as affirming

---

in the late orthodoxy period (1725–1780), but it was not universal. He gives Ridgley and Gill as examples of theologians who were not philosophical. Muller, *Triunity of God*, 138–39.

60. Ridgley, *Body of Divinity*, 67.
61. Ridgley, *Body of Divinity*, 67–68.
62. Ridgley, *Body of Divinity*, 68.
63. Ridgley, *Body of Divinity*, 73. Ridgley states in the preface to *Body of Divinity*, "As to what I have advanced concerning the eternal generation of the Son, and the procession of the Holy Ghost, I have thought myself obliged to recede from some common modes of explication, which have been used, both by ancient and modern writers, in insisting on these mysterious doctrines, which, probably, will appear, if duly weighed, not to have done any great service to the cause, which, with convincing evidence, they have maintained." Ridgley, *Body of Divinity*, iii.
64. Ridgley, *Body of Divinity*, 74.
65. Ridgley, *Body of Divinity*, 74.
66. Ridgley, *Body of Divinity*, 74.

the Son as Mediator.[67] The term "Mediator" for Ridgley effectively resolved all ambiguities surrounding the eternal generation of the Son. "That when we read of the Son of God as dependent on the Father, inferior and obedient to him, and yet as being equal with him, and having the same divine nature, we cannot conceive of any character which answers to all these ideas of sonship, except that of Mediator."[68] As the Mediator, the Son is both truly divine and truly human.[69] Ridgley knew others would be suspect of his questioning, but not denying, the usefulness of eternal generation of the Son.[70] Yet, he was fully persuaded that he affirmed what the church fathers before him had affirmed regarding the Trinity.[71]

Though Ridgley affirmed stating the Trinity in terms of confessional language, as evidenced by Salters' Hall and lecturing on the *Larger Catechism*, he was hesitant of philosophical methods and terms to define the Trinity and of language used by the early church fathers. He sought to explain the Trinity from the revelation of Scripture without dependence upon classical language or philosophical language. This does not place Ridgley among those who adhered to the Protestant Principle. But his reluctance to fully employ the language of the early confessions and his skepticism of philosophical language does alter his explanation of the Trinity, especially in regard to the eternal generation of the Son.

John Gill, A Complete Body of Doctrinal and Practical Divinity

John Gill (1697–1771) pastored the Baptist church Horsleydown in Southwark, London, from 1720 until his death in 1771. He was a popular

---

67. "I cannot but conclude that those I have mentioned, and all others of a similar nature, which are brought to prove the eternal generation or sonship of Christ, respect him as God-man, Mediator." Ridgley, *Body of Divinity*, 76.

68. Ridgley, *Body of Divinity*, 77.

69. Muller comments, "The logic of his argument must be traced to his debate with the Socinians, who assigned sonship entirely to the human Jesus: in response, Ridgley argues that sonship properly indicates divinity and humanity together in the person of the Mediator, while never setting aside the extended usage of 'Son' as rightful title of the second person of the Trinity." Muller, *Triunity of God*, 140.

70. Muller says Ridgley's position "presses on the boundaries of orthodoxy and leans towards Sabellianism, largely because of his desire to avoid the subordinationistic pitfalls of his day." Muller, *Triunity of God*, 332.

71. "Whether my method of explaining these doctrines be reckoned just, or no, I cannot but persuade myself, that what I have said, concerning the subordination of these divine persons, be considered in any other view, than as an explication of the Sonship of Christ, and the procession of the Holy Ghost, it will not be reckoned a deviating from the common faith of those who have defended the doctrine of the ever-blessed Trinity." Ridgley, *Body of Divinity*, iii–iv.

theologian among and for Particular Baptists in England. Though he had no formal education after the age of eleven, Gill was a masterful linguist in the original Scripture languages, especially Hebrew, and a skilled exegete and theologian.[72] He turned his attention to matters of the Trinity three separate times. In 1731, he wrote *Doctrine of the Trinity Stated and Vindicated*. In 1767 he published "A Dissertation Concerning the Eternal Sonship of Christ," then in 1769 came his *magnum opus* of systematic theology, *A Complete Body of Doctrinal and Practical Divinity*.

As early as 1770, Bristol Academy used Gill's *A Complete Body of Divinity* as noted above with Dunscomb's and Sutcliff's references. Haykin surmises that it became the "academy's main textbook in dogmatic theology."[73] That the academy utilized Gill is significant. First, *Complete Body of Divinity* was the first systematic theology used by the academy that was written by a Baptist. From its inception, Bristol Academy sought to be a Baptist academy for Baptist students.[74] Until Gill published his work, there were no written Baptist systematic theology works available. Gill was the first Baptist to do so.[75] Second, *Complete Body of Divinity* was a new work, only published a year before Dunscomb entered the academy in 1770. Gill was not an unknown author to the academy. Caleb Evans recommended Gill's *Doctrine of the Trinity Stated and Vindicated* in his *Scripture Doctrine of the Deity of the Son and Holy Spirit*.[76] Having affirmed Gill's writings from earlier, the academy adopted *Complete Body of Divinity* from its first publication.[77] And, third, Gill was opposed to Ridgley whom the academy had used since as early as 1744 as noted by Ryland. In "A Dissertation Concerning the Eternal Sonship of Christ" Gill says of Ridgley, "The other person, who has objected to the eternal generation of the Son of God, is Dr Thomas Ridgley, Professor of Divinity in London, towards the beginning of the present century: who strongly asserts, and contends for the doctrine of a Trinity of divine distinct persons in the Godhead, and yet strangely adopts the Socinian notion of Sonship by office, and makes the eternal Sonship of Christ to be what he

---

72. Haykin, "Gill, John," para. 1.

73. Haykin, *One Heart*, 54.

74. For a history of Bristol Baptist Academy, see chapter 5.

75. George, "John Gill," in George and Dockery, *Theologians of the Baptist Tradition*, 12.

76. Evans, *Scripture Doctrine*, 41.

77. John Rippon in the *Baptist Annual Register* for the years 1790 to 1793 relays a list of useful books recommended by Caleb Evans in the year 1773. In this list of authors and books, Evans says Gill is a "touchstone of orthodoxy." Rippon, *Baptist Annual Register, 1790–1793*, 254.

calls his mediatorial Sonship."[78] That the academy replaced Ridgley with Gill is no indication that the academy therefore rejected Ridgley. Again, the Baptist academy switched authors from an Independent theologian to an admired Baptist theologian.

After noting Gill's position on the use of confessions and the early church writings, attention will be given to Gill's affirmation of the eternal generation of the Son since that is where Gill and Ridgley disagreed.

Gill on Confessions and the Early Church Writings

Gill was not opposed to the use of confessional language to state doctrine. In the introduction to *Complete Body of Divinity*, Gill writes:

> It is strongly pleaded that articles and confessions of faith, in which men are to agree, should be expressed in the bare words of the sacred Scriptures, and that nothing should be considered as a fundamental article that is matter of controversy: as to the latter, if that was admitted, there would be scarce any article at all left us to believe; for what is there almost that is believed, but what is controverted by some, nor any passage of Scripture brought in support of it, but the sense of it is called in question, or perverted?[79]

This statement demonstrates that Gill was not an advocate of the Protestant Principle. He affirms that doctrine can and ought to be stated in confessional language. By this statement Gill would not have been among the nonsubscribers at Salters' Hall.[80] Gill determines that confessional language was not only permissible but also necessary for "the sentiments of one man in any point of religion cannot be distinguished from those of another, though diametrically opposite; so an Arian cannot be known from an Athanasian."[81] Confessional language to explain scriptural language is what discerns orthodoxy from unorthodoxy.

Gill also appeals to the writings of the early church fathers. In his dissertation on the trinitarian theology of Gill, Steven Godet demonstrates that

---

78. Gill, "Eternal Sonship," in Gill, *Collection*, 2:562–63.

79. Gill, *Complete Body*, 1:vi.

80. Gill was not present at the Salters' Hall Debates. Contra the nonsubscribers, Gill wrote, "Words and phrases, though not literally expressed in Scripture, yet if what is meant by them is to be found there, they may be lawfully made use of; as some respecting the doctrine of the Trinity." Gill, *Complete Body*, 1:ix.

81. Gill, *Complete Body*, 1:viii.

Gill was a Patristic scholar.[82] He finds that Gill, in *Complete Body of Divinity*, cited twenty-two Patristic authors.[83] For a work that originally extended to three volumes, twenty-two Patristic references are relatively few. However, in "A Dissertation on the Eternal Sonship of Christ," which is only thirty pages in length, Gill references the Patristics nearly as much as in *Complete Body of Divinity*.[84]

Regarding trinitarian matters, Gill appeals many times to the church fathers in reference to the eternal generation of the Son. In "A Dissertation on the Eternal Sonship of Christ" Gill demonstrates, by tracing church history from the first century up to the Reformation of the sixteenth century, that the church has always held to the eternal generation of the Son in opposition to those who have opposed it. Gill notes the position of creeds and confessions of faith in the times of the early church that "all agreed in inserting the clause respecting their faith in Christ, the only begotten Son, as *begotten of the Father before all ages*, or the *world was*."[85]

Gill on the Trinity and the Eternal Generation of the Son

Book 1 of *A Complete Body of Divinity* concerns theology proper. Chapters 26 and 28 will only be considered as these relate to the unity of God and the personal relations in the Deity. Gill sets out in chapter 26 to prove the unity of God; that is, that there is but one God. After a logical defense of monotheism, Gill warns of three false ways to understand God's unity when considering the Trinity. The first is Arianism, which only affirms the Father as the supreme God and the Son and Spirit as inferior gods. The second erroneous view is that of Sabellianism among whom Gill places Socinians and Unitarians.[86] These deny the three Persons within the godhead and only affirm God as a singular person. Third is Tritheism that affirms three Persons in the godhead and concludes that there are three gods. Gill counters each false way with a common truth. The common truth is that God as a Trinity is one because there is "one divine essence, undivided, and common to Father, Son, and Spirit . . . since there is but one essence, though there are different modes of subsisting in it which are called persons."[87] Contra the Arians, each person of the Trinity possesses the divine nature so the Son

---

82. See chapter 4 in Godet, "Trinitarian Theology."
83. Gill, *Complete Body*, 134.
84. Godet, "Trinitarian Theology," 134.
85. Gill, "Eternal Sonship," in Gill, *Collection*, 2:556.
86. Gill, *Complete Body*, 1:187.
87. Gill, *Complete Body*, 1:187.

and the Spirit are consubstantial with the Father. Contra the Sabellians, the divine nature unites three Persons without merging them. And contra the Tritheists, the divine nature can be possessed by the three persons without being divided itself.

In chapter 28, Gill addresses the relative properties that distinguish the three divine persons in the godhead. Concerning the Son, Gill argues that the eternal generation of the Son is the only proper understanding to distinguish the second person of the Trinity. He is the only one of whom in the Scriptures it is said is the Son, begotten by the Father. The Son's "distinctive relative property and character is, that he is begotten, which is never said of the other two Persons, and so distinguishes him from them."[88] And so to deny eternal generation would in effect lead to the Socinian error of Sabellianism; that is, the Son is only God in name but not in nature. Also, the denial of the eternal generation of the Son leads to the Arian error of denying the Son's full divine nature. Gill stresses not just that the Son is generated but that He is *eternally* generated. The emphasis on eternally signifies that since the Son is God, He possesses the attribute of eternality. Gill concludes, "There being nothing in the divine nature but what is eternal, then this generation must be eternal."[89]

Gill confronts Ridgley at this point. Since Ridgley objected to eternal generation, Gill accuses him of either affirming Arianism as "without his eternal generation no proof can be made of his being a distinct divine Person *in the Godhead,* and so not of his Deity,"[90] or Ridgley is guilty of Sabellianism as "no other in the divine nature can be substituted in its [eternal generation] room; not the office of Christ, as Mediator; for he must first be proved to be a distinct divine Person, before he can be considered as Mediator."[91] Gill had cause to critique and question Ridgley's apprehension to the phrase "eternal generation of the Son." Ridgley had already acknowledged that some would object to his position, but whether Gill rightly understood Ridgley or unjustly accused Ridgley is another matter. As evidenced earlier, Ridgley affirmed that God is one in three distinct persons who are co-equal in nature and co-eternal in existence.[92]

---

88. Gill, *Complete Body*, 1:209.

89. Gill, *Complete Body*, 1:211. Gill posits that the Father "may be considered in priority of order previous the Son generated by him, though not in priority of time, of which there can be none in eternity." Gill, *Complete Body*, 211.

90. Gill, *Complete Body*, 1:210.

91. Gill, *Complete Body*, 1:210.

92. The purpose of this section is not to compare and contrast Gill and Ridgley; the purpose is to demonstrate that Bristol Academy used two authors who agreed on the Trinity but had disagreements with how to express the relations within the Trinity.

Complete Body of Divinity provided Bristol Academy with Baptist theology by a trusted Baptist theologian. Gill's explanation and defense of the Trinity and trinitarian issues were already known by those at the academy. If the academy was concerned with Ridgley's objection to classical language concerning eternal sonship, then in Gill they found one who not only affirmed the use of confessions but also language of classical confessions.

By examining Vincent, Ridgley, and Gill, it is evident that Bristol Academy educated the students with orthodox and confessional trinitarian writings by trusted authors. Prior to Gill, the academy was not hesitant to use Presbyterian or Independent authors as they and the academy agreed in scriptural teaching of the Trinity. Gill provided the Baptist academy with an orthodox Baptist author.

The Trinitarianism of Caleb Evans

The previous sections have highlighted certain works used by the tutors and students at the academy. Attention now will be given to the tutors of the academy, specifically one, Caleb Evans (1737–1791). Evans served at Bristol Academy for a total of thirty-three years, from 1758 to 1791, first as a tutor (1758–1781) and then as principal (1781–1791).[93] During his tenure as tutor and principal, he helped train 105 students, which is 55 percent of the academy's student body from 1720 to 1791.[94] Having published over thirty works and sermons, Evans published more works than the previous two principals, Bernard Foskett and Hugh Evans.[95] For these reasons, Evans will be used to demonstrate the trinitarian teaching of Bristol Academy by one of its own faculty members. Three of his works will be considered: *The Scripture Doctrine of the Deity of the Son and Holy Spirit* (1766), his Confession of Faith before Broadmead Baptist Church (1767), and *An Address to the Serious and Candid Professors of Christianity* (1773).

---

93. For a biography of Caleb Evan, see Wellum and Salley, "Caleb Evans," in Haykin and Wolever, *British Particular Baptists*, 5:115–51; Hayden, *Continuity and Change*, 121–31; "Evans, Caleb." Along with his service during these year, Evans was the assistant pastor (1758–1781) and then pastor (1781–1791) at Broadmead.

94. Hayden, *Continuity and Change*, 135–36. The total number of students from 1720 to 1791 was 189 (see list of students from 1720 to 1791 in Hayden, *Continuity and Change*, 222–49). Foskett, the first principal, trained 73 students. Because Hugh Evans's tenure overlapped with both Foskett and his son, Caleb, he trained 128 students.

95. Wellum and Salley, "Caleb Evans," in Haykin and Wolever, *British Particular Baptists*, 5:123. If Hugh Evans, Caleb's father, is referenced, he will be cited by H. Evans.

The Scripture Doctrine of the Deity of the Son and Holy Spirit

In 1766, Evans published two sermons he delivered to Broadmead in the previous year.[96] The occasion for publishing these sermons was the recent release of a second edition of George Williams's *An Attempt to Restore the Supreme Worship of God the Father Almighty* in 1765. The first edition of this work was published only a year before in 1764. What incited Evans is that the second edition hit too close to his home, Bristol. The second edition was published by a local Bristol publisher, T. Cadell. Also, Edward Harwood, who had recently moved to Bristol in 1765 to be the minister at the Presbyterian chapel on Tucker Street, wrote the preface to the second edition of *An Attempt*.

Harwood authored *An Account of the Conversion of a Deist* in 1762. In *An Account*, Harwood tells the journey of an anonymous person who once held to orthodox Christian teaching, then became a deist, and later settled on being a rationalist Christian. The moral of the story, according to Harwood, is that Christian ministers and parents ought not to teach "the absurd and irrational Opinions of Systematic Divines, which have really no Foundation at all in Christianity," but should rather "with Minds free from Partiality, and open to Conviction, examine the *Truth, as it is in Jesus*, and not in human Creeds."[97] Among the irrational doctrines and creeds, Harwood includes the Trinity as defended by Athanasius, "which is a real Insult to all common Sense and Reason, and subverts the very first Principle of all natural and revealed Religion—I mean, the Unity of God."[98] Harwood's thesis is that most people who reject Christianity do not reject true Christianity but an irrational Christianity defended by creeds and confessions. Therefore, Christians ought to remove all such stumbling blocks, like the Trinity in Unity, that prevent reasonable people from accepting true Christianity. For Harwood, an Arian understanding of the Trinity is what is most reasonable and unobstructive to the Christian faith.

Evans's preface and the first sermon, on the deity of Christ, will only be considered.[99] Evans prefaces the two sermons with a thirty-two-page

---

96. The two sermons are "On the Deity of Christ. This Is the True God" from 1 John 5:20, delivered at Broadmead on March 24, 1765, and "Thou Hast Not Lied unto Men, but unto God" from Acts 5:4, delivered at Broadmead on April 21, 1765. See Evans, *Scripture Doctrine*, 1–46, 47–80.

97. Harwood, *Account*, 49.

98. Harwood, *Account*, 61.

99. The reason is that this book has not been considering writings and positions on the deity of the Holy Spirit, but only on the deity of Christ as it relates to trinitarian matters.

refutation of Harwood's preface to *An Attempt*.[100] Three convictions of Evans concerning the Trinity will be taken from the preface. The first is Evans's conviction of the importance of trinitarian doctrine. In the opening paragraph, Evans writes, "And I could now no longer, with a good conscience, venture to remain silent. What I plead for appears to me *important truth*: whilst I cannot therefore but regret the prevalence of what is opposite to it, I am bound to do all I can in my narrow sphere, to prevent its further progress."[101] Evans observed the widespread dissemination of Harwood's opinions and convictions throughout the church during his era. For him, the doctrine of the Trinity was of such importance to the Christian faith that to remain silent would almost make him culpable in the decline of orthodox trinitarianism.

Evans's second conviction is that classical trinitarianism is not based on confessions but on Scripture. Throughout the preface, Evans refers to Harwood's claim that Christians must give up the "athanasian impiety" in order to convert Jews, Muslims, and Deists.[102] But Evans could no more give up classical trinitarianism, or Athanasianism, to appeal to Jews than he could give up the atoning sacrifice of Christ, which is also a stumbling block for them.[103] Evans argues that Christian truth is not to be based on popular opinions or rational acceptance; rather, it is the Scripture from which Christians derive truth. While confessions and creeds are useful, for Evans, "if the *athanasian* impiety as it is styl'd, be not a scripture doctrine, let it be rejected; but if it be, the aversion of the *Jews* or of all the world, can be no reason why it should be cancell'd."[104]

The third conviction of Evans is that Christians must in their own conscience hold to the trinitarian doctrine. Evans cites Harwood as arguing that the dissenters rebelled against the Church of England because of immoral and unscriptural practices, and since "Athanasian" dissenters have committed similar acts, the people should rebel against them.[105] Evans corrects Harwood by affirming that the dissenters removed themselves from the Church of England based on religious liberty. By religious liberty, Evans

---

100. Evans's preface is a summarization of the arguments for the deity of Christ and the Spirit as found in the two sermons. Evans, *Scripture Doctrine*, iii–xxxv.

101. Evans, *Scripture Doctrine*, iii–iv.

102. Because of Harwood's appeal to rationalism, he understood classical trinitarianism, like that of Athanasius, as not affirming three Persons in one God but asserting three Gods. Evans, *Scripture Doctrine*, vii.

103. Evans, *Scripture Doctrine*, xi.

104. Evans, *Scripture Doctrine*, x–xi.

105. Evans, *Scripture Doctrine*, xxvi–xxvii.

was not addressing such liberty as politically but ecclesiastically.[106] The church has no power to command the obedience of Christians' consciences to articles of faith; rather, "it is the duty of every one to think, judge and act for himself, according to the dictates of his own conscience."[107] By this, Evans is not stating that everyone's understanding of the Trinity is valid or true; he is rather affirming the authority of Scripture over Christians and their responsibility to submit to it.

Turning to the sermon on the deity of Christ, Evans informs his readers of his purposes for the sermon.[108] One purpose is to reclaim those who have left the truth of Christ's deity. The other purpose is to preserve those in the faith who affirm Christ's deity. To do this, Evans divides his sermon into two parts, preliminary observations and scriptural proof of Christ's deity. Under the preliminary observations, two topics of Evans will be considered—the unity of God and the humanity of Christ.

Evans devotes most of his attention to the second of four preliminary observations, "that the doctrine of Christ's true and proper Deity, is by no means set in opposition to the unity of God."[109] Here, Evans counters the argument that those who uphold the deity of Christ do so at the cost of losing the unity of God. In fact, he asserts that the unity of God is a main pillar upon which "we build the doctrine now pleaded for, of the true and proper Deity of the Lord Jesus Christ."[110] The reason is that the unity of God is a first-principal doctrine of the Christian faith. The Scriptures clearly declare there is but one God; therefore, no other doctrine can contradict this truth and be true itself.[111] The three Persons of the godhead are not divided in the divine nature, but they are united by the divine nature, "these three are one as to their divine nature and essence."[112] Upon this principle, Evans then affirms classical trinitarianism by asserting the unity of God.

From the unity of God Evans turns to the divinity of the Son. Evans demonstrates from Scripture that the Son possesses the divine nature as that of the Father. He contends "all those passages concerning the unity of

---

106. For Evans's position on religious liberty within a nation, see Evans, *British Constitutional Liberty*.

107. Evans, *Scripture Doctrine*, xxvii.

108. Evans, *Scripture Doctrine*, 5.

109. Evans, *Scripture Doctrine*, 7.

110. Evans, *Scripture Doctrine*, 12.

111. Evans argues that it is the Arians who violate and contradict the unity of God by insisting that there is a superior God and an inferior God. Evans, *Scripture Doctrine*, 14.

112. Evans, *Scripture Doctrine*, 8.

God . . . support it [the divinity of Christ] in the strongest manner."[113] Such passages include Jesus being attributed with divine names, divine attributes, divine works, and divine worship.[114] Evans concludes that if the deity of the Father is proved "by those names titles attributes works, &c," then "surely they cannot but be *equal proofs* of *his* [the Son's] *Deity* also."[115]

Returning to the preface to the sermons, Evans appeals to the full deity of the Son by the designation "*only-begotten* Son *of GOD*."[116] This phrase is as close as Evans gets to using the designation "eternal Son of God," but by "only-begotten Son" Evans intends the same: "It is suggested to us he is fully of the same nature with his Divine Father. And if necessary eternal existence be essential to the divine nature, this must belong to the Son as well as the Father."[117]

The third preliminary observation of the sermon addresses Christ's humanity. Evans clearly states that "the doctrine of Christ's true and proper Deity, does by no means interfere with his true and proper humanity, or with his inferiority to the Father as man and mediator."[118] Under this observation, Evans counters the Arian argument that in Scripture the Son in His humanity is inferior to the Father; therefore, the Son in His deity is inferior to the Father. Evans agrees that the Son in His humanity was inferior to the Father, "We do not deny the *superiority* of the Father to the Son as man and mediator, because the Father was never incarnate nor sustain'd the office of mediator in the oeconomy of man's redemption."[119] Yet, the inferiority of the Son to the Father was only in His humanity because "we maintain there is also a sense in which they *are one*, and consequently *equal* in power and glory."[120] By this, Evans infers that the roles assumed by the Father and Son, and the relationships had between them as Father and Son, in no way makes one inferior to the other. The reason is that the deity of the Father and the Son is not based on function but upon essence. They each have different functions, but they possess the same essence.

---

113. Evans, *Scripture Doctrine*, 21–22.
114. Evans, *Scripture Doctrine*, 22–27.
115. Evans, *Scripture Doctrine*, 27.
116. Evans, *Scripture Doctrine*, xix.
117. Evans, *Scripture Doctrine*, xix.
118. Evans, *Scripture Doctrine*, 16.
119. Evans, *Scripture Doctrine*, 18. Though Evans is not addressing the issue of Sabellianism, he clearly denied a modalistic understanding of the Trinity for he denies that the Father was the one incarnate.
120. Evans, *Scripture Doctrine*, 18.

So, how are the passages to be interpreted that speak of the Son as inferior to the Father? Evans appeals to partitive exegesis,[121] "For it is most clear and evident, that not only all the passages which are brought by the writer [Harwood] before mentioned, in proof of the inferiority of Christ to the Father, but every such passage that is to be met with, refers to Christ *as man and mediator*; in which respect and capacity his *inferiority* is by himself and all his followers *acknowledged*."[122] The incarnation of the Son of God was a true act of humility by which he assumed human flesh and a human nature that are inferior to the divine nature. Therefore, those passages that speak of the Son, or where the Son speaks of Himself, as inferior must only refer to Him in His human nature.

The Scripture Doctrine of the Deity of the Son and Holy Spirit demonstrates Evans's commitment to orthodox trinitarianism. Evans was not hesitant to affirm confessions of the Trinity, but he maintained that the Trinity and the deity of the Son is firmly grounded in Scripture. He showed how those who use Scripture to make the Son both in His deity and humanity inferior to the Father are not interpreting Scripture rightly. Evans sided with the early church's use of partitive exegesis to rightly understand the Son in His humanity and His divinity.

A Confession of Faith before Broadmead Church

Upon his ordination at Broadmead on August 18, 1767, Evans wrote a confession of faith so that the members of his church would know his understanding of certain doctrines.[123] The confession consists of nine main doctrines with subtopics under each.[124] Only the second of the doctrines, which is on God, will be considered.

---

121. By partitive exegesis is meant the method of interpretation employed by the pro-Nicenes in the fourth century to counter the Arians' explanation of Christ's mutability and, therefore, inferiority to God the Father. Partitive exegesis presumes that the incarnation was "the intermingling of the immutable, divine nature proper to the eternal *Logos* with a mutable and passible human nature." With this presumption, the reader of Scripture "must distinguish the lofty expressions that are attributable to Christ's divinity from the lowly descriptions that must be ascribed to Christ's humanity." See Smith, "Trinity," 117.

122. Evans, *Scripture Doctrine*, 16–17.

123. Evans's ordination address and his understanding of confessions are discussed in chapter 5.

124. The number of main doctrines considered in the confession are that of this author. The confession is not numbered according to doctrine nor is it headed with titles of doctrines.

Regarding the Trinity, Evans simply states that, "*In the unity of the Godhead there are three divine persons, the Father, the Son, and the Holy Ghost, into whose name therefore we are commanded to be baptized, and who are all spoken of as possessing divine attributes, and partaking of divine honors, and consequently must be one in nature and essence, however inferior in office in the oeconomy of redemption, or there cannot be but one God.*"[125] What Evans states in his confession is a distillation of the sermon he preached over two years earlier on the deity of Christ. He affirms the true distinction of the three Persons who fulfill different offices, and though the offices may be ranked from superior to inferior, each person of the godhead is equal in essence, and therefore one in nature. Interestingly, Evans does not say more about the Trinity in his confession since he knew of the spread of antitrinitarian views.

An Address to the Serious and Candid Professors of Christianity

In 1772, Evans again responded publicly to a published work that attacked historic orthodox Christian doctrine. The pamphlet was *An Appeal to the Serious and Candid Professors of Christianity* by Joseph Priestley, the provocative Unitarian.[126] The pamphlet is brief, only twenty-four pages in length, and covers six topics: of reason, the ability of man, original sin, election, the divinity of Christ, and the atonement. Priestley presents a view for each of these doctrines that is in opposition to the majority understanding within the church. He says of those who embrace his teaching that "you will be called Arminians and Socinians by your adversaries"; and those who are deemed such should "think yourselves happy, as being reproached for the name of Christ."[127]

Following suit, Evans published his response with a similar title, *An Address to the Serious and Candid Professors of Christianity*, and he also published it anonymously.[128] Evans was compelled to respond to Priestley for several reasons. Of utmost concern to him was the possibility that many people might actually be misled by Priestley. Evans perceived his era as

---

125. Evans et al., *Charge and Sermon*, 21.

126. The work was published under the pseudonym "A Lover of the Gospel." For attribution to Priestley as the author, see Schofield, "Priestley, Joseph," para. 21.

127. Priestley, *Appeal*, 23.

128. That Evans is the author of *Address*, see Cross, *Useful Learning*, 89–90; Wellum and Salley, "Caleb Evans," in Haykin and Wolever, *British Particular Baptists*, 5:137. The decisive factor to attribute authorship to Evans is that Samuel Stennett, a close friend of Evans, attributes the work to Evans when he delivers the sermon at Evans's funeral. See Stennett, *Mortality of Ministers*, 28.

a "superficial age" characterized by the "readiness of the multitude to be swayed and carried about by every passing doctrine, influenced by the whims of men."[129] He also considered the topics appealed to by Priestley as some of the most important topics to the Christian faith. Evans writes, "The manifest design of the Appeal which hath been circulated amongst you with such uncommon assiduity, is to overturn the very *foundations* of your faith and hope. It is not levelled merely against some of the less important and more *disputable* points of Christianity, but at those *capital, essential* truths, which have hitherto been esteemed the *distinguishing peculiarities* of the gospel."[130] Among the topics that are distinguishing of the gospel is included the doctrine of the divinity of Christ, which directly relates to the Trinity. And, last, Evans sought to defend the historic orthodox doctrines of Christianity as given throughout church history. Evans warned that Priestley sought "to excite you to reject with *abhorrence* that faith for which your pious ancestors earnestly contended."[131] Evans defended the historic orthodox teachings of the church and advocated for its validity and truthfulness. Of the six topics, only the deity of Christ will be considered.

The divinity of Christ is the fifth of six doctrines covered in *An Address*. Evans begins by recounting three historic Christological heresies: that Christ only possessed a divine nature, that Christ only possessed a human nature, and that Christ possessed a composite divine-human nature.[132] Priestley certainly did not advocate for the first heresy that may be styled Docetism because he denied that Christ was God.[133] And though he heavily leaned toward the second heresy of Ebionism, because he did favor the term "mere man" to describe Christ, Priestley probably would have rejected it as he believed Christ did have some divine communication from the Father.[134] Priestley may have affirmed a form of Adoptionism, but he did believe that Christ was born by supernatural generation and not by natural generation.[135]

---

129. Evans, *Address*, 5, 6. Evans summarizes what Priestley tries to draw Christians both away from and toward: "The intention of it, is to persuade you, that you are *not*, in consequence of the original apostasy, become *guilty* and, in yourselves, *helpless sinners*. That Jesus Christ is *not* the person you have hitherto supposed him to be, but a *mere man* like yourselves. That you are *not* to be saved by *his merits*, but merely by your own *repentance and reformation*." Evans, *Address*, 6.

130. Evans, *Address*, 6.

131. Evans, *Address*, 5.

132. Evans, *Address*, 37.

133. Priestley, *Appeal*, 14.

134. Priestley, *Appeal*, 14, 16.

135. Priestley, *Appeal*, 16.

The third heresy given by Evans appears to be Apollinarianism. Whether Priestley argued for the third heresy is uncertain as he never argued in *An Appeal* for a composite nature of Christ. However, Evans later refers to it as Arianism, but then later he uses the term Socinian and Unitarian to describe this third heresy.[136] For Evans, there is a common thread amongst these three heresies. They do not attribute "to Christ neither *Deity* nor *humanity*, but makes him a strange *mysterious compound of both*, and at the same time does not admit him to be, properly speaking, possessed of either."[137] Evans concluded that these three schemes conjoined the divine and human natures of Christ into one nature since they attempted to affirm to some degree that Christ was human and divine. Priestley was once an Arian, then a Socinian, and finally a Unitarian.[138] Evans might be converging on the vast ground of these three schemes because Priestley had traveled through all three.

Evans puts most of his attention on the refutation of the second and third heresies as these are the ones most closely aligned with Priestley, though possibly not perfectly aligned with him. To refute the second heresy, that Christ only possessed a human nature, Evans places attention on the incarnation. His argument is that the incarnation is only an act of humiliation if Christ existed in an exalted state prior to the incarnation. Evans acknowledges that Christ was a man because He did possess a human nature at conception and birth. However, Evans does not accept the term "mere man" to describe Christ's humanity as that means "he had no existence till born of the virgin."[139] Central to his argument is that it is the preexistence of Christ that makes the incarnation a defense of Christ's divinity. Evans turns his attention to Philippians 2:5–11. From this passage Evans says, "Now these expressions seem naturally to intimate, that the form of a servant was a form that did not originally belong to him, but a form which he *voluntarily assumed*."[140] Those who insist Christ was no more than a mere man cannot affirm that Christ "took the form of servant." Evans asks, "If he [Christ] was

---

136. Evans, *Address*, 42, 47, 53. Evans is wrong to insinuate that any of these schemes of Christology affirmed an Apollinarian position. And though the three schemes do share some commonalities, Evans is wrong to speak of these three schemes as synonymous as they are distinct from one another.

137. Evans, *Address*, 42.

138. For a description of Priestley's theological journey from Arianism to Unitarianism, see Wiles, *Archetypal Heresy*, 47–58.

139. Evans, *Address*, 38. In defense of Christ's preexistence, Evans cites John 1:1–3; 8:58.

140. Evans, *Address*, 39. By "form of a servant" is meant the inferiority of man to God.

no more than a *mere man*, what form *but* that of a servant could belong to him; or with what propriety could he be represented as *taking* this form upon him, and his doing so be mentioned as an instance of his *humility*?"[141] Evans point is that the incarnation is only an act of humiliation if Christ existed in the form of God prior to the incarnation.[142]

To refute the third heresy, that Christ possessed a composite divine-human nature, Evans affirms Chalcedonian Christology. He begins by affirming the full divinity of Christ. Under the refutation of the second heresy, Evans had argued that Christ had to be preexistent for the incarnation to be an act of humility. Now, he argues that Christ was not just preexistent, as an Arian would also assert, but that Christ is the eternal Son of God. The crucial turning point for Evans in the debate about the divinity of Christ was "who became man?"[143] He answers the question, "The scriptures are indeed very full and express in assuring us, that he who *took human nature into union* with that *original nature* he possessed before, was the *eternal Son of God, the Son of the Father in truth, the only-begotten Son of God*, not the *person* of the Father, but fully of the *same nature and essence*."[144] The answer provides two fundamental points for Evans.

The first point is that Christ is the eternal Son of God by His very nature. He has argued this already in *Scripture Doctrine*. However, he adds a phrase to express what is not meant by "Son of God." The phrase is "not the person of the Father." Evans makes an observation from Scripture. The Son is not referred to as "the Son of the Father" but as "the Son of God." If he were "the Son of the Father," then the Son would receive His divine nature from the Father. And if the Son had received His divine nature from the Father, then the Son would be eternally dependent upon and subordinate to the Father, which was a prominent teaching of Socinians and Unitarians.[145]

---

141. Evans, *Address*, 39.

142. Evans, *Address*, 39. "If he was no more than a *mere man like ourselves*, and had no *existence* till born of the virgin, how could he be *in the form of God antecedently* to his taking upon him the form of a servant? which yet he is expressly said to have been." Evans, *Address*, 39.

143. Evans, *Address*, 43.

144. Evans, *Address*, 44. Of the extant writings of Evans, this may be the first time in print that he used the phrase "eternal Son of God." As noted earlier, Evans used the phrase "only begotten Son of God" and not "eternal Son of God" in his 1765 sermon on the deity of the Son. But now in 1773 Evans uses the phrase "eternal Son of God." This is not a change in doctrine for Evans as he has always affirmed the eternality of the Son; it does appear, however, to be a change in terminology.

145. Priestley states, "The apostles, notwithstanding their attachment to their Lord and Master, always preserve the idea of his subordination to the Father, and consider all his honour and power as derived from him." Priestley, *Appeal*, 13.

Rather than receiving His divine nature from the Father, Evans positively affirms that Christ is "the *literal* Son of the divine nature" because He is the "Son of God."[146] Evans's point is that the Son's divinity is not derived but is innate, Himself being very God.

Evans's assertation that Christ is the "literal Son of the divine nature" could lead the reader to make two conclusions that Evans does not intend. The first is that the reader might conclude the Son is a separate God from the Father and thereby undo God's unity. But that is not Evans's intent. The unity of God is maintained by the Father and the Son both being coequal in essence.[147] He makes this argument in *Scripture Doctrine*. The second wrong conclusion would be that Evans denies the eternal generation of the Son by the Father. However, in the answer above Evans states that the Son is eternally "the Son of the Father in truth." Evans affirms that the Father and the Son are truly and eternally related as Father and Son because the Son is the only begotten of the Father. Thereby, Evans upholds the eternal relative properties of the Father and the Son.[148]

Having argued for the full divine nature of the Son prior to his incarnation, Evans turns his attention to how the two natures, divine and human, dwell in the one person, Christ. Evans addressed the issue of Christ's inferiority to the Father in His humanity in *Scripture Doctrine*. He brings it up in *An Address* because Socinians attempted to prove the inferiority of the Son by appealing to Jesus' own statements of inferiority to the Father.[149]

To counter the Socinian argument, Evans appeals to the hypostatic union. In the one person of Christ there were the two natures of divinity and humanity. The statements by Christ must be understood in the light of this reality. Evans says, "But to imagine that what is said of him *in the form of a servant*, implies that *no other form belongs* to him, is to overturn from the very foundation the whole of that *amazing love* which the scriptures constantly represent as being strikingly exhibited in the *incarnation and obedience* of the Son of God."[150] Christ in His humanity is inferior to the Father, but He remains equal with the Father because He still possesses

---

146. Evans, *Address*, 45. Evans is quoting in the affirmative an unnamed author.

147. Evans, *Address*, 50. "Yet in the most essential respect, even as to their *nature* or *essence*, they are one." Evans, *Address*, 50.

148. Evans, *Address*, 50. "They are distinct in *person* and relative character." Evans, *Address*, 50.

149. Priestley had argued that Jesus acknowledged the superiority of the Father to Himself in John 10:29, which overrode Jesus' statement that He and the Father are one in John 10:30, "But how could the Father be greater than all, if there was any other, who was so much one with him, as to be, in all respects, equal to him." Priestley, *Appeal*, 14.

150. Evans, *Address*, 47.

the divine nature in His person. And this distinction must be maintained because the two natures in Christ are joined in Him "without confounding the two distinct natures."[151] By this phrase, Evans is alluding back to the Chalcedonian Definition.[152] He is upholding the historic doctrine that Christ was one person with two natures. For Evans, the appeal to the two natures in the one person of Christ is scripturally warranted, "by having recourse to the distinction of the two natures in the person of Christ, 'tis a distinction the scripture authorizes, and there are many passages which cannot be consistently explained without it."[153] Evans maintains that partitive exegesis is to be a hermeneutical tool that the reader must use to rightly understand Scripture.

Evans had a great influence upon the students of the academy because of his tenure at the academy. Though the class notes Evans may have used during his time of teaching are no longer extant, he has left behind writings that give insight into how he would have instructed the students in the doctrine of the Trinity and Christology. From the consideration of three of his writings, it is known that Evans upheld an orthodox trinitarianism. The doctrine of the Trinity was of such importance to Evans that he was compelled to write against modern authors who attempted to lead others away from a classical trinitarianism and into Arianism or Socinianism.

Conclusion

Bristol Academy, from its inception to the end of the eighteenth century, affirmed and taught orthodox trinitarianism. The library demonstrates that the academy made trinitarian books available to the students. The curriculum of the academy was designed around authors who affirmed orthodox trinitarianism. Caleb Evans, the third principal of the academy, publicly defended orthodox trinitarianism against those who denied it.

---

151. Evans, *Address*, 48.

152. "We also teach that we apprehend this one and only Christ-Son, Lord, only-begotten-in two natures; and we do this *without confusing the two natures*, without transmuting one nature into the other, without dividing them into two separate categories, without contrasting them according to area or function." Leith, *Creeds of the Churches*, 36 (emphasis added).

153. Evans, *Address*, 47.

7

"You Will Save Both Yourself and Your Hearers"

The Trinitarianism of Bristol Baptist Academy Alumni

THE OPENING OF THE constitution of the Bristol Education Society (BES) states the purpose of the society, "To the end that dissenting congregations, especially of the Baptist denomination . . . be more effectually supplied with a succession of *able and evangelical ministers*."[1] Although written in 1770, this encapsulated Bristol Academy's founding purpose. Bristol Academy sought to strengthen local Particular Baptist churches with ministers who had been taught by the academy. Thereby, the trinitarian teaching of Bristol Academy would reach and influence local Baptist churches through the students of the academy who would pastor these churches. However, not all alumni of Bristol Academy held to the trinitarian doctrine they had received. This chapter will explore two alumni who affirmed Bristol Academy's trinitarianism as evidenced by their writings. Next will be considered an alumnus and tutor of the academy who was suspected of antitrinitarianism. And, last, the chapter will explore an alumnus who later rejected the academy's trinitarianism.

---

1. Swaine, *Faithful Men*, 72 (emphasis added). Swaine's citation of the BES constitution is the only known earliest source for the document. The citation spans pp. 72–74. He dates the constitution as June 7, 1770. Hugh and Caleb Evans are the likely authors of the constitution.

Alumni Who Affirmed Orthodox Trinitarianism

Two alumni of Bristol Academy will be considered to demonstrate how local Particular Baptist churches received orthodox trinitarianism. The students are Benjamin Beddome and John Reynolds.

Benjamin Beddome

Benjamin Beddome (1717–1795) studied at Bristol Academy for two years (1736–1737) under Bernard Foskett and Hugh Evans.[2] He finished his training at the Independent academy Tenter Alley, Moorfields, in London, led by John Eames.[3] The Bourton-on-the-Water church in Gloucestershire called Beddome in 1740 (ordained in 1743) where he served until his death in 1795.[4] Beddome nurtured his church in orthodox trinitarianism as evidenced by a sermon he preached, hymns he composed, and a catechism he wrote.

Beddome's Trinitarianism in a Sermon

One of Beddome's sermons will be considered, "The Mutual Glory of Christ and His People" taken from John 17:22, "And the glory which thou hast given me have I given unto them."[5] Only the first point of the sermon will be observed, which addresses the nature of Christ's glory.[6] Beddome articulates three glories related to Christ—his essential glory, his mediatorial glory, and his remunerative glory.

The essential glory of Christ relates to the glory he has "as the second Person of the ever-blessed and adorable Trinity."[7] Interestingly, Beddome does not refer to Scripture that speaks of the deity of the Son prior to the incarnation. Rather, the focus is on the "glory of deity shown through the veil of humanity" ensuing at the incarnation.[8] Beddome's purpose for directing attention on the incarnate Christ is to demonstrate that the words and works of Christ show him to be the God-Man. Beddome says, "God and man, finite and infinite, temporal and eternal, met in conjunction, that the

2. Hayden, *Continuity and Change*, 224.
3. Montgomery, "Benjamin Beddome, 102.
4. Montgomery, "Benjamin Beddome," 121.
5. Beddome, *Sermons*, 81–88. The sermon is undated but listed as Sermon XIII in the published collection of sermons.
6. Beddome, *Sermons*, 82–85.
7. Beddome, *Sermons*, 82.
8. Beddome, *Sermons*, 83.

human nature of Christ might be *the theatre for the divine nature to show its perfections in*."[9] Socinians used the life of Christ to deny His deity, while Beddome uses Christ's life to affirm His deity.

It might appear that Beddome would fall trapped before the Socinians for using a text where Christ states that his glory was given him from the Father, as well as a glory he may give to others. Beddome makes clear, however, that such is not the case, "But this glory cannot be intended in my text; for it was neither derived by Christ from another, nor could it be communicated by him to others; it was alike essential and peculiar to himself."[10] Beddome here is affirming that Christ's glory is not a derived glory, even from the Father. Christ as the second person of the Trinity possesses the eternal glory of God ontologically.[11]

The glory given to Christ by the Father is the second glory, mediatorial glory. By this, Beddome refers to Christ's miraculous works, efficacious teachings, and sonship that resulted as one anointed with the Spirit of God. Beddome says, "But the glory spoken of in my text was the glory which the Father had given him,—the glory of working miracles,—which he imparted to his immediate followers; the glory of preaching the gospel, and thereby converting sinners to himself, which he bestows on his faithful ministers; and the glory of sonship, of which all the saints are made partakers."[12] Two observations are made from this quotation. First, the glory received from the Father by the Son is in reference to Christ's human nature. Beddome's previous attention on the deity of Christ as the essential glory of Christ has affirmed that Christ possessed fully the divine nature because he is God. So, the glory received is not a derived glory but an imparted glory because Christ is also man. The imparted glory is the work of miracles Christ performed as a man anointed with the Holy Spirit. Therefore, second, this is a glory that Christ may impart to men by the Spirit. Beddome says, "The Spirit of God and of glory rests upon them, as it did upon him. They partake of the same anointing, though not in the same measure."[13] As Christ was anointed with the Holy Spirit, so disciples of Christ are given the Holy Spirit. Thereby, the disciples may demonstrate the glory of God through their lives as they seek to follow Christ.

9. Beddome, *Sermons*, 83 (emphasis added). Beddome is quoting an unnamed author.

10. Beddome, *Sermons*, 83.

11. In another sermon, "Christ Manifested to the Soul," Beddome unequivocally states in affirmation of Christ's divinity, "Now this Son, this *coessential, coeternal*, Son of God was revealed in the Apostle Paul." Beddome, *Sermons*, 119–20 (emphasis added).

12. Beddome, *Sermons*, 83.

13. Beddome, *Sermons*, 84.

The third glory spoken of by Beddome is Christ's remunerative glory. Whereas Beddome has focused on Christ's incarnation, he now switches to Christ's exaltation. This is the glory Christ received as reward by the Father for his suffering and death. "All power and authority is given to him; all other power and authority subjected to him."[14] By this, Beddome is not referring to Christ returning to the glory he had prior to his incarnation. This is another state of glory God the Father gives to Christ due primarily to his humanity. That is, Christ, now the God-Man, is exalted to a place of authority over all creation; it is a state of glory to which his disciples will share with him for "in this all the members of his mystical body shall be conformed to their glorious Head."[15]

Beddome's sermon, "The Mutual Glory of Christ and His People," demonstrates his trinitarianism via his Christology. Beddome acknowledges that Christ was the second person of the Trinity who possessed an underived divine glory. At his incarnation, Christ did not diminish his deity, but evidenced it through his works and teachings; and because the Son became incarnate, taking human nature to himself, he was then able to receive glory from the Father as Man and to be exalted to authority as the God-Man.

Beddome's Trinitarianism in Hymns

Beddome grew up in the tradition of singing hymns at church. His father, John, led his church at Alcester in Warwickshire to include hymn singing in the church service, which he continued when he moved to the Pithay church in Bristol.[16] Beddome continued the practice of his father. Hymns serve as a valuable tool for the congregation to learn theology. And so, Beddome composed hymns to complement the teachings of his sermons.[17]

While some of Beddome's hymns had been included in other collections during his life, Beddome had not intended to publish them.[18] After his death, 830 of his compositions were collected and published in 1818. The topical arrangement of the hymns is that of the editor of the collection.[19]

---

14. Beddome, *Sermons*, 84.

15. Beddome, *Sermons*, 84.

16. Connell, "Such Wondrous Grace Demands a Song," in Haykin et al., *Glory to the Three Eternal*, 119.

17. The editor of the collection of Beddome's hymns says, "During a long-continued and highly useful ministry, he was in the habit of preparing a few verses suited to the subject of his pulpit discourses, and which were sung in his own congregation, more or less frequently, at the close of the public service." Beddome, *Hymns*, ix.

18. Beddome, *Hymns*, ix.

19. Beddome, *Hymns*, viii.

The collection of Beddome's hymns lists five hymns associated with the doctrine of the Trinity.[20]

Hymn #255 conveys the unique work of each of the three Persons of the godhead while also affirming the divine will of the one God. The hymn begins with three stanza's that each focus on the common work in salvation by the Father, the Son, and the Holy Spirit. These stanzas affirm the three Persons of the Triune God. The Father saves sinners by grace, the Son saves sinners by giving himself as a sacrifice, and the Holy Spirit saves sinners by humbling them and renewing them. Yet, Beddome would not let the hymn conclude with doubt regarding the oneness of God. The fourth stanza concludes, "Glory to the Three eternal, Yet the great mysterious One, Author of all bliss supernal, Be unceasing honors done." This stanza affirms the coeternality of each of the three Persons. Also, it affirms that the three Persons are the one God. And, interestingly, Beddome, having articulated the salvific work of each of the three Persons, states that the one God is the author of salvation. By this, Beddome demonstrates that the three Persons have their unique work, but they share the divine will.

Hymn #256 is praise to the one God. This hymn consists of three stanzas. Stanzas two and three address God in the singular. However, Beddome began the hymn with, "To God the Father, and the Son, And God the Spirit too, The One in three, and Three in one, Ascribe the honours due." Beddome makes clear that the one God he praises is a Triune God consisting of the three persons—Father, Son, and Holy Spirit.

Hymn #257, three stanzas in length, is a call to praise the Father, the Son, and the Spirit for their work in salvation. The first line of the hymn and the final line of the hymn stand in poetical parallelism. The first line of the hymn opens with "To Father, Son, and Holy Ghost." The final line of the hymn closes with "And bless and praise the triune God." Beddome artfully opens with the diversity of Persons in the godhead and closes with the unity of the Persons in the godhead.

Hymn #599 ascribes equal praise to the three Persons because each share coequally the divine nature. The first three stanzas of the hymn are similar to hymn #255 in that each stanza focuses on one of the three Persons in the work of salvation. The fourth and final stanza states, "Give to each the highest praise, Lofty hallelujahs raise; One in nature, persons three, Bless the sacred Trinity." Beddome affirms that the Son and Spirit are owed equal praise as to the Father because each of the Three share the same divine nature.

---

20. The five hymns associated with the doctrine of the Trinity include hymns #255, #256, #257, #599, and #823. Pages are not numbered in the collection.

The final trinitarian hymn, #823, is listed among doxologies in the collection. This hymn is composed of three stanzas, one stanza each devoted to one of the three Persons of the godhead. The common refrain is that each of the Persons is owed glory. The second stanza focuses on the Son. The first half of the stanza states, "Glory to his co-equal Son, In feeble flesh arrayed." Beddome affirms the full equality of the Son with the Father in the divine nature even in His incarnation. The second half of the stanza states, "That he might all our sins atone, He suffered in our stead." The second half concludes that the Son had to be fully divine, coequal with the Father, in order to atone for sin.

These five hymns of Beddome's demonstrate his classical trinitarianism. He affirmed that the godhead consisted of three coessential and coeternal Persons who shared the common will of God.

Beddome's Trinitarianism in a Catechism

After being persuaded by many of his friends, in February 1752 Beddome published a catechism.[21] Beddome states that he followed the lead of Matthew Henry's catechism in the formation of his own.[22] Henry, in 1702, had expounded on the Westminster *Shorter Catechism* by adding additional questions and answers under each of the catechism's questions and answers.[23] Beddome followed the same format as Henry but he used the catechism produced by the Particular Baptists.[24]

Beddome's catechism was republished in 1776, evidencing its popularity among Baptists. The 1776 circular letter of the Western Association advertised that at the "repeated requests" of Baptist churches, a new edition of Beddome's catechism, which had been out of print for several years, had been reprinted that year at the expense of the author.[25] Haykin says the second edition of Beddome's catechism was "widely used" by Bristol Academy though he does not cite evidence of it.[26]

---

21. Beddome, *Scriptural Exposition*, A2.
22. Beddome, *Scriptural Exposition*, A2.
23. Henry and Tong, *Works*, 82. For the catechism, see pp. 672–720.
24. Beddome also utilized some of the same additional questions and answers as that of Henry. Haykin, "Glory to the Three Eternal," in Haykin et al., *Glory to the Three Eternal*, 43.
25. Gibbs, *Elders and Messengers*, 7.
26. Haykin, "Glory to the Three Eternal," in Haykin et al., *Glory to the Three Eternal*, 43. The *Alphabetical Catalogue of All the Books in the Library: Belonging to the Bristol Education Society* (1795) does not include Beddome's catechism. Though not listed in the catalogue, it is possible Bristol Academy had and used Beddome's catechism. The

Beddome's treatment of Questions 8 and 9 will be considered. Question 8 of the *Baptist Catechism* asks, "Are there more Gods than one?" The answer given is, "There is but one only, the living and *true God.*" The theme of this question is the unity, or oneness, of God. Beddome follows Question 8 with four additional paragraphs that each contain multiple questions and answers totaling seventeen in all.[27] The first paragraph of questions affirms and expounds the answer that God is the *living God.*[28] Beddome's emphasis is that God is the only being who has life in himself. Here, Beddome is making a distinction between Creator and creation. Since God is the only one who has life in himself, all else is dependent and, therefore, subordinate to him. The second paragraph affirms and expounds the answer that God is the true God.[29] Since God is the only true God, Beddome emphasizes that anyone or anything else that is deemed God is nothing more than an idol, a false god.

In the third paragraph, Beddome affirms and expounds the answer that God is *one only.*[30] Of the five questions in this paragraph, three of them underscore the fact that the Scriptures teach there is but only one God. The fifth question, however, shifts towards Christology. The question asks, "But do not those who assert the deity of Christ destroy the unity of the godhead?" The answer is, "No. For he [Christ] says, *I and my Father are one,* John x.30." By this answer, Beddome affirms that Christ, the Son of God, is coessential with the Father in deity. Therefore, the Son is not a creature dependent upon the Father nor is the Son to be considered as a false god.

In paragraph four, Beddome expounds beyond the answer to Question 8.[31] Here, he stresses the impiety of worshiping false gods. An affirmative answer is given to the first of the five questions, which asks, "Are there many Gods in name?" Then, the second of the questions is answered in the negative, which asks, "But are these gods by nature?" That this paragraph and these questions follow immediately after Beddome's question about

---

current library of Bristol Baptist Academy, now College, lists among its Special Collections both the first and second editions of Beddome's catechism. Whether these editions were held by the Academy in the eighteenth century is not known by this author. This is not intended to cast doubt on Haykin's claim, just that this author was not able to confirm his claim.

27. The first paragraph contains four questions, the second paragraph contains three questions, the third paragraph contains five questions, and the fourth paragraph contains five questions.

28. Beddome, *Scriptural Exposition*, 23.

29. Beddome, *Scriptural Exposition*, 23.

30. Beddome, *Scriptural Exposition*, 23.

31. Beddome, *Scriptural Exposition*, 23.

Christology is telling. Again, the paragraph is not addressing a given statement from the answer to Question 8, as did the previous three paragraphs. So, Beddome intends to convey something more to his readers. Beddome seems to be critiquing those who would say the Son of God is divine but not coessential with the Father, not of the same nature. If the Son is not of the same nature as the Father, then the Son is nothing more than a false god, which Christians are prohibited to worship.

Question 9 of the *Baptist Catechism* asks, "How many persons are there in the godhead?" The answer given is, "There are three Persons in the godhead, the Father, the Son, and the Holy Ghost, and these three are one God, the same in essence, equal in power and glory." The theme of this question is the plurality of persons within the godhead. Following his format, Beddome expands upon the answer in five paragraphs totaling thirty additional questions.[32] The first paragraph asserts the distinction of persons within the godhead.[33] The opening two questions affirm a plurality of three Persons in the godhead. Questions three, four, and five answer in the affirmative whether the Father, Son, and Holy Spirit are distinct from one another. Then it is affirmed in question six that these three Persons are the same in essence, affection, and operation. The paragraph closes with the denial that the three Persons of the godhead imply that there are three Gods.

The second paragraph affirms the codivinity of the Son and the Spirit with the Father.[34] Beddome demonstrates this by implication of the names used in reference to the Son and the Spirit. Questions one, two, three, and four affirmingly answer whether the Son and the Spirit are both referred to as God and Jehovah in the Scriptures.[35] The final question then indicates that the Son and the Spirit are both coequally divine since these names, especially Jehovah, are used in reference to none other than the one true God.

Paragraph three asserts the coequality of the three Persons by means of common divine attributes and activity stated of each.[36] Questions one and two affirm the coeternality of the three Persons. The attribute of omnipresence is the focus of questions three and four; and omniscience is the

---

32. Paragraph one contains seven questions, paragraph two contains five questions, paragraph three contains nine questions, paragraph four contains five questions, and paragraph five contains four questions.

33. Beddome, *Scriptural Exposition*, 23–24.

34. Beddome, *Scriptural Exposition*, 24.

35. Beddome, *Scriptural Exposition*, 5–12. Beddome indicates that the name Jehovah is the name Lord, or Yhwh, as used in Jeremiah 23:6 for the Son and Exodus 17:7, to which he cross references Isaiah 63:10, for the Spirit. Beddome, *Scriptural Exposition*, 24.

36. Beddome, *Scriptural Exposition*, 24–25.

focus of questions five and six. The common activity by each in creation finishes out the paragraph in questions seven, eight, and nine.

Paragraph four demonstrates that the three Persons are equally worthy of worship.[37] The acts of worship highlighted by Beddome are prayer and baptism. Questions one, two, and three affirm that each of the Persons are prayed to by man. Question four affirms that disciples are baptized in the name of the Father, Son, and Holy Spirit. Such acts of worship are only the prerogatives of God, question five.

The final paragraph serves as final implications for the saints in reference to the unity of the distinct Persons in the godhead.[38] Question one shows that saints receive distinct blessings from each Person—grace of the Son, love of the Father, and communion of the Holy Spirit. The saints are saved by the distinct work of each Person in salvation, question two. And as the three Persons are united in the godhead, so, as question three maintains, saints are to be united. Beddome then closes the paragraph with the assertion that saints are to hold fast to this sound doctrine of the Triune God.

The *Baptist Catechism* already upheld the Triunity of God. Beddome's additional questions and answers served both to affirm and to expand upon the answers to Questions 8 and 9. Thereby readers of Beddome's catechism were further instructed and grounded in classical and confessional trinitarianism.

John Reynolds

Compared to Beddome, John Reynolds (1731–1792) is the least known as Beddome had certain notoriety in his own day and to the present day. Reynolds's lack of notoriety provides a good example of how an "average" alumni of Bristol Academy proclaimed the Trinity.

Reynolds was converted and called to ministry under Benjamin Beddome at Bourton-on-the-Water.[39] Reynolds matriculated at Bristol Academy in 1748 during Foskett's principalship.[40] In 1766, John Brine, prior to his death, requested Reynolds to succeed him as pastor at Cripplegate, London, which Reynolds accepted and served at until his death.[41] Rip-

37. Beddome, *Scriptural Exposition*, 25.
38. Beddome, *Scriptural Exposition*, 25.
39. Rippon, *Baptist Annual Register, 1794–1797*, 41.
40. Reynolds more than likely remained at Bristol Academy until 1750. Rippon states that Reynolds entered the academy at age eighteen and then two years later, at age twenty, he was preaching mainly at Bromsgrove, Bratton, Cirencester, and Cheltenham. Rippon, *Baptist Register, 1794–1797*, 41.
41. Rippon, *Baptist Register, 1794–1797*, 41.

pon says of Reynolds's ministry and preaching, "Nothing very remarkable attended Mr. Reynolds's labours among his people. His sermons were orthodox and methodical."[42]

Of the decades of sermons Reynolds delivered, only one sermon survives to the present time. This sermon was not delivered at Cripplegate, but was one he preached at Broadmead in 1782 before the BES on August 28.[43] His text that day was Ephesians 3:8, "The Unsearchable Riches of Christ." The sermon has three points relating to the riches of Christ. Only the first point will be considered in which Reynolds addresses the glories and perfections of Christ's person.[44]

In the sermon, Reynolds affirms the Trinity through Christology. He takes this route because he recognized that the opposition to orthodox trinitarianism stems from denying orthodox Christology.[45] He does not name the opponents, but it appears he is referencing Socinianism. Many of his arguments are directed toward those who confess Jesus as a mere man who attained to deity.

Reynolds concludes that the opponents came to this conclusion because they were confused by "not distinguishing between what is said in Scripture of Christ as a divine person; what is said of him as man; and what is affirmed of him as God-man, the great Mediator."[46] By this statement, Reynolds appeals to partitive exegesis. Some Scriptures speak of Christ as God, as man, and as the God-man; however, Christ is always to be understood as a single person with two natures. Regarding Christ as a divine person, "he was rich in the infinite glories and perfections."[47] Regarding Christ as a man, he was not "divested of his perfections" but they were only veiled by the human nature, which he assumed at the incarnation.[48] Regarding Christ as the God-man and mediator, he has ascended to the right hand of the Father and bestowed with "dignity and glory as are not conferred on any mere creature whatsoever."[49] From these affirmations, Reynolds upholds the deity of Christ from eternity past, continuing into his incarnation, and remaining so at his exaltation.

42. Rippon, *Baptist Register, 1794–1797*, 42.

43. Though the sermon was not preached at Cripplegate, it still serves as an example of how Reynolds would have upheld orthodox trinitarianism at his church.

44. Reynolds, *Unsearchable Riches*, 6–8.

45. "The doctrine of Christ's proper deity is opposed by many in our day, and treated with contempt." Reynolds, *Unsearchable Riches*, 6.

46. Reynolds, *Unsearchable Riches*, 8.

47. Reynolds, *Unsearchable Riches*, 8.

48. Reynolds, *Unsearchable Riches*, 8.

49. Reynolds, *Unsearchable Riches*, 8.

Reynolds's main argument is that Christ is "truly and properly God."[50] By this declaration he does not intend to affirm that there is a plurality of Gods for "the notion of a plurality of Gods is *contrary to reason and revelation*."[51] This is an interesting phrase for Reynolds to use because Socinians denied orthodox trinitarianism based on the appeal to reason, but Reynolds would not separate reason and revelation. If Scripture revealed the deity of Christ, then through one's use of reason the deity of Christ would be affirmed. He goes on to state logical consequences of revelational truth concerning the deity of Christ. One logical consequence is in regard to the worship of Christ. Reynolds states, without citation but by example of the angels, that Christ is upheld as the object of worship in Scripture. However, if Christ is not God, then, reasons Reynolds, the Bible affirms idolatry.[52] He then gives the logical consequence of salvation in regard to Christ. If Christ is not God, then, warns Reynolds, men are trusting in a mere man for salvation, which is no salvation.[53]

Beddome provided a thorough grounding of the Trinity to the Bourton-on-the-Water church. The Bourton church heard the coessence of the Son with the Father in his sermons, the church praised the one God in Three by songs Beddome composed, and the church held fast to the Trinity through the catechism Beddome wrote. The sermon, "The Unsearchable Riches of Christ," clearly illustrates that the church at Cripplegate during Reynolds's tenure would have upheld and maintained orthodox trinitarianism. Reynolds achieved this by employing a classical approach to exegesis and employing logical reasoning to affirm the divinity of Christ as presented in Scripture.

Robert Hall Jr. and Accusation of Trinitarian Downgrade at Bristol Academy

Some authors have insinuated that during the years of Hugh and Caleb Evans, Socinianism began to enter the teaching of the academy. Jerom Murch in 1835 was an early promoter of this allegation. He says, "But there had been noticed in the Principality, several years before, *a spirit of inquiry* amongst some of the leading teachers in the Calvinistic Baptist connexion, which led many to doubt the truth of some popular opinions."[54] And then

---

50. Reynolds, *Unsearchable Riches*, 6.
51. Reynolds, *Unsearchable Riches*, 6 (emphasis added).
52. Reynolds, *Unsearchable Riches*, 7.
53. Reynolds, *Unsearchable Riches*, 7.

54. Murch, *History*, 80–81 (emphasis added). The "Principality" are Hugh and Caleb Evans.

later he says, "Although educated in a Calvinistic academy, Mr. Freeman partook of *the spirit of inquiry* which prevailed among the students, and, before he left, became a decided Unitarian."[55] W. T. Whitley, speaking of a Bristol Academy alumnus, said, "William Richards is a fair specimen of what Bristol had become under Hugh Evans, when Welshmen flocked in, and the miasma of Socinianism tainted not the Established Church alone."[56] Even as late as 2009, some have questioned the trinitarian orthodoxy of Bristol Academy in the late eighteenth century. John H. Y. Briggs states, "What the General Baptists experienced at the beginning of the eighteenth century was mirrored among the Particular Baptists at the end of the century especially amongst those with Bristol connexions."[57] Neither Murch, Whitley, nor Briggs provide evidence for their claims of a trinitarian downgrade at Bristol Academy other than students who later rejected orthodox trinitarianism.

There's one instance that could potentially lead to accusations of a trinitarian downgrade. Robert Hall Jr. (1764–1831) attended Bristol Academy as a student from 1778 to 1780.[58] He then returned to Bristol in 1785, at the age of twenty-one, to serve as both Broadmead's associate pastor to Caleb Evans and as a tutor of classical studies at Bristol Academy.[59] Hall served in these roles until his resignation in late 1790.

Hall's tenure at the church and the academy were met with suspicion in the later years of his service. According to the Broadmead historians, C. Sidney Hall and Harry Mowvley, some members of Broadmead "were apprehensive that he [Hall] would lapse into Unitarianism, or worse into Socinianism."[60] The cause for concern stemmed from Hall's theological speculation and enthusiasm as a young man. The Bristol Academy historians, Ruth Gouldbourne and Anthony R. Cross, state that Hall was committed to "the practical expression of Christian love and acceptance," which led him to speak "warmly of those who were not orthodoxly trinitarian."[61]

---

55. Murch, *History*, 321 (emphasis added). The "Calvinistic academy" is Bristol Academy.

56. Mann, "Calendar of Letters," 184.

57. Briggs, "Changing Pattern," in Briggs, *Pulpit and People*, 5. The comparison between the General Baptists and the Particular Baptists is that of Christological heresy.

58. Hayden, *Continuity and Change*, 235.

59. Hayden, *Continuity and Change*, 139. Hall would later serve as Broadmead's pastor from 1826 to 1831.

60. Hall and Mowvley, *Tradition and Challenge*, 35.

61. Gouldbourne and Cross, *Story of Bristol*, 34. Chadwick says that Hall's "love of speculative conversation, his open admiration for Joseph Priestley, his 'advanced' views on some theological points, and a tendency to make rash remarks fuelled their [Broadmead members'] suspicions." Chadwick, "Hall, Robert," para. 2.

Also, Hall did not affirm the "distinct personality of the Holy Spirit."[62] Hall spoke of the Holy Spirit as an influence or power of God, which is a Socinian belief.[63]

Hall, being an eloquent and persuasive speaker, had great influence upon the students of the academy, especially since they were close in age to him.[64] Roger Hayden reports that both Andrew Fuller and John Ryland Jr. expressed their concerns to Hall regarding his trinitarian theology.[65] These concerns, along with a personal dispute between he and Evans, led to his resignation.

Though Hall legitimately gave others concern about his trinitarian theology, it is questionable whether he held to Socinian or Unitarian views. Soon after his resignation, Hall wrote a letter, at the request of some Broadmead members, in which he affirmed the deity of Christ.[66] Gouldbourne and Cross state that after 1799, Hall "was explicitly trinitarian, and he even spoke of becoming 'more settled' in his views."[67] This comment seems to suggest that Hall was not a firm orthodox trinitarian in his earlier years. Walker agrees with Gouldbourne and Cross that Hall became a convinced trinitarian by 1800.[68]

From this survey of Hall's time at Broadmead and Bristol Academy it can be concluded that he provided an opening for a discussion of a more liberal trinitarianism at the academy among the students, though he most likely did not hold to such views himself. This could be the "spirit of inquiry" of which Murch spoke. At best, this speculation was merely a tolerance of other trinitarian perspectives to be discussed within an academic setting. Though some students after leaving Bristol Academy became Socinian or Unitarian, it is no indication that Bristol Academy was affirming of such positions.[69] As has been shown from the writings of Foskett and Caleb Evans,

62. Walker, *Theology of Robert Hall Jr.*, 17.

63. Stephen Nye in his history of Socinians demonstrated that the Socinian doctrine of the Holy Spirit as being "only the Power or Inspiration of God" thereby denying the Spirit's divinity and personality. Nye, *Brief History*, 17. Contra Nye, Biddle denied the Holy Spirit to be God but did affirm the Spirit's personality and referred to him as only a "Ministering Spirit." Biddle, *Confession of Faith*, 49.

64. Moon, *Education for Ministry*, 25.

65. Hayden, *Continuity and Change*, 139–40.

66. Hall and Mowvley, *Tradition and Challenge*, 36.

67. Gouldbourne and Cross, *Story of Bristol*, 35.

68. Walker, *Theology of Rober Hall Jr.*, 17.

69. Manley and Ballard come to the same conclusion when addressing Whitley's accusation of a trinitarian downgrade at Bristol Academy. "Others [students of Bristol Academy] later became Socinians, but in no case is there evidence of a link with the Academy's teaching. Certainly both Hugh and Caleb were tolerant. But after carefully

along with the reading materials used by the academy, Bristol Academy was firmly orthodox in its trinitarianism.

Job David, An Alumnus Who Denied Orthodox Trinitarianism

Not all the alumni of Bristol Academy held to the trinitarianism of which they were taught during their tenure at the academy. At least seven Bristol Academy alumni during the tenures of Hugh and Caleb Evans either rejected, or are alleged to have rejected, orthodox trinitarianism.[70] One of these seven will be considered, Job David.

Job David (1746–1813) was admitted to Bristol Academy in 1768.[71] His time at the academy precedes the tenure of Hall. His father was a Baptist pastor at Pen-y-sai, near Bridgend where David ministered for a short time after Bristol Academy. He then was called to the church in Frome, in Somersetshire, where he was ordained on October 7, 1773, and remained for thirty years.[72] Afterwards, David pastored at a church in Taunton before retiring due to his health.[73]

When and how David came to hold antitrinitarian views is not known. But by David's death in 1813 he had written "five small publications on controversial subjects."[74] Whether David began to hold some form of antitrini-

---

examining all the publications of both the Evans, and reading memoirs of several Bristol men, the inescapable conclusion has been that both men were strictly orthodox in their Christology, and believers in a moderate Calvinism." Manley and Ballard, "Making of an Evangelical Baptist Leader," 266.

70. The seven are Robert Aspland (1798), who founded a Unitarian Academy in Hackney (Gouldbourne and Cross, *Story of Bristol*, 34); Job David (1768), who pastored a Unitarian church in Taunton (Hayden, *Continuity and Change*, 228); John Evans (1784), the grandson of Caleb Evans, denied distinct personhood of the Holy Spirit (Briggs, "Changing Pattern," in Briggs, *Pulpit and People*, 5 [however, both Moon and Hayden say Evans became a General Baptist (Moon, *Education for Ministry*, 117; Hayden, *Continuity and Change*, 233)]); Stephen Freeman (1783), who became Unitarian (Murch, *History*, 348); Daniel Jones, who became Unitarian (1788) (Murch, *History*, 80–81); William Richards (1775), who became Socinian (Mann, "Calendar of Letters," 184); and Anthony Robinson (1784), who became Unitarian (Song, "When They Know Only," 85). The years in parenthesis are when the students were admitted to the academy.

71. Hayden, *Continuity and Change*, 228. Murch records that David was admitted in 1766. Murch, *History*, 207.

72. Murch, *History*, 207.

73. Murch, *History*, 207–8.

74. Murch, *History*, 207–8. Two of these writings were his letters to the churches of the Western Association, and another is an address he gave before the Society of Unitarian Christians in 1803.

tarian views while at Bristol Academy is not known, but it is doubtful. It is doubtful because Caleb Evans delivered the sermon at David's ordination at the church in Frome.[75] Evans, by this date, had already shown himself to be an orthodox trinitarian, so it is unlikely that he would participate in an ordination of one suspected of antitrinitarian views. In neither the charge given by Daniel Turner nor the sermon delivered by Evans at the ordination does trinitarian doctrine occur as something to which David should return or affirm.

The church in Frome which David pastored was a member of the Western Association. As has been seen in earlier chapters, the Western Association did have churches that either refused to affirm confessional trinitarianism or may have denied orthodox trinitarianism.[76] Whether the church in Frome did either of these is not known. The church in Taunton, however, was a decidedly Unitarian church. David replaced the Unitarian pastor Joshua Toulmin at the Mary Street General Baptist Chapel in Taunton.[77]

David's Orthodoxy in 1780

In 1780, David participated with Toulmin in the ordination of Samuel Evans at the Wedmore church in Somersetshire. David's charge to Evans is his earliest known writing. In the charge, David exhorts Evans to avoid two extremes found in the dissenting churches. Of the first extreme, David says, "Such on the one hand as would degrade Christ in the economy of redemption, depreciate the merit of his life and the efficacy of his sufferings, trample under foot the blood of the covenant, and do despite to the spirit of grace; that would represent the Deity as an idle spectator of the concerns of mortals, either incapable or unwilling to succor them, unless impelled by necessity."[78] The last half of David's description of those whom to avoid sounds like David is warning against Deism. Deists viewed God as distant from creation. However, the first half of his description sounds like David is warning against Socinianism. Socinians degraded Christ in His redemption as being only illustrative and not efficacious. Of the second extreme, David says, "And on the other all those misrepresentations of the gospel which feed the principles of malevolence in the breast; which promote spiritual pride; circumscribe the compassion and love of God; release the

---

75. Turner and Evans, *Charge and Sermon*.
76. See chapters 4 and 5.
77. J. Evans, *Memoirs*, 247; Ditchfield, "Toulmin, Joshua," para. 2.
78. David et al., *Duty of the Christian Minister*, 10.

obligations of holiness, and render useless the preaching of repentance."[79] This description of those whom Evans is to avoid sounds like Calvinism, or hyper-Calvinism.[80]

David later charges Evans to think for himself when it comes to the doctrines of the Bible.[81] In this section of the charge, David upholds the Protestant Principle. He warns Evans to not be like "the minister that will strenuously contend for unscriptural phrases as making an essential part of his devotion, because the ignorance or impiety of men have sanctified the use of them."[82]

Though it may be disconcerting that David would participate with a Unitarian in an ordination service, David shows himself to be a minister who seeks not to be led astray by doctrinal extremes or factions, Socinianism or hyper-Calvinism. However, while one may hold to the Protestant Principle and remain doctrinally sound as evidenced by many nonsubscribers at Salters' Hall, it is a door that can lead to Socinian views as evidenced by some General Baptists in the late seventeenth century.

David's Unorthodoxy in 1788

The next available writing of David is eight years later. In 1788, David wrote a letter to admonish the Calvinistic Baptist churches of the Western Association.[83] His opening and main charge against the Western Association churches is as follows, "Yet these Baptists themselves, use a form of human invention that is full as destitute of any countenance in the Bible as infant baptism, in which they ascribe all honour and glory to three distinct persons in the Deity; each of these persons, according to their plan of devotion, having supreme, distinct honours ascribed to him!"[84] David's comparison to infant baptism is that Baptists reject paedobaptism as being not explicitly found in the Scriptures but something that Paedobaptists conclude by inference. David brings the same charge against trinitarian Baptists, that the

---

79. David et al., *Duty of the Christian Minister*, 10.

80. By hyper-Calvinism is meant those who did not see the need to call men to repentance as that was a work of the Holy Spirit.

81. David et al., *Duty of the Christian Minister*, 11.

82. David et al., *Duty of the Christian Minister*, 10.

83. David does not identify himself as the author of the letter. The letter simply says "By One of Their Brethren." Caleb Evans, however, identifies David as the author when he wrote the response on behalf of the Western Association. See Evans, *Remarks on a Letter*, A2.

84. David, *Letter Addressed*, 6.

Trinity is not explicitly found in the Scriptures and is only an inference that ought to be rejected.

David began his letter with a definition of the "Rational Christian." A rational Christian is one whose "general rule of interpreting Scripture is to explain distinct propositions of ambiguous interpretation by the general and plain sense of the word of God."[85] While this is a valid form of interpretation, interpreting Scripture with Scripture, for David he could not reconcile the texts that affirm God as one along with texts that seemingly affirm the deity of the Son and the Holy Spirit. David asks the question regarding the Trinity whether it teaches "the people the knowledge and worship of the *one true God*, by one Mediator; or doth it teach them the worship of three Gods?"[86] As for confessional trinitarianism that would explain texts that affirm one God and the deity of the three persons, David rejects them because those who use confessions "leave the light of Christ, and prefer human inventions to the plain truth, of scripture!"[87]

By 1788, it is evident that David had come to deny orthodox trinitarianism.[88] David's reliance on the Protestant Principle appears to have led him to this conclusion. His refusal of confessional trinitarianism as unscriptural left him without a means to reconcile texts of Scripture that appeared to him a contradiction.

Conclusion

Four alumni of Bristol Academy have been considered—Benjamin Beddome, John Reynolds, Robert Hall Jr., and Job David. Though separated by a few decades as alumni attending the academy, all received orthodox trinitarian teaching. Two alumni, Beddome and Reynolds, upheld orthodox trinitarianism in their ministries. Consequently, both of their churches were rooted in the trinitarian teachings they had acquired at Bristol Academy.

85. David, *Letter Addressed*, 6.
86. David, *Letter Addressed*, 9–10.
87. David, *Letter Addressed*, 14.

88. In 1803, David delivered an address to the Society of Unitarian Christians in which he argues Jesus was a man approved of God. His stress is the humanity of Jesus and the denial of His deity. Of orthodox trinitarianism, he says, "The idea of the second person in the Trinity being united to, and incorporated with the man Jesus, so as to make only one person, is a sentiment so novel and so unlike all that God had before revealed to men, as to destroy all our other ideas of objects we had been in the habit of considering as necessarily distinct, that one might be tempted to think it must stagger even the strongest faith." And then he later asserts, "To obviate this difficulty by calling it a great mystery, is to confess it is not a revealed truth, consequently not an article of Christian faith." David, *Wisdom and Benevolence*, 13–14, 15.

Hall's teachings at the academy raised some questions about his doctrine of the Trinity. While his trinitarian views may not have perfectly aligned with the academy's during his tenure as a faculty member, he later fully embraced orthodox trinitarianism. Job David exemplifies the rare individuals who renounced orthodox trinitarianism upon leaving the academy. David's subsequent denial of the Trinity was not a consequence of his education at Bristol Academy. Instead, the combination of the Protestant Principle and rationalism led him to embrace Unitarianism.

8

Conclusion

BRISTOL BAPTIST ACADEMY IN the eighteenth century played a crucial role in safeguarding English Baptist churches from drifting towards antitrinitarianism. In response to the Salters' Hall Debate, the academy diligently taught its students orthodox trinitarianism, effectively preventing the churches from succumbing to such heresies.

Review

Antitrinitarianism flourished in seventeenth-century England, fueled by the dissemination of Socinian doctrine and the application of the Protestant Principle. The spread of Socinianism can be attributed to two key factors. Firstly, Richard Muller demonstrated how Socinians effectively challenged orthodox trinitarianism in England using the same tools employed by trinitarians to defend the Trinity. Socinians strategically selected patristic authors, particularly pre-Nicaea figures, to highlight the absence of unanimous agreement among early church fathers regarding Nicene trinitarian doctrine. Their objective was to present a balanced perspective, showing that church history equally supports non-orthodox trinitarians as it does orthodox ones. Secondly, Socinians turned to the Scriptures to counter the claims of orthodox trinitarians. While they acknowledged the revelational truth of Scripture, they employed reason to interpret and resolve apparent contradictions, such as the deity of the Son alongside the oneness of God.

Second, Francis Cheynell testified about the spread of Socinianism in the wake of Arminian growth within the Church of England. One aspect of Arminian doctrine is its emphasis on the freedom of human will in determining salvation. This emphasis on human free will lent credibility to the notion of human freedom of reason. Even those who opposed Socinianism, such as William Chillingworth, elevated reason over revelation in determining truth from Scripture. The reliance on Scripture and the elevation of reason led to the development of the Protestant Principle, which is the second cause for the spread of seventeenth-century England's antitrinitarianism.

The Protestant Principle, championed by Chillingworth, challenged the notion that any individual could derive an infallible deduction from Scripture. This notion undermined the foundation of confessional doctrine. According to this principle, only Scripture itself can infallibly articulate doctrine, and such articulations are limited to matters clearly articulated in the Scriptures. Consequently, all Christians must adhere to these unambiguous scriptural doctrines. However, when the Scriptures are unclear on certain matters, such as the Trinity, individuals may hold their own opinions, which are not necessarily testable for the orthodoxy of others.

English Baptists, both General and Particular, faced the rise of antitrinitarianism within their ranks during the seventeenth century. The two groups responded differently. The General Baptists had to confront Matthew Caffyn, who held a Christology that rejected the notion of two distinct natures within Christ. Caffyn believed that the Son of God possessed an eternal form of celestial flesh before the incarnation. Consequently, he denied that the Son of God could share an equal divine nature with God the Father. Several General Baptists accused Caffyn of heresy before five different General Assemblies. Each assembly denounced the heterodox claims alleged of Caffyn but also denied that Caffyn held such views. Their denial was based on the fact that Caffyn consistently affirmed clear scriptural teachings about Christ. The assembly's primary conviction was that discussions about the Trinity and Christology should be confined to the scriptures. Their stance was similar to that of Chillingworth.

The Particular Baptists addressed Thomas Collier, who held a flawed Christology that distorted his understanding of the Trinity. Collier couldn't grasp that the Son could only possess a divine nature before the incarnation and then acquire a human nature without any transformation within Him. Collier asserted that the Son eternally possessed both a divine and a human nature, leading him to conclude that the Son was creation, albeit an eternal creation. The Particular Baptists, particularly those from London, were compelled to confront and correct Collier's beliefs. After an unsuccessful meeting with him, the Particular Baptists from the Petty France church, led by Nehemiah Coxe and William Collins, issued a confession of faith in 1677 that affirmed orthodox trinitarianism in opposition to Collier. This confession was subsequently subscribed to and recommended by the messengers to the Baptist General Assembly in 1689, which was known as the *Second London Baptist Confession of Faith* (2LCF).

The Salters' Hall Debates of 1719 revealed that the General and Particular Baptists' responses to antitrinitarianism, whether in scriptural or confessional terms, during the seventeenth century mirrored their responses in the eighteenth century. Among the non-subscribers at Salters' Hall were fourteen General Baptists and two Particular Baptists. Conversely, among the subscribers at Salters' Hall were fourteen Particular Baptists and one General Baptist.

Bristol Baptist Academy, established after the Salters' Hall Debates, manifested itself as a confessional Particular Baptist Academy. This confessional identity can be attributed to its founding church, Broadmead. Broadmead, established in 1640, began as a Reformed church but gradually transitioned over the next five decades into Baptist practice and adopting Particular Baptist doctrine. Bernard Foskett, the inaugural principal of Bristol Academy, played a pivotal role in leading the Western Association of Baptist churches to adopt the 2LCF as a means of achieving doctrinal unity in the aftermath of Salters' Hall.

Bristol Academy, throughout the eighteenth century, adhered to and taught orthodox trinitarianism. Students' accounts reveal that the academy employed authors who taught through catechisms that affirmed classical trinitarianism. The academy's principals, as evidenced by Foskett and Caleb Evans, promoted confessions that upheld classical trinitarianism as a means to foster doctrinal unity. While some alumni would later reject the teachings they had received, the majority of Bristol Academy alumni went on to establish local Particular Baptist churches based on orthodox trinitarianism.

Reflections

The Protestant Principle and the Sufficiency of Scripture

The Protestant Principle is a common factor among those who moved toward and adopted antitrinitarian views. A question arises whether the Protestant Principle is a necessary condition that naturally leads one to antitrinitarianism. Two examples have been attested to where employment of the principle led to antitrinitarianism. Both James Peirce and Job David were men who once held to classical trinitarianism. Their movement away from classical trinitarianism included the practice of the Protestant Principle. Though no explicit example was given among the General Baptists in the seventeenth century, the orthodox General Baptists of the day were concerned that antitrinitarian views were being tolerated within the assembly because of its use and defense of the Protestant Principle.[1]

However, examples have also been given of those who held to the Protestant Principle and yet did not become antitrinitarian. Though the orthodox General Baptists were concerned, the vast majority of those who comprised the General Assembly were not antitrinitarian. In hopes to reunite with the General Association, the General Assembly approved *The Treaty of Union* in the 1704 assembly. In part, it states, "We do believe and are very Confident . . . in this Divine & Infinite Being or Unity of the Godhead there are three persons The Father the Word and the Holy Ghost of one Substance Power and Eternity."[2] The language certainly is not scriptural but confessional. Yet, the approval of the treaty by the assembly demonstrates that though the General Assembly was Protestant Principle by conviction, they did affirm classical trinitarianism.

Another example is the nonsubscribers at Salters' Hall. Though a few who refused subscription may have been antitrinitarian, the nonsubscribers by far affirmed classical trinitarianism. In their advices to the Exeter churches, the nonsubscribers state that they "sincerely believe the Doctrine of the Blessed Trinity, and the proper Divinity of our Lord Jesus Christ, which we apprehend to be clearly revealed in the Holy Scriptures."[3] This is not confessional language, but it is sufficient to accept their genuine affirmation of the Trinity.

Based on this evidence, it must be concluded that the Protestant Principle is not a necessary condition that leads to antitrinitarianism. However, the principle is a sufficient condition for antitrinitarianism. That is, those who deny orthodox trinitarianism will not affirm confessional trinitarian language but only scriptural language. Their antitrinitarianism may not be caused by the Protestant Principle, but it is employed in their antitrinitarianism.

Modern-day Baptists may not use the phrase "Protestant Principle," but they have been described as a "people of the Book." This means that Baptists look to the Scriptures, not tradition or creeds, for their source and foundation of their beliefs and practices. However, Baptists must learn from the past. For this reason, the use of the Protestant Principle needs to be

---

1. Since so little of Matthew Caffyn's writings are extant, it is difficult to assert whether he adhered to the Protestant Principle. As has been demonstrated, Caffyn could and would affirm the confessions of the General Baptists since the confessions were written in purely scriptural terms.

2. Whitley, *MGA*, 1:97.

3. *Authentick Account*, 15.

carefully understood and rightly employed. The principle is not a replacement of the sufficiency of Scripture that affirms that Scripture alone is perfectly adequate to determine, understand, and defend revelational truth. The sufficiency of Scripture does not deny the use of reason and deductions to articulate and explain revelational truth in other than scriptural terms. The sufficiency of Scripture affirms Scripture as authoritative and the alone normative of truth. When understood this way, the Protestant Principle is rightly employed and will guard against heterodoxy.

Confessions and Conscience

Baptists, from their inception in seventeenth-century England, have upheld the conscience of individuals in regard to religious belief and practice. They themselves were among the dissenters from the Church of England, and even among their fellow dissenters due to their practice of credobaptism. Through acts such as the Act of Uniformity passed by English parliament, the Baptists experienced the attempt to force beliefs and practices upon them from others. The General Baptists declared in the 1660 *Brief Confession of Faith* that "all men should have the free liberty of their own Consciences in matters of Religion, or Worship."[4] The Particular Baptists in the 2LCF stated, "God alone is the Lord of the Conscience, and hath left it free from the Doctrines and Commandments of Men, which are in any thing contrary to his Word, or not contained in it."[5]

Interestingly, however, when questionable doctrine or questions of doctrine arose, both the General and Particular Baptists reverted to their confessions. The General Baptists in their 1691 General Assembly directed attention to the 1660 *Brief Confession of Faith* to settle, or at least attempt to settle, a Christological dispute.[6] The Particular Baptists called the 1689 General Assembly for many reasons. The main tenor of the reasons was the decay and defects within Particular Baptist churches that occurred during the decades of oppression.[7] To help cure the decay, the assembly recommended other Particular Baptist churches to furnish themselves with the 2LCF.[8] Though both groups of Baptists affirmed liberty of conscience, neither retreated from the use of confessions.

---

4. *Brief Confession* (1660), 10.
5. *Confession of Faith* (1688), 71.
6. Whitley, *MGA*, 1:30.
7. Renihan, *Faith and Life*, 27–32.
8. Renihan, *Faith and Life*, 42.

Modern-day Baptists still affirm the liberty of conscience. For some Baptists this leads them to deny the use of confessions, or even to denounce confessions. But modern-day Baptists can learn from those in the past. Baptists have never held that confessions of faith are authoritative over the conscience of a Christian. That right belongs to Scripture alone. Yet, confessions are helpful, even a necessary consequence of freedom of conscience, in order to express what a particular group holds as right and accurate expressions of scriptural doctrine. It is no denial of one's conscience to direct them to a confession and even to give assent unto it. No confession will perfectly articulate such doctrine. A person may agree with the substance of the confession and yet question certain words or phrases that express the substance.

Recommendations

1. Bristol Academy in the eighteenth century was Particular Baptist in confession and conviction. Bristol College (its present designation) in the twenty-first century appears that it is not. Ruth Gouldbourne describes the history of Bristol College as that of catholicity, which is "the refusal of a narrow denominational (or, within the denomination, a party) position, and a willingness to embrace all those who embrace the Saviour."[9] This appears to be a shift in the school's confessional identity over the centuries. A study could be made of the academy's confessional heritage in the nineteenth and twentieth centuries to determine whether a shift in confessional identity has occurred and, if so, when and how that shift occurred.

2. Of the seven alumni mentioned in chapter 7 who either rejected or are alleged to have rejected orthodox trinitarianism, four attended Bristol Academy during the five-year tenure of Robert Hall Jr. A study could be made concerning the years 1785–1790 to determine whether Hall introduced teaching that compromised orthodox trinitarianism that might have been a factor in these alumni later denying orthodox trinitarianism. Also, a study could be made concerning these alumni post-Bristol Academy to determine whether other factors may have led to their rejection.

3. Caleb Evans is not a well-known Baptist figure in the modern day. There are just over thirty extant writings of Evans held by the Bristol Baptist College library. His writings cover doctrinal, pastoral, political, and educational topics. While he may not be on the same level of eloquence as other eighteenth-century Baptist writers, Evans's writings would benefit modern day readers. He models how local pastors can address prevalent heterodoxies of the day. Evans demonstrates Baptist political engagement as

---

9. Gouldbourne and Cross, *Story of Bristol*, 14.

he defends religious freedom in the years leading up to Revolutionary War. He also writes of the need for religious education to equip church pastors for the work of the ministry. A study could be made of the works of Evans to show their context in his day and application for the modern day.

Bibliography

An Account of the Reasons Why Many Citizens of Exon Have Withdrawn from the Ministry of Mr. Joseph Hallet and Mr. James Peirce. 2nd ed. London: Printed for John Clark, at the Bible and Crown in the Poultry, near Cheapside, 1719.

An Alphabetical Catalogue of All the Books in the Library: Belonging to the Bristol Education Society. Bristol: Printed by W. Pine and Son, Wine-Street, 1795.

Aretius, Benedictus, and Robert South. *A Short History of Valentinus Gentilis, the Tritheist, Tryed, Condemned.* London: Printed by E. Whitlock, 1696.

Ascol, Thomas K., and Nathan A. Finn, eds. *Ministry by His Grace and for His Glory: Essays in Honor of Thomas J. Nettles.* Cape Coral, FL: Founders, 2011.

An Authentick Account of Several Things Done and Agreed upon by the Dissenting Ministers Lately Assembled at Salters-Hall. London: Printed for John Clark, at the Bible and Crown in the Poultry near Cheapside; E. Matthews, at the Bible in Paternoster-Row; and R. Ford, at the Angel in the Poultry, 1719.

Ayres, Lewis. *Nicaea and Its Legacy: An Approach to Fourth-Century Trinitarian Theology.* New York: Oxford University Press, 2004.

Barrington, John Shute. *An Account of the Late Proceedings of the Dissenting Ministers at Salters-Hall: Occasioned by the Differences Amongst Their Brethren in the Country: With Some Thoughts Concerning the Imposition of Humane Forms for Articles of Faith. In a Letter to the Revd. Dr. Gale. With a Postscript to Mr. Bradbury.* 3rd ed. London: Printed for J. Roberts, near the Oxford-Arms in Warwick-Lane, 1719.

Bass, Clint C. *The Caffynite Controversy.* Centre for Baptist Studies in Oxford 19. Oxford: Regent's Park College, 2020.

———. *Thomas Grantham (1633-1692) and General Baptist Theology.* Centre for Baptist Studies in Oxford 10. Oxford: Regent's Park College, 2019.

Bebbington, David W. *Baptists through the Centuries: A History of a Global People.* Waco, TX: Baylor University Press, 2010.

———. "The Significance of Bristol Baptist College." *Baptist Quarterly* 53.4 (2022) 149–66.

Beddome, Benjamin. *Hymns Adapted to Public Worship, or Family Devotion: Now First Published, from the Manuscripts of the Late B. Beddome.* London: E. W. Morris, Printer, Wycomb. Sold by Burton and Briggs, Leadenhall Street; and Button and Son, Paternoster Row, 1818.

———. *A Scriptural Exposition of the Baptist Catechism by Way of Question and Answer.* 2nd corrected ed. Bristol: Printed by W. Pine, 1776.

———. *Sermons Printed from the Manuscripts of the Late Rev. Benjamin Beddome, A. M. of Bourton-on-the-Water, Gloucestershire; with a Brief Memoir of the Author.* London: William Ball, Aldine Chambers, 13, Paternoster Row, 1835.

Biddle, John. *A Confession of Faith Touching the Holy Trinity, According to the Scripture.* London, 1648.

Brackney, William H., Paul S. Fiddes, and John H. Y. Briggs, eds. *Pilgrim Pathways: Essays in Baptist History in Honour of B. R. White.* Macon, GA: Mercer University Press, 1999.

A Brief Confession or Declaration of Faith. (Lately Presented to King Charles the Second) Set Forth by Many of Us, Who Are (Falsely) Called Ana-Baptists, to Inform All Men (in These Days of Scandal and Reproach) of Our Innocent Beleef and Practise; for Which Wee Are Not Only Resolved to Suffer Persecution, to the Losse of Our Goods, but Also Life It Self, Rather Than to Decline the Same. Subscribed by Certain Elders, Deacons, and Brethren, Met at London, in the Behalf of Themselves, and Many Others unto Whom They Belong; in London, and in Several Counties of This Nation, Who Are of the Same Faith with Us. London: Printed for Francis Smith at the Elephant and Castle neer the Temple-Barre, 1660.

A Brief Confession or Declaration of Faith, Set Forth by Many of Us, Who Are (Falsly) Called Ana-Baptists, to Inform All Men of Our Innocent Belief and Practice. Subscribed by Certain Elders, Deacons, and Brethren, in the Behalf of Themselves, and Many Others unto Whom They Belong, in London, and in Several Counties of This Nation, Who Are of the Same Faith with Us. London: n.p., 1691.

A Brief Confession or Declaration of Faith Set Forth by Many of Us, Who Are (Falsely) Called Ana-Baptists, to Inform All Men (in These Dayes of Scandal and Reproach) of Our Innocent Belief and Practise; for Which We Are Not Only Resolved to Suffer Persecution, to the Loss of Our Goods, but Also Life It Self, Rather Than to Decline the Same. Subscribed by Certain Elders, Deacons, and Brethren, Met at London, in the First Month (Called March, 1660.) in the Behalf of Themselves, and Many Others unto Whom They Belong, in London, and in Several Counties of This Nation, Who Are of the Same Faith with Us. London: Printed by G. D. for F. Smith, at the Elephant and Castle, near Temple-Barr, 1660.

A Brief Instruction in the Principles of Christian Religion Agreeable to the Confession of Faith, Put Forth by the Elders and Brethren of Many Congregations of Christians, (Baptized upon Profession of Their Faith) in London and the Country, Owning the Doctrine of Personal Election, and Final Perseverance. 5th ed. London: n.p., 1695.

Briggs, John H. Y., ed. *Pulpit and People: Studies in Eighteenth-Century Baptist Life and Thought.* Studies in Baptist History and Thought 28. Eugene, OR: Wipf & Stock, 2009.

Bristol Baptist College. *Bristol Baptist College: 250 Years, 1679–1929.* Bristol: Rankins Brothers Limited, 1929.

Brown, Raymond Edward. *The English Baptists of the Eighteenth Century.* Vol. 2 of *A History of the English Baptists.* London: Baptist Historical Society, 1986.

Bustin, Dennis C. *Paradox and Perseverance: Hanserd Knollys, Particular Baptist Pioneer in Seventeenth-Century England.* Studies in Baptist History and Thought 23. Eugene, OR: Wipf & Stock, 2006.

Caffyn, Matthew. *Envy's Bitterness Corrected with the Rod of Shame: Or, an Answer to a Book Lately Published by Richard Haines (a Person Withdrawn from) Entituled, New Lords, New Laws; Wherein Is Shewed Such an Image of Envy, as in Late Ages*

Have Not Appeared, by His Heaping up False Accusations, and Abusive Expressions to a Great Number, with Malicious Insinuations, Thereby to Provoke (If Possible) the Civil Magistrate to Have Suspitious Thoughts of the Innocent, with a Great Out-cry of Usurpation and Tyranny, Proved to Have No Other Foundation but His Own Evil Imaginations, and so, Neither Lords, nor New Laws. Wherein Also the Several Persons Therein Accused, Are in Righteousness Quitted, to the Shame of the Accuser. London: n.p., 1674.

Chadwick, Rosemary. "Hall, Robert (1764–1831)." In *Oxford Dictionary of National Biography*. Oxford: Oxford University Press, 2004. https://doi.org/10.1093/ref:odnb/11982.

Chandler, Kegan A. "Unorthodox Christology in General Baptist History: The Legacy of Matthew Caffyn." *Journal of European Baptist Studies* 19.2 (2019) 140–51.

Chernaik, Warren. "Chillingworth, William (1602–1644)." In *Oxford Dictionary of National Biography*. Oxford: Oxford University Press, 2010. https://doi.org/10.1093/ref:odnb/5308.

Cheynell, Francis. *The Divine Trinunity of the Father, Son, and Holy Spirit: Or, The Blessed Doctrine of the Three Coessentiall Subsistents in the Eternall Godhead Etc*. London: T. R. and E. M. for Samuel Gellibrand at the Ball in Pauls Church-Yard, 1650.

———. *The Rise, Growth and Danger of Socinianisme together with a Plaine Discovery of a Desperate Designe of Corrupting the Protestant Religion, Whereby It Appears that the Religion Which Hath Been So Violently Contended for (by the Acrchbishop of Canterbury and His Adherents) Is Not the True Pure Protestant Religion, but an Hotchpotch of Arminianisme, Socinianisme and Popery. It Is Lkewise Made, That the Atheists, Anabaptists, and Sectaries So Much Complained of, Have Been Raised or Encouraged by the Doctrines and Practises of the Arminian, Socinian and Popish Party*. London: Printed for Samuel Gellibrand, at the Brazen Serpent in Pauls Church-Yard, 1643.

Child, Robert L., and C. E. Shipley. *Broadmead Origins: An Account of the Rise of Puritanism in England and of the Early Days of Broadmead Baptist Church, Bristol, Issued for the Tercentenary, 1940*. London: Kingsgate, 1940.

Chillingworth, William. *The Religion of Protestants a Safe Way to Salvation. Or an Answer to a Booke Entitled Mercy and Truth, Or, Charity Maintain'd by Catholiques, Which Pretends to Prove the Contrary*. Oxford: Printed by Leonard Lichfield, and are to be sold by John Clarke under St Peter's Church in Corn-Hill, 1638.

Churchill, Winston S. *The New World*. Vol. 2 of *A History of the English-Speaking People*. New York: Dodd, Mead & Company, 1956.

Clements, K. W. "The Significance of 1679." *Baptist Quarterly* 28.1 (1979) 2–6.

Coffey, John. *John Goodwin and the Puritan Revolution: Religion and Intellectual Change in Seventeenth-Century England*. Woodbridge, Suffolk, UK: Boydell, 2006.

Collier, Thomas. *An Additional Word to the Body of Divinity, or Confession of Faith; Being the Substance of Christianity. Added on Special Occasion, Tending Further to Confirm Some Truths Therein. With a Further Discourse about the Doctrine of Election, Universal, and Special Grace, &c. All Which Were Touched in the Said Confession of Faith, but in This More Plainy and Fully (Though Briefly) Discoursed and Designed for the Good of All. Whereunto Is Annexed a Seasonable Word of Advice, Being an Essay for Peace and Union Among All the Sons and Daughters of Peace*. London: Printed for the author, 1676.

———. *The Body of Divinity, Or, A Confession of Faith, Being the Substance of Christianity: Containing the Most Material Things Relating to Matters Both of Faith and Practise*. London: Printed for Nath. Crouch in Exchange Ally, over against the Royal-Exchange in Corn-Hill, 1674.

———. *A Brief and True NARRATIVE of the Unrighteous Dealings with Thomas Collier, a Member and Minister of the Church Usually Assembling at Southwick in the County of Wilts*. n.p., 1677.

———. *The Heads and Substance of a Discourse; First Private, and Afterwards Publike; Held in Axbridge, in the County of Somerset, about the 6th of March, 1650. Between John Smith of Badgworth, and Charls Carlile of Bitsham, &c. on the One Part; and Thomas Collier of Westbury on the Other. Things They Are of Weight and Highest Concernment*. London: Printed for Giles Calvert, at the Black Spred-Eagle at the West end of Pauls, 1651.

———. *The Second Volume of the Works of Thomas Collier*. London: Printed for Giles Calvert, 1649.

———. *The Titles of the Severall Pieces Written by Thomas Collier*. London: Printed for Giles Calvert, at the Black Spred-Eagle at the West-End of Pauls, 1647.

Colligan, James Hay. *The Arian Movement in England*. Manchester, England: Sherratt & Hughes, 1913.

A Confession of Faith Put Forth by the Elders and Brethren of Many Congregations of Christians (Baptized upon Profession of Their Faith) in London and the Country. London, 1677.

A Confession of Faith Put Forth by the Elders and Brethren of Many Congregations of Christians, (Baptized upon Profession of Their Faith) in London and the Country: With an Appendix Concerning Baptism. London, England: Printed for John Harris, at the Harrow against the Church in the Poultrey, 1688.

A Confession of Faith of Seven Congregations or Churches of Christ in London, Which Are Commonly (but Uniustly) Called Anabaptists. Published for the Vindication of the Truth, and Information of the Ignorant; Likewise for the Taking off of Those Aspersions Which Are Frequently Both in Pulpit and Print Unjustly Cast upon Them. London: Printed by Matth. Simmons, and are to be sold by John Hancock in Popes-Head Alley, 1646.

A Confession of the Faith of Several Churches of Christ, in the County of Somerset, and of Some Churches in the Counties Neer Adjacent. London: Printed by Henry Hills, and are to be Sold by Thomas Brewster, at the Three Bibles at the West End of Pauls, 1656.

The Confession of Faith of Those Churches Which Are Commonly, Though Falsly, Called Anabaptists Presented to the View of All That Feare God to Examine by the Touchstone of the Word of Truth, as Likewise for the Taking off Those Aspersions Which Are Frequently Both in Pulpit and Print, Although Unjustly, Cast upon Them. London, 1644.

Copson, Stephen, ed. *Trinity, Creed and Confusion: The Salters' Hall Debate of 1719*. Centre for Baptist Studies in Oxford 20. Oxford: Regent's Park College, 2020.

Copson, Stephen L., and Peter J. Morden, eds. *Challenge and Change: English Baptist Life in the Eighteenth Century*. Didcot, Oxon: Baptist Historical Society, 2017.

Coxe, Nehemiah. *A Believers Triumph over Death Exemplified in a Relation of the Last Hours of Dr. Andrew Rivet and an Account of Divers Other Remarkable Instances: Being an History of the Comfortable End and Dying Words of Several Eminent*

Men, with Other Occasional Passages, All Tending to Comfort Christians against the Fear of Death and Prepare Them for a Like Happy Change. London: Printed for Benjamin Alsop at the Angel and Bible in the Poultrey, 1682.

———. *A Discourse of the Covenants That God Made with Men before the Law. Wherein the Covenant of Circumcision Is More Largely Handled, and the Invalidity of the Plea for Pædobaptism Taken from Thence Discovered.* London: Printed by J. D. and are to be sold by Nathaniel Ponder at the Peacock in the Poultry; and Benjamin Alsop at the Angel and Bible in the Poultry, 1681.

———. "Inaugral Medical Dissertation on Gout, Which with God on the Authority of the Great Doctor Rector, Doctor Melchoir Leydecker Doctor of Sacred Theology, and Ordinary Professor of the Same Faculty in the Most Renowned University of Utrecht, and Also by Agreement of the Most Illustrious Academic Senate & by Decree of the Most Noble Faculty of Medicine for the Degree of Doctor and the Highest Honors and Privileges in Medicine Rightly to Follow Was Submitted to the Examination of Learned People [by] Nehemiah Cox, an Englishman from London." MD thesis, University of Utrecht, 1684.

———. *Nehemiah Coxe's Vindiciæ Veritatis: "A Vindication of the Truth."* Edited by James M. Renihan. Macclesfield, UK: Broken Wharfe, 2023.

———. *A Sermon Preached at the Ordinatoin of an Elder and Deacons in a Baptized Congregation in London.* London: Printed for Tho. Fabian, at the Bible in Saint Paul's Church-Yard, a corner Shop next Cheap-Side, 1681.

———. *Vindiciæ Veritatis, or, A Confutation of the Heresies and Gross Errours Asserted by Thomas Collier in His Additinal Word to His Body of Divinity.* London: Printed for Nath. Ponder, at the Peacock in the Poultry near Corn-Hill and in Chancery-Lane near Fleet-Street, 1677.

Crosby, Thomas. *The History of the English Baptists.* Vols. 3–4. Bellingham, WA: Logos Bible Software, 2011.

Cross, Anthony R. "'To Communicate Simply You Must Understand Profoundly': The Necessity of Theological Education for Deepening Ministerial Formation." *Journal of European Baptist Studies* 19.1 (2019) 54–67.

———. *"To Communicate Simply You Must Understand Profoundly": Preparation for Ministry Among British Baptists.* Didcot, Oxon: Baptist Historical Society, 2016.

———. *Useful Learning: Neglected Means of Grace in the Reception of the Evangelical Revival Among English Particular Baptists.* Eugene, OR: Pickwick, 2017.

Cross, Anthony R., Nicholas J. Wood, and John H. Y. Briggs, eds. *Exploring Baptist Origins.* Center for Baptist History and Heritage 1. Oxford: Regent's Park College, 2010.

David, Job. *A Letter Addressed to the Ministers of the Orthodox, or Calvinistic Baptists; Particularly Those of the Western Association, Shewing the Inconsistency of Their Conduct and Worship, and Proposing a Remedy. By One of Their Brethren.* London: Printed for the Author. Sold by J. Johnson, St. Paul's Church Yard; J. Buckland, Paternoster Row; and the Booksellers at Bristol, 1788.

———. *A Vindication of a Printed Letter Addressed to the Calvinistic Baptists of the Western Association, on the Subject of Doxologies: From the Remarks of a Member of the Western Association. By a Baptist.* Trowbridge: Abraham Small, 1789.

———. *The Wisdom and Benevolence of the Deity Displayed in the Appointment of the Man Christ Jesus, to Be the Mediator of the New Covenant, in a Discourse Delivered at Taunton, July 6, 1803, before the Society of Unitarian Christians, Established in* the West of England, for Promoting Christian Knowledge, and the Practice of Piety and Virtue. London: Printed by C. Stower, Charles-Street, Hatton-Garden. And Sold by W. Vidler, No. 349, Strand, 1803.

David, Job, Joshua Toulmin, and Philip Jones. *The Duty of the Christian Minister Recommended in a Charge; and Christ's Compassion on the Multitude Considered in a Sermon, Delivered at the Ordination of the Rev. Samuel Evans, December 27th, 1780, at Wedmore Somersetshire.* Taunton: Printed and Sold by J. Poole. Sold also by J. Johnson. No. 72 St. Paul's Church-Yard, London, 1781.

Davies, G. Henton. "Bristol Baptist College: Three Hundredth Birthday." *Baptist History and Heritage* 14.2 (1979) 8–14.

Dennison, James T. *Reformed Confessions of the Sixteenth and Seventeenth Century in English Translation.* Vol. 2. Grand Rapids: Reformation Heritage, 2008.

Ditchfield, G. M. "Toulmin, Joshua (1740–1815)." In *Oxford Dictionary of National Biography.* Oxford: Oxford University Press, 2004. https://doi.org/10.1093/ref:odnb/27579.

Dixon, Philip. *Nice and Hot Disputes: The Doctrine of the Trinity in the Seventeenth Century.* London: T&T Clark, 2003.

Dowley, Timothy Edward. "The History of the English Baptists During the Great Persecution, 1660–1688." PhD diss., University of Manchester, 1976.

Edwards, Thomas. *The Third Part of Gangræna, or, A New and Higher Discovery of the Errors, Heresies, Blasphemies, and Insolent Proceedings of the Sectaries of These Times with some Animadversions by Way of Confutation upon Many of the Errors and Heresies Named.* London: Printed by T. R. and E. M. for Ralph Smith, at the Sign of the Bible in Cornhill near the Royall Exchange, 1646.

Emery, Giles, and Matthew Levering. *The Oxford Handbook of the Trinity.* Oxford: Oxford University Press, 2011.

Evans, Caleb. *An Address to the Serious and Candid Professors of Christianity on the Following Subjects, Viz. I. The Use of Reason in Matters of Religion, II. The Power of Man to Do the Will of God, III. Original Sin, IV. Election and Reprobation, V. The Divinity of Christ, and VI. Atonement for Sin by the Death of Christ. Occasioned by an Appeal, Lately Published, on the Same Subjects.* 2nd ed. London: Printed for J. Buckland, and to be had of any of the Booksellers in Town or Country, 1773.

———. *Brief Remarks upon the Rev. Mr. Harwood's Late Extraordinary Letter.* Bristol: Printed and sold by S. Farley, in Castle-Green; Sold also by J. Buckland, in Paternoster-Row, and G. Keith, in Gracechurch-Street, London, 1767.

———. *British Constitutional Liberty: A Sermon, Preached in Broad-Mead, Bristol, November 5, 1775.* W. Pine, T. Cadell, M. Ward. And in London, by J. Buckland, G. Keith, E. and C. Dilly, and W. Harris, 1775.

———. *Christ Crucified: Or the Scripture Doctrine of the Atonement Briefly Illustrated and Defended. In Four Discourses upon That Subject.* Bristol: Printed by William Pine. Sold in London by Buckland, Button and Reynolds and in Bristol by Browne, Evans and Allen, James at the Circulating Library, and the other booksellers, 1789.

———. *Elisha's Exclamation! A Sermon Occasioned by the Death of the Rev. Hugh Evans, M. A., Who Departed This Life, March 28, 1781, in the 69th Year of His Age. Preached at Broadmead, Bristol, April 8, 1781.* Bristol: Printed by W. Pine, in Wine-Street: Sold by Cadell, Mills, Evans, and other Booksellers in Bristol; And by Buckland, MacGowan and Carter in London, 1781.

———. *Remarks on a Letter Addressed to the Ministers of the Orthodox or Calvinistic Baptists, Particularly Those of the Western Association. By a Member of the Western Association.* London: Printed for the Editor. Sold by Johnson, St. Paul's Churchyard. J. Buckland, Paternoster-Row, and the Booksellers at Bristol, 1789.

———. *The Scripture Doctrine of the Deity of the Son and Holy Spirit, Represented in Two Sermons Preached at Bristol, March 24, and April 21, 1765: Occasioned by a Pamphlet, Entitled an Attempt to Restore the Supreme Worship of God, By George Williams. Together with Some Animadversions on the Preface to the Second Edition by TAOTCOAD.* Bristol: Printed and Sold by S. Farley, Castle-Green. Sold also by J. Buckland, in Pater-noster-Row, and G. Keith, in Gracechurch-Street, London, 1766.

Evans, Caleb, Samuel Stennett, John Tommas, and Hugh Evans. *A Charge and Sermon together with an Introductory Discourse and Confession of Faith Delivered at the Ordination of the Rev. Mr. Caleb Evans, August 18, 1767, in Broad-Mead, Bristol.* Bristol: Printed and Sold by S. Farley, in Castle-Green; sold also by J. Buckland, in Pater-noster-Row, and G. Keith, in Gracechurch-street, London, 1767.

Evans, John. *Memoirs of the Life and Writings of the Rev. William Richards, LLD.* Chiswick: Printed by Charles Whittingham, College House. Sold by Sherwood, Neely, and Jones, Paternoster Row; T. Wiche, Beech-Street, Barbican; and D. Eaton, High Holborn, London, 1819.

Foreman, Harry. "Baptist Provision for Ministerial Education in the Eighteenth Century." *Baptist Quarterly* 27.8 (1978) 358–69.

Fuller, J. G. *The Rise and Progress of Dissent in Bristol; Chiefly in Relation to the Broadmead Church.* London: Hamilton, Adams and Co., 1840.

Gale, Nathaniel. *Brief Remarks upon Dr. Russel's Brief Account of Mr. Caffin's Several Opinions, of the Person of the Messiah.* London: N.p., 1700.

Gascoigne, John. "Clarke, Samuel (1675–1729)." In *Oxford Dictionary of National Biography.* Oxford: Oxford University Press, 2004. https://doi.org/10.1093/ref:odnb/5530.

George, Timothy, and David S. Dockery, eds. *Theologians of the Baptist Tradition.* Nashville: Broadman & Holman, 2001.

Gibbs, Philip. *The Elders and Messengers of the Several Baptist Churches, Being Met in Association at Kingsbridge, Devon, May 29 and 30, 1776.* N.p.: 1776.

Gill, John. *A Collection of Sermons and Tracts.* Vol. 2. London: Printed for George Keith in Gracechurch-Street, 1773.

———. *A Complete Body of Doctrinal and Practical Divinity; Or, A System of Evangelical Truths, Deduced from the Sacred Scriptures.* Vol. 1. New ed. London: Printed for W. Winterbotham, and Sold by J. Ridgway, York Street, St. James Square, and W. Button, Paternoster Row, 1796.

———. *The Doctrine of the Trinity Stated and Vindicated. Being the Substance of Several Discourses on That Important Subject; Reduc'd into the Form of a Treatise.* London: Aaron Ward at the King's-Arms in Little-Britain, 1731.

Godet, Steven Tshombe. "The Trinitarian Theology of John Gill (1697–1771): Context, Sources, and Controversy." PhD diss., Southern Baptist Theological Seminary, 2015.

Gordon, Alexander, and Alan Ruston. "Ridgley, Thomas (1667–1734)." In *Oxford Dictionary of National Biography.* Oxford: Oxford University Press, 2008. https://doi.org/10.1093/ref:odnb/23625.

Gouldbourne, Ruth, and Anthony R. Cross. *The Story of Bristol Baptist College: Three Hundred Years of Ministerial Formation*. Eugene, OR: Wipf & Stock, 2022.

Grantham, Thomas. *Christianismus Primitivus, or, the Ancient Christian Religion, in Its Nature, Certainty, Excellency, and Beauty, (Internal and External) Particularly Considered, Asserted, and Vindicated from the Many Abuses Which Have Invaded That Sacred Profession, by Humane Innovation, or Pretended Revelation Comprehending Likewise the General Duties of Mankind, in Their Respective Relations: And Particularly the Obedience of All Christians to Magistrates, and the Necessity of Christian-Moderation about Things Dispensible in Matters of Religion: With Divers Cases of Conscience Discussed and Resolved*. London: Printed for Francis Smith, at the Elephant and Castle at Cornhill, near the Royal-Exchange, 1678.

Haines, Richard. *New Lords, New Laws, or, A Discovery of a Grand Usurpation, in Opposition to the Holy Laws of God, and Contempt of the Good Laws, and Royal Prerogative of the Supream Magistrate, as It Hath Been Lately Practised by the Lordly Matthew Caffin, a Pretended True Apostle of Our Blessed Lord and Saviour, and Ruling Head of His Congregation, Usually Meeting at Southwater Near Horsham in Sussex*. London: N.p., 1674.

Hall, C. Sidney, and Harry Mowvley. *Tradition and Challenge: The Story of Broadmead Baptist Church, Bristol from 1685 to 1991*. Bristol: Broadmead Baptist Church, 1991.

Harwood, Edward. *An Account of the Conversion of a Deist. With an Appendix, Containing Reflections on Deism and Christianity*. London: Printed for R. Griffiths in Strand, and C. Henderson at the Royal-Exchange, 1762.

———. *A Letter to the Reverend Mr. Caleb Evans of Bristol; Occasioned by His Two Sermons on the Deity of the Son and the Holy Spirit*. London: Printed for J. Johnson and B. Davenport, at the Globe in Pater-noster Row; and N. Young, under the Royal Exchange: and Sold, in Bristol, by T. Caddel, J. Palmer, and E. Ward, 1766.

Hayden, Roger. "Bristol Baptist College and America." *Baptist History and Heritage* 14.4 (1979) 26–33.

———. "Bristol Baptist Academy (1720 to Present)." Dissenting Academies Online, 2004. https://dissacad.english.qmul.ac.uk/sample1.php?parameter=academyretrieve&alpha=26#tabs-2 (page discontinued).

———. "Broadmead, Bristol in the Seventeenth Century." *Baptist Quarterly* 23.8 (1970) 348–59.

———. *Continuity and Change: Evangelical Calvinism Among Eighteenth-Century Baptist Ministers Trained at Bristol Academy, 1690–1791*. Occasional Publications Series. Oxford: Nigel Lynn, 2006.

———. *English Baptist History and Heritage*. London: Baptist Union of Great Britain, 2005.

———. "Evangelical Calvinism Among Eighteenth-Century British Baptists with Particular Reference to Bernard Foskett, Hugh and Caleb Evans and the Bristol Baptist Academy, 1690–1791." PhD diss., Keele University, 1991.

———. "Evans, Caleb (1737–1791)." In *Oxford Dictionary of National Biography*. Oxford: Oxford University Press, 2004. https://doi.org/10.1093/ref:odnb/40192.

Haykin, Michael A. G. "Gill, John (1697–1771)." In *Oxford Dictionary of National Biography*. Oxford: Oxford University Press, 2004. https://doi.org/10.1093/ref:odnb/10731.

———. *Kiffin, Knollys, and Keach: Rediscovering English Baptist Heritage*. Leeds, England: Reformation Today Trust, 1996.

———. *One Heart and One Soul: John Sutcliff of Olney, His Friends and His Times*. Durham, UK: Evangelical, 1995.

Haykin, Michael A. G., and Roy M. Paul, eds. *In Essence One, in Persons Three: The Doctrine of the Trinity in Particular Baptist Life and Thought, 1640s–1840s*. West Lorne, ON: H&E Academic, 2022.

Haykin, Michael A. G., Roy M. Paul, and Jeongmoo Yoo, eds. *Glory to the Three Eternal: Tercentennial Essays on the Life and Writings of Benjamin Beddome*. Eugene, OR: Pickwick, 2019.

Haykin, Michael A. G., and Terry Wolever, eds. *The British Particular Baptists*. Vol. 1. Rev. ed. Springfield, MS: Particular Baptist, 2019.

———. *The British Particular Baptists*. Vol. 4. Springfield, MS: Particular Baptist, 2018.

———. *The British Particular Baptists*. Vol. 5. Springfield, MS: Particular Baptist, 2019.

Henry, Matthew, and William Tong. *The Works of the Late Reverend Matthew Henry: Being a Complete Collection of All the Discourses, Sermons and Other Tracts That Were Published by Himself. Together with an Account of His Life, and a Sermon, Preached on the Occasion of His Death Both by the Reverend Mr. William Tong*. London: Emanuel Matthews in Pater-Noster Row, 1726.

"History of the Conference at Salters' Hall on the Doctrine of the Trinity, in 1719." *Baptist Magazine* 11 (1819) 1–6, 49–56, 106–10.

Holmes, Stephen R. "General Baptist 'Primitivism,' the Radical Reformation, and Matthew Caffyn: A Response to Kegan A. Chandler." *Journal of European Baptist Studies* 21.1 (2021) 123–39.

———. "A Note Concerning the Text, Editions, and Authorship of the 1660 Standard Confession of the General Baptists." *Baptist Quarterly* 47.1 (2016) 1–7.

———. *The Quest for the Trinity: the Doctrine of God in Scripture, History and Modernity*. Downers Grove, IL: IVP Academic, 2012.

Ivimey, Joseph. *A History of the English Baptists: Comprising the Principal Events of the History of Protestant Dissenters, from the Revolution 1668 Till 1760; and of the London Baptist Churches, during That Period*. Vol. 3. London: Printed for B. J. Holdsworth, 18, St. Paul's Church-Yard, 1823.

———. *A History of the English Baptists: Containing Biographical Sketches and Notices of above Three Hundred Ministers, and Historical Accounts, Alphabetically Arranged, of One Hundred and Thirty Churches, in the Different Counties in England: From about the Year 1610 Till 1700*. Vol. 2. London: Printed for the Author; and sold by Button and Son, Baynes, Gale, Curtis, and Fenner, Paternoster Row; Williams, Stationers' Court; Otridge and Bagster Strand; and Gardiner, Princes Street, Cavendish Square, 1814.

———. *A History of the English Baptists: Including an Investigation of Baptism in England from the Earliest Period to Which It Can Be Traced to the Close of the Seventeenth Century*. Vol. 1. London: Printed for the Author, and Sold by Burditt, Button, Baynes, and Gale and Curtis, Paternoster-Row; Williams, Stationers' Court; Otridge, and Bagster, Strand; Miller and People, Chancery Lane; and Gardiner, Prince-Street, Cavendish Square, 1811.

———. *A History of the English Baptists: The Principal Events of the History of the Protestant Dissenters, during the Reign of Geo. III and of the Baptist Churches in London, with Notices of the Principal Churches in the Country during the Same*

Period. Vol. 4. London: Isaac Taylor Hinton, Warwick Square; and Holdsworth & Ball, St. Pauls' Church-Yard, 1830.

Kelly, J. N. D. *Early Christian Doctrines.* Rev. ed. San Francisco: HarperOne, 1978.

Knollys, Hanserd. *The Gospel Minister's Maintenance Vindicated. Wherein, a Regular Ministry in the Churches, Is First Asserted, and the Objections against a Gospel Maintenance for Ministers, Answered. Also, the Dignity, Necessity, Difficulty, Use and Excellency of the Ministry of Christ Is Opened. Likewise, the Nature and Weightiness of That Sacred Work and Office Clearly Evinc'd. Recommended to the Baptized Congregations, by Several Elders in and about the City of London.* London: John Harris, 1689.

Land, Richard D. "Doctrinal Controversies of English Particular Baptists (1644–1691) as Illustrated by the Career and Writings of Thomas Collier." DPhil diss., University of Oxford, 1979.

Leith, John H., ed. *Creeds of the Churches: A Reader in Christian Doctrine, from the Bible to the Present.* 3rd ed. Louisville, KY: John Knox, 1982.

Lim, Paul Chang-Ha. *Mystery Unveiled: The Crisis of the Trinity in Early Modern England.* Oxford: Oxford University Press, 2012.

Lumpkin, William Latane. *Baptist Confessions of Faith.* Rev. ed. Chicago: Judson, 1969.

Manley, K. R., and Paul. H. Ballard. "The Making of an Evangelical Baptist Leader: John Rippon's Early Years, 1751–1773." *Baptist Quarterly* 26.6 (1976) 254–74.

Mann, Isaac. "Calendar of Letters, 1742–1831." *Baptist Quarterly* 6.4 (1932) 173–86.

McBeth, Leon. *The Baptist Heritage.* Nashville: Broadman, 1987.

McGlothlin, William Joseph. *Baptist Confessions of Faith.* Philadelphia: American Baptist, 1911.

McLachlan, Herbert J. *English Education under the Test Acts: Being the History of the Noncomformist Academies 1662–1820.* Vol. 59. Historical Series. Manchester: University of Manchester, 1931.

———. *Socinianism in Seventeenth-Century England.* London: Oxford University Press, 1951.

Milton, Anthony. "Laud, William (1573–1645)." In *Oxford Dictionary of National Biography.* Oxford: Oxford University Press, 2004. https://doi.org/10.1093/ref:odnb/16112.

Monck, Thomas. *A Cure for the Cankering Error of the New Eutychians: Who (Concerning the Truth) have Erred Saying, That Our Blessed Mediator Did Not Take His Flesh of the Virgin Mary, Neither Was He Made of the Seed of David According to the Flesh; and Thereby Have Overthrown the Faith of Some.* London: Printed for the Author, 1673.

Montgomery, Jason C. "Benjamin Beddome: The Fruitful Life and Evangelical Labor of a Forgotten Village Preacher." PhD diss., Southwestern Baptist Theological Seminary, 2018.

Moon, Norman S. "Caleb Evans, Founder of the Bristol Education Society." *Baptist Quarterly* 24.4 (1972) 175–90.

———. *Education for Ministry: Bristol Baptist College, 1679–1979.* Bristol: Stanley L. Hunt Ltd., 1979.

Moon, Norman S., L. G. Champion, and Harry Mowvley. *The Bristol Education Society 1770–1970.* Bristol: Bristol Baptist College, 1970.

Muller, Richard A. "Review of 'Commentary on the Larger Catechism—Previously Entitled A Body of Divinity—Wherein the Doctrines of the Christian Religion

Are Explained and Defended, Being the Substance of Several Lectures on the Assembly's Larger Catechism,' by Thomas Ridgley." *Calvin Theological Journal* 29.2 (1994) 607–9.

———. *Prolegomena to Theology.* Vol. 1 of *Post-Reformation Reformed Dogmatics: The Rise and Development of Reformed Orthodoxy, ca. 1520 to ca. 1725.* 2nd ed. Grand Rapids: Baker Academics, 2003.

———. *The Triunity of God.* Vol. 4 of *Post-Reformation Reformed Dogmatics: The Rise and Development of Reformed Orthodoxy, ca. 1520 to ca. 1725.* 2nd ed. Grand Rapids: Baker Academics, 2003.

Murch, Jerom. *A History of the Presbyterian and General Baptist Churches in the West of England; with Memoirs of Some of Their Pastors.* London: R. Hunter, 72, St. Paul's Churchyard, 1835.

Newton, James. *A Reply to a Letter to the Reverend Mr. C. Evans of Bristol; Occasioned by His Two Sermons on the Deity of the Son and Holy Spirit.* Bristol: Printed and Sold by S. Farley, in Castle-Green; Sold also by T. Cadell, Palmer and Becket, in Wine-Street, 1766.

Nye, Stephen. *A Brief History of the Unitarians, Called Also Socinians: In Four Letters, Written to a Friend.* William Kienton, 1687.

Oliver, Robert W. "Baptist Confession Making 1644 and 1689 (Revised)." Presented to the Strict Baptist Historical Society, March 17, 1989. *Reformation Today.* https://reformation-today.org/articles-of-interest/455.

Oliver, Willem H. "Sola Scriptura: Authority Versus Interpretation?" *Acta Theologica* 40.1 (2020) 102–23.

An Orthodox Creed, or, A Protestant Confession of Faith Being an Essay to Unite, and Confirm All True Protestants in the Fundamental Articles of the Christian Religion, against the Errors and Heresies of the Church of Rome. London: N.p., 1679.

Owens, Jesse. "Matthew Caffyn, Thomas Monck, and English General Baptist Creedalism." *Criswell Theological Review* 18.1 (2020) 39–55.

———. "The Salters' Hall Controversy of 1719." PhD diss., Southern Baptist Theological Seminary, 2021.

———. "Scripture Consequences." *Helwys Society Forum* (blog), April 5, 2021. http://www.helwyssocietyforum.com/scripture-consequences.

Peirce, James. *The Evil and Cure of Divisions. A Sermon Preach'd at Exon, at the Opening of a New Meeting-house, March 15. 1718/9.* Exon: Printed by Andrew Brice, at the Head of the Serge-Market, 1719.

———. *Plain Christianity Defended: Being an Answer to a Pamphlet Lately Printed at Exon, Intitled, Arius Detected and Confuted, &c. Part I.* London: Printed for J. Noon at the White-Hart near Mercers-Chappel in Cheapside, 1719.

———. *Propositions Relating to the Controversy Among the Dissenters in the West: Concerning the Trinity. In a Letter to the Revd. Mr. John Enty.* T. Bickerton, at the Crown in Pater-noster-row, and A. Dodd, at the Peacock without Temple-Bar, 1720.

———. *The Western Inquisition: Or, A Relation of the Controversy, Which Has Been Lately Among the Dissenters in the West of England.* London: Bible and Crown in the Poultry, 1720.

Pooley, Roger. "Cheynell, Francis (*bap.* 1608, *d.* 1665)." In *Oxford Dictionary of National Biography.* Oxford: Oxford University Press, 2004. https://doi.org/10.1093/ref:odnb/5266.

Powicke, Fred J. "The Salters' Hall Controversy." *Transactions of the Congregational Historical Society* 7.2 (1916) 110–24.

Priestley, Joseph. *An Appeal to the Serious and Candid Professors of Christianity, on the Following Subjects, Viz. I. the Use of Reason in Matters of Religion, II. The Power of Man to Do the Will of God, III. Original Sin, IV. Election and Reprobation, V. the Divinity of Christ, and VI. Atonement for Sin by the Death of Christ.* 3rd ed. Printed for J. Johnson, No. 72, St. Paul's Church-yard. Sold also by T. Cadell, at Bristol, J. Gore at Liverpool, J. Grigg, at Exeter, J. Harrop, at Manchester, T. Banks and W. Eyres, at Warrington, W. Edwards, at Halifax, and B. Binns, at Leeds, 1771.

Purnell, Robert. *The Way to Heaven Discovered: And, the Stumbling-Blocks (Cast Therein by the World, Flesh, and Devill) Removed. Or, the Ready Way to True Happines: Leading to the Gate of Full Assurance. with a Word of Reproof to the Scattered, Discontented Members of the Late Parliament. and a Word of Advise to the Present Supreme Authority of England.* Bristol: Printed for William Ballard of Bristol, 1655.

Renihan, James M. "An Excellent and Judicious Divine: Nehemiah Coxe." *Reformed Baptist Theological Review* 4.2 (2007) 62–78.

———. *Faith and Life for Baptists: The Documents of the London Particular Baptist General Assemblies, 1689–1694.* Palmdale, CA: Reformed Baptist Academic, 2016.

———. *For the Vindication of the Truth: A Brief Exposition of the First London Baptist Confession of Faith.* Vol. 1. Baptist Symbolics. Cape Coral, FL: Founders, 2021.

———. "God Freely Justifieth . . . by Imputing Christ's Active . . . and Passive Obedience." *Master's Seminary Journal* 32.1 (2021) 61–75.

———. *To the Judicious and Impartial Reader: A Contextual-Historical Exposition of the Second London Baptist Confession of Faith.* Vol. 2. Baptist Symbolics. Cape Coral, FL: Founders, 2022.

———. "Thomas Collier's Descent into Error: Collier, Calvinism, and the Second London Confession." *The Reformed Baptist Theological Review* 1.1 (2004) 67–83.

Renihan, Samuel D. *The Petty France Church (Part 1).* Re-Sourcing Baptist History: Seventeenth Century Series 9. Oxford: Centre for Baptist Studies, 2019.

A Reply to the Subscribing Ministers Reasons in Their Vindication, for Declaring Their Faith at This Critical Juncture: And, in Other Than Express Scripture Words. Publish'd by Agreement of a Committee of the Non-subscribing Ministers. London: Printed for John Clark, at the Bible and Crown in the Poultry, near Cheapside; E. Matthews, at the Bible in Pater-Noster-Row; and R. Ford, at the Angel in the Poultry, 1719.

Reynolds, John. *The Unsearchable Riches of Christ. A Sermon Preached in Broad-Mead, Bristol, Before the Bristol Education Society, August 28, 1782.* Bristol: Printed by William Pine, Wine-Street, 1782.

Ridgley, Thomas. *A Body of Divinity: Wherein the Doctrines of the Christian Religion, Are Explained and Defended. Being the Substance of Several Lectures on the Assembly's Larger Catechism.* 3rd ed. Glasgow: Printed by John Bryce, and Sold by him at his Shop in the Salt-Market, 1770.

Rippon, John. *The Baptist Annual Register for 1790, 1791, 1792, and Part of 1793. Including Sketches of the State of Religion Among Different Denominations of Good Men at Home and Abroad.* Sold by Messrs Dilly, Button, and Thomas, London; Brown, James, and Cottle, Bristol; Ogle, Edinburgh; Allein, Dublin, and may be had of the Baptist Ministers in New York, Philadelphia, Boston, Richmond, Savanah, and Charleston, in America, 1793.

———. *The Baptist Annual Register, for 1794, 1795, 1796–1797, Including Sketches of the State of Religion Among Different Denominations of Good Men at Home and Abroad*. Sold by Messrs. Dilly, Button, and Thomas, London; Brown, James, and Cottle, Bristol, Ogle, Edinburgh; Allein, Dublin; and may be had at the Baptist Ministers in New York, Philadelphia, Boston, Richmond, Savannah, and Charleston, in America, 1797.

———. *A Brief Essay towards an History of the Baptist Academy at Bristol: Read before the Bristol Education Society, at Their Anniversary Meeting, in Broadmead, August 26th, 1795*. London: Sold by Messrs. Dilly and Button, London; and by Brown, James, and Cottel, Bristol, 1796.

Ryland, John Collett. "A Student's Programme in 1744." *Baptist Quarterly* 2.6 (1925) 249–52.

Schofield, Robert. "Priestley, Joseph (1733–1804)." In *Oxford Dictionary of National Biography*. Oxford: Oxford University Press, 2013. https://doi.org/10.1093/ref:odnb/22788.

Song, Baiyu Andrew. "'When They Know Only or Chiefly Its Language, Not Its Spirit': Joseph Kinghorn (1766–1832) and Socinianism." *Puritan Reformed Journal* 12.2 (2020) 81–99.

Spivey, Jim. "Caffyn, Matthew (*bap.* 1628, *d.* 1714)." In *Oxford Dictionary of National Biography*. Oxford: Oxford University Press, 2004. https://doi.org/10.1093/ref:odnb/4332.

Stennett, Samuel. *The Mortality of Ministers Contrasted with the Unchangeableness of Christ: In a Sermon Occasioned by the Decease of the Rev. C. Evans, DD, Who Departed This Life Aug. 9, 1791, in the 54th Year of His Age: Preached at Broad-Mead, Bristol Aug. 21, 1791, by Samuel Stennett, DD, to Which Is Added the Address Delivered at His Interment, by the Rev. J. Tommas*. London: Printed by Rivington and Marshall: And Sold by T. Cadell, in the Strand; C. Dilly, in the Poultry; R. Bishop, Newport-Street, Leicester-Fields; and T. Knott, Lombard-Street. And Sold by W. Browne, and J. Cottle, and the Other Booksellers in Bristol, 1791.

Swaine, Stephen Albert. *Faithful Men: Or, Memorials of Bristol Baptist College, and Some of Its Most Distinguished Alumni*. London: Alexander & Shepheard, 1884.

Swaish, John. *Chronicles of Broadmead Church, Bristol, 1640–1923*. Bristol: Young & Humphry, 1927.

Taylor, Abraham. *The Scripture Doctrine of the Trinity Vindicated: In Opposition to Mr. Watts's Scheme of One Divine Person and Two Divine Powers*. 2nd ed. Printed for J. Roberts, near the Oxford-Arms in Warwick-Lane, 1728.

Taylor, Adam. *The History of the English General Baptists*. 2 vols. London: T. Bore, Raven Row, Mile-End Turnpike, 1818.

Terrill, Edward. "Introduction." In *The Records of a Church of Christ in Bristol, 1640–1687*, edited by Roger Hayden, 1–78. Bristol Record Society 27. Gateshead: Northumberland Limited, 1974.

———. *The Records of a Church of Christ in Bristol, 1640–1687*. Edited by Roger Hayden. Bristol Record Society 27. Gateshead, England: Northumberland Limited, 1974.

———. *The Records of a Church of Christ Meeting Broadmead, Bristol, AD 1640 to AD 1688*. Edited by Nathaniel Haycroft. London: J. Heaton & Son, 42 Paternoster Row, 1865.

———. *The Records of a Church of Christ, Meeting in Broadmead, Bristol. 1640–1687.* Edited by Edward Bean Underhill. Hanserd Knollys Society. London: J. Haddon, Castle Street, Finsbury, 1847.

Thomas, Roger. "The Non-Subscription Controversy Amongst Dissenters in 1719: The Salters' Hall Debate." *Journal of Ecclesiastical History* 4.2 (1953) 162–86.

A True Relation of Some Proceedings at Salters-Hall: By Those Ministers Who Sign'd the First Article of the Church of England, and the Answers to the Fifth and Sixth Questions in the Assemblies Shorter Catechism. London: Printed for John Clark, at the Bible and Crown in the Poultry; and E. Matthews, at the Bible in Pater-Noster-Row, 1719.

Turner, Daniel, and Caleb Evans. *A Charge and Sermon, Delivered at the Ordination of the Rev. Mr. Job David, October 7, 1773, at Frome, Somersetshire.* Bristol: Printed and Sold by W. Pine, T. Cadell, M. Ward. And by J. Buckland, in London, 1773.

Underhill, Edward Bean, ed. *Confessions of Faith, and Other Public Documents, Illustrative of the History of the Baptist Churches of England in the Seventeenth Century.* The Hanserd Knollys Society Publications of the Works of Early English and Other Baptist Writers 8. London: Haddon, Brothers, and Co. Castle Street, Finsbury, 1854.

———. "An Historical Introduction." In *The Records of a Church of Christ, Meeting in Broadmead, Bristol. 1640–1687*, by Edward Terrill, xi–xcvi. The Hanserd Knollys Society Publications of the Works of Early English and Other Baptist Writers 2. London: Printed for the Society, by J. Haddon, Castle Street, Finsbury, 1847.

Vincent, Thomas. *An Explicatory Catechism: Or an Explanation of the Assembly's Shorter Catechism.* Glasgow: Printed by William Duncan, and are to be Sold at his Shop in the Salt mercat, in Gibson's Land, 1744.

A Vindication of the Subscribing Ministers, in Answer to a Late Paper, Entitled, an Authentick Account. London: Printed for John Clark, at the Bible and Crown in the Poultry: And R. Cruttenden, at the Bible and Three Crowns in Cheapside, 1719.

Walker, Austin R. *The Theology of Robert Hall Jr.: The Undermining of Calvinism Among the English Particular Baptists.* Studies in Baptist History 3. Ontario: H&E Academic, 2024.

Waller, J. "William Chillingworth: A Study." *The Journal of Ecclesiastical History* 6.2 (1955) 175–89.

Watts, Isaac. *The Christian Doctrine of the Trinity: Or Father, Son, and Spirit, Three Persons and One God, Asserted and Prov'd, with Their Divine Rights and Honors Vindicated by Plain Evidence of Scripture without the Aid or Incumbrance of Human Schemes: Written Chiefly for the Use of Private Christians.* London: Printed for J. Clark at the Bible and Crown in the Poultry near Cheapside; E. Matthews at the Bible in Pater-noster-Row; and R. Ford at the Angel in the Poultry, 1722.

Watts, Michael R. *From the Reformation to the French Revolution.* Vol. 1 of *The Dissenters.* Oxford: Clarendon, 1978.

Weaver, Garry Stephen. "Hercules Collins: Orthodox, Puritan, Baptist." PhD diss., Southern Baptist Theological Seminary, 2013.

Weaver, Steve. "'Three Subsistences . . . One Substance': The Doctrine of the Trinity in the Second London Confession." *Perichoresis* 20.1 (2022) 9–21.

Wheeler, H. "A Baptist Student—John Collett Ryland." *Baptist Quarterly* 3.1 (1926) 25–33.

Whelan, Timothy. "A Glance at the 1795 Catalogue of Books in the Library of the Bristol Baptist Academy and Museum." *Baptist Quarterly* 39.1 (2001) 35–38.

White, B. R. *Association Records of the Particular Baptists of England, Wales, and Ireland to 1660*. London: Baptist Historical Society, 1971.

———. *The English Baptists of the Seventeenth Century*. Rev. ed. Vol. 1 of *A History of the English Baptists*. Edited by Roger Hayden. Didcot, Oxon: Baptist Historical Society, 1996.

———. "Thomas Collier and Gangræna Edwards." *Baptist Quarterly* 24.3 (1971) 99–110.

Whitley, W. T. "Benjamin Cox." *Transactions of the Baptist Historical Society* 6.1 (1918) 50–59.

———. *Minutes of the General Assembly of the General Baptist Churches in England: With Kindred Records*. 2 vols. N.p.: Alpha, 2019.

———. "Salters' Hall 1719 and the Baptists." *Transactions of the Baptist Historical Society* 5.3 (1917) 172–89.

Wiles, Maurice F. *Archetypal Heresy: Arianism through the Centuries*. Oxford: Oxford University Press, 2001.

Williams, George. *An Attempt to Restore the Supreme Worship of God the Father Almighty: To Which Is Now Added, a Dialogue Between an Athanasian and a Unitarian. Written for the Use of Poor Christians, by George Williams, a Livery-Servant. Second Edition, with Additions and a Preface, by TAOTCOAD*. 2nd ed. N.p.: T. Becket and P. A. de Hondt, in the Strand and T. Cadell, in Bristol, 1765.

Wilmer, Richard H. "Chillingworth on Infallibility." *Anglican Theological Review* 36.2 (1954) 99–104.

Wilson, Walter. *The History and Antiquities of Dissenting Churches and Meeting Houses, in London, Westminster, and Southwark: Including the Lives Their Ministers, from the Rise of Noncomformity to the Present Time*. Vol. 1. N.p.: Printed for the Author; Sold by W. Button and Son, Paternoster Row; T. Williams and Son, Stationers' Court; J. Conder, Bucklersbury, 1808.

Wright, Joseph. *Speculum Haereticis: Or, A Looking-glass for Hereticks. A True Relation of the Apostacy, Allegations, Uncertainties and Falsehoods of Matthew Caffen, a Ringleader, First of the Apollinarian Sect for Near Twenty Years; and Afterwards and Hitherto Denying the Holy Trinity, and the Divine and Human Nature of Our Lord and Saviour Jesus Christ, Wandering Stillin the Misty Fogs, and Mystical Woods, and Desolate Subterfuges of Arianism and Socinianism, & c*. London: Printed for the Author, 1691.

Wright, Stephen. "Collier, Thomas (d. 1691)." In *Oxford Dictionary of National Biography*. Oxford: Oxford University Press, 2004. https://doi.org/10.1093/ref:odnb/5922.

———. "Cox [Coxe], Benjamin (bap. 1595, d. in or after 1663?)." In *Oxford Dictionary of National Biography*. Oxford: Oxford University Press, 2004. https://doi.org/10.1093/ref:odnb/6518.

Wykes, David L. "Peirce, James (1674–1726)." In *Oxford Dictionary of National Biography*. Oxford: Oxford University Press, 2004. https://doi.org/10.1093/ref:odnb/21782.

———. "Subscribers and Non-Subscribers at the Salters' Hall Debate (Act. 1719)." In *Oxford Dictionary of National Biography*. Oxford: Oxford University Press, 2009. https://doi.org/10.1093/ref:odnb/95681.

Subject Index

Antitrinitarianism,
    def. of, 7
    presence of in in seventeenth-
        century England, 12–25

Beddome, Benjamin, 154–61
    alumnus of Bristol Baptist
        Academy, 154
    trinitarianism of in catechism,
        158–61
    trinitarianism of in hymns,
        156–58
    trinitarianism of in sermon,
        154–56

Bristol Baptist Academy, 103–13
    accusation of trinitarian
        downgrade, 163–66
    beginning of, 105–7
    confessional doctrine of, 107–13
    curriculum of, 130–41
    history of, 103–13
    library catalogues of, 127–30
    students' records of studies,
        131–32

Bristol Education Society, 128

Broadmead Baptist Church, 91–103
    confessional doctrine of, 99–
        101, 110–11
    founding of Bristol Baptist
        Academy, 101–3

    reformed Baptist development
        of, 96–101
    reformed separatist origin of,
        93–96

Caffyn, Matthew, 32–40
    Christology of, 36–39
    heterodoxy of, 33–36
    trinitarianism of, 39–40

Cheynell, Francis, 15–25

Chillingworth, William
    articulation of Protestant
        principle, 27–29
    use of Socinian principle, 23–24

Collier, Thomas, 61–77
    trinitarianism in confessions,
        63–68
    trinitarianism in writings, 68–76

Confessions,
    1660 Brief Confession, 40–48
    1691 Brief Confession, 48–49
    1703 Brief Confession, 49–51
    Alcester Confession, 108–10
    First London Baptist Confession
        of Faith, 63–64
    Second London Baptist
        Confession of Faith, 86–90
    Somerset Confession, 65–68

SUBJECT INDEX

Coxe, Nehemiah, 77–86
    author of Second London
        Baptist Confession of Faith,
        86–88
    biography of, 77–80
    Vindiciæ Veritatis, 80–86

David, Job, 166–69
    alumnus of Bristol Baptist
        Academy, 166
    orthodoxy of, 167–68
    unorthodoxy of, 168–69

Evans, Caleb,
    An Address, 147–52
    confession of faith before
        Broadmead Baptist Church,
        146–47
    confessionalism of, 111–13
    principal of Bristol Baptist
        Academy, 111
    Scripture Doctrine, 142–46
    trinitarianism of, 141–52

Foskett, Bernard
    confessionalism of, 108–11
    principal of Bristol Baptist
        Academy, 106–7
    trinitarianism of, 110

General Baptists,
    assemblies of, 51–60
    confessions of, 40–51
    def. of, 8
    dispute with Caffyn, 32–33
    response to Caffyn, 40
    use of Protestant principle, 42,
        55

Gill, John, 136–41
    on confessional language,
        138–39
    on eternal generation of the Son,
        139–41

Hall, Robert Jr., 163–66
    alumnus and tutor of Bristol
        Baptist Academy, 164
    accusation of nontrinitarianism,
        164–66

Nonsubscribers,
    advices of at Salters' Hall
        Debates, 123–25
    def of, 8

Particular Baptists,
    def. of, 8
    dispute with Collier, 61–76
    response to Collier, 77–90
    trinitarian confession, 86–90
    trinitarian writing, 80–86

Protestant Principle, 25–29
    def. of, 8
    contrasted with sola scriptura,
        26–27
    articulated by Chillingworth,
        27–29
    General Baptist use of, 42, 55

Reynolds, John, 161–63
    alumnus of Bristol Baptist
        Academy, 161
    trinitarianism in sermon,
        162–63

Ridgley, Thomas, 133–36

Salters' Hall Debates, 113–25
    debates of, 120–25
    key issues, 119
    origin of, 116–19

Socinianism,
    def. of, 8–9
    presence of in in seventeenth-
        century England, 20–25
    principle of, 22
    rise of in in seventeenth-century
        England, 16–20

Subscribers,
    advices of at Salters' Hall
        Debates, 121–23
    def of, 9

Trinitarianism,
    challenges to in seventeenth-
        century England, 14–15
    def. of classical, 8
    def. confessional, 8
    def. of nonconfessional, 8
    def. of orthodox, 8
    trajectory of in seventeenth-
        century England, 13–14

Vincent, Thomas, 132–33

www.ingramcontent.com/pod-product-compliance
Lightning Source LLC
Chambersburg PA
CBHW051739230426
43670CB00012B/2078